God on the Mountain

THE SOCIETY OF BIBLICAL LITERATURE
MONOGRAPH SERIES

Adela Yarbro Collins, Editor
E.F. Campbell, Associate Editor

Number 37
GOD ON THE MOUNTAIN

by
Thomas B. Dozeman

Thomas B. Dozeman

GOD ON THE MOUNTAIN
A Study of Redaction, Theology and Canon in Exodus 19-24

Scholars Press
Atlanta, Georgia

GOD ON THE MOUNTAIN

by
Thomas B. Dozeman

© 1989
The Society of Biblical Literature

Library of Congress Cataloging in Publication Data

Dozeman, Thomas B.
  God on the mountain : a study of redaction, theology, and canon in
Exodus 19-24 / Thomas B. Dozeman.
    p. cm. -- (Monograph series / the Society of Biblical
Literature ; no. 37)
    Bibliography: p.
    ISBN 1-55540-358-1 (alk. paper) -- ISBN 1-55540-359-X (pbk. :
alk. paper)
    1. Bible. O.T. Exodus XIX-XXIV--Criticism, Redaction. 2. Bible.
I. Title. II. Series: Monograph series (Society of Biblical
Literature) : no. 37.
BS1245.2.D67 1989
222'.12066--dc20   89-33590
                                                        CIP

Printed in the United States of America
on acid-free paper

CONTENTS

ABBREVIATIONS

AB	Anchor Bible
AcOr	*Acta orientalia*
AnBib	Analecta biblica
ANET	J.B. Pritchard (ed.). *Ancient Near Eastern Texts*
AnOr	Analecta orientalia
ATANT	Abhandlungen zur Theologie des Alten and Neuen Testaments
BAG	W. Bauer, W.F. Arndt, and F.W. Gingrich, *Greek-English Lexicon of the NT*
BAR	*Biblical Archaeologist Reader*
BASOR	*Bulletin of the American Schools of Oriental Research*
BBB	Bonner biblische Beiträge
BETL	Bibliotheca ephemeridum theologicarum lovaniensium
BEvT	Bieträge zur evangelischen Theologie
Bib	*Biblica*
BWANT	Beiträge zur Wissenschaft vom Alten and Neuen Testament
BZ	*Biblische Zietschrift*
BZAW	Beihefte zur *Zeitschrift für die alttestamentliche Wissenschaft*
CAT	Commentaire de l'Ancien Testament
CBQ	*Catholic Biblical Quarterly*
ConBOT	Coniectanea biblica, Old Testament
CTA	A. Herdner, *Corpus des tablettes en cunéiformes alphabétiques*
ETL	*Ephemerides theologicae lovanienses*
EvT	*Evangelische Theologie*
FRLANT	Forschugen zur Religion und Literatur des Alten und Neuen Testaments
Fs.	Festschrift
GKC	*Gesenius' Hebrew Grammar*, ed. E. Kautzsch, tr. A.E. Cowley
HAT	Hundbuch zum Alten Testament
HKAT	Handkommentar zum Alten Testament

HSM	Harvard Semitic Monographs
HTR	*Harvard Theological Review*
HUCA	*Hebrew Union College Annual*
IDBSup	K. Crim (ed.), Supplementary volume to *Interpreter's Dictionary of the Bible*, 1976
Int	*Interpretation*
JANESCU	*Journal of the Ancient Near Eastern Society of Columbia University*
JAOS	*Journal of the American Oriental Society*
JBL	*Journal of Biblical Literature*
JCS	*Journal of Cuneiform Studies*
JHNES	Johns Hopkins Near Eastern Studies
JPOS	*Journal of the Palestine Oriental Society*
JSNTSup	Journal for the Study of the New Testament— Supplement Series
JSOT	*Journal for the Study of the Old Testament*
JSOTSup	Journal for the Study of the Old Testament— Supplement Series
JSS	*Journal of Semitic Studies*
JTS	*Journal of Theological Studies*
KAT	Kommentar zum Alten Testament
KB	L. Koehler and W. Baumgartner, *Lexicon in Veteris Testamenti libros*
NCB	New Century Bible
OBO	Orbis biblicus et orientalis
OTL	Old Testament Library
OTS	*Oudtestamentische Studiën*
PRU	*Le Palais royal d'Ugarit*
RB	*Revue biblique*
SANT	Studien zum Alten und Neuen Testament
SBLASP	Society of Biblical Literature Abstracts and Seminar Papers
SBT	Studies in Biblical Theology
ScEs	*Science et esprit*
SOTSMS	Society for Old Testament Study Monograph Series
ST	*Studia theologica*
TBl	*Theologische Blätter*
TBü	Theologische Bücherei
TDOT	G.J. Botterweck and H. Ringgren (eds.), *Theological Dictionary of the Old Testament*
TSK	*Theologische Studien und Kritiken*
TToday	*Theology Today*
TTZ	*Trierer theologische Zeitschrift*
TZ	*Theologische Zeitschrift*
UF	*Ugarit-Forschungen*

VF	*Verkündigung und Forschung*
VT	*Vetus Testamentum*
VTSup	Vetus Testamentum, Supplements
WMANT	Wissenschaftliche Monographien zum Alten and Neuen Testament
ZA	*Zeitschrift für Assyriologie*
ZAW	*Zeitschrift für die alttestamentliche Wissenschaft*
ZTK	*Zeitschrift für Theologie und Kirche*

Chapter 1

REDACTION AND THEOLOGY IN
THE SINAI COMPLEX

Pentateuchal studies are presently going through a creative period. Past solutions concerning the formation and character of the literature are being reevaluated and new avenues of interpretation are being explored. Such scholars as Van Seters,[1] Rendtorff,[2] Thompson,[3] Schmid,[4] Coats,[5] Damrosch[6] and others[7] are pushing pentateuchal studies in new directions by evaluating past source-critical and form-critical models for interpretation, while also exploring new solutions for dating distinct traditions and for describing their interrelationship within the canonical Pentateuch. Thus it is a time of taking stock in the impressive work of past generations of biblical scholars to determine what will endure into the next century of interpretation. I hope to contribute to the current discussion with a study on redaction and theology in the canonical Sinai Complex.

My use of the designation "canonical Sinai Complex" re-

---

[1] J. Van Seters, *Abraham in History and Tradition* (New Haven: Yale University Press, 1975); *In Search of History: Historiography in the Ancient World and the Origins of Biblical History* (New Haven: Yale University Press, 1983).

[2] R. Rendtorff, *Das überlieferungsgeschichtliche Problem des Pentateuch*, BZAW 147 (Berlin: de Gruyter, 1977).

[3] T. L. Thompson, *The Historicity of the Patriarchal Narratives: The Quest for the Historical Abraham*, BZAW 133 (Berlin: de Gruyter, 1974); and *The Origin Tradition of Ancient Israel: I. The Literary Formation of Genesis and Exodus 1-23*, JSOTSup 55 (Sheffield: JSOT Pres, 1988).

[4] H. H. Schmid, *Der sogenannte Jahwist: Beobachtungen und Fragen zur Pentateuchforschung* (Zürich: Theologischer Verlag, 1976).

[5] G. W. Coats, *Moses: Heroic Man, Man of God*, JSOTSup 57 (Sheffield: JSOT Press, 1988).

[6] D. Damrosch, *The Narrative Covenant: Transformations of Genre in the Growth of Biblical Literature* (New York: Harper and Row, 1987).

[7] For a current bibliography on pentateuchal research see S. J. De Vries, "A Review of Recent Research in the Tradition History of the Pentateuch," *SBLASP* 26 (1987): 459-502. See also R. N. Whybray, *The Making of the Pentateuch: A Methodological Study* JSOTSup 53 (Sheffield: JSOT Press, 1987); and E. Blum, *Die Komposition der Vätergeschichte*, WMANT 57 (Neukirchen-Vluyn: Neukirchener Verlag, 1984).

quires definition. When the Sinai Complex is defined as broadly
as possible, it comprises over half of the canonical Pentateuch,
since it not only includes the interweaving of narrative and law
in Exodus 19-34, but also the priestly (Exodus 35-Numbers 10)
and deuteronomic (Deuteronomy) legislations which are
anchored in the events of Exodus 19-34. Thus the canonical Sinai Complex consists primarily of law. However, the central
event that has attracted nearly one hundred chapters of legislation is the revelation of God on the mountain in Exodus 19-24,
and it is this core story that will be the primary subject matter
for study. This is a study, therefore, in pentateuchal narrative.
Yet having said this, we must continually remind ourselves in
the following chapters that narrative in the Sinai Complex functions to provide a context for legislation, so that it is never an
end in itself, but a means for directing the reader's attention to
law. In view of the close interrelationship between law and narrative, the canonical Sinai Complex might best be characterized
as a narrative of law.

The subtitle of this monograph, *A Study of Redaction, Theology and Canon*, indicates two primary aims of the following
chapters. They are to describe the tradition-historical development of the Sinai Complex as a process of redaction and to
probe the theology of divine presence that is embedded in the
imagery of theophany on the mountain. An overview of the
place of redaction in modern biblical scholarship and a definition of symbol will provide a point of departure for our study of
redaction and theology in the canonical Sinai Complex.

I
THE ROLE OF REDACTORS IN THE HISTORY
OF SCHOLARSHIP ON THE SINAI
COMPLEX

The dominant theory in the last century concerning the formation of the Sinai Complex has been the Documentary Hypothesis, and redactors have occupied a central place within this
theory. However, their central role has been judged to be essentially negative. In particular, the predominant view of redactors has been that they are passive tradents, whose primary
aim was to preserve tradition, rather than creative theologians
who critically transformed tradition. This assessment of redactors has had two important results in most modern biblical scholarship on the Sinai Complex. First, it has implied a negative
literary judgment concerning the canonical text, since the preservation of tradition was believed to take precedence over the

literary quality of the canonical story itself. Thus modern scholars have frequently judged the canonical Sinai Complex to be "incomprehensible" precisely because of the influence of redactors. Second, the negative literary judgment concerning the canonical text has allowed past biblical scholars to bypass the work of redactors in order to recreate the source documents whose preservation was considered to be the goal of the redactors. In this way, the "incomprehensible" quality of the canonical Sinai Complex has actually been a pivotal link in allowing past scholars to reconstruct parallel literary sources that reflect an earlier stage of tradition.

Wellhausen, Gressmann, and von Rad each illustrate this negative judgment of redactors in a somewhat different way, and thus they also illustrate how such a view of redactors as passive tradents necessitates the loss of the canonical Sinai Complex for the present reader. A review of their work will provide background for reassessing the role of redactors in the formation of the canonical Sinai Complex.

A. Wellhausen and the Role of Redactors in Source Criticism

Wellhausen has set much of the agenda concerning the negative assessment of redactors in the Sinai Complex. He described two central problems that had to be overcome in any interpretation of the Sinai Complex, namely the predominance of legislation over narrative and the lack of logical sequence within the narratives themselves.[8] His solution, of course, was the Documentary Hypothesis. The most significant literary feature of this hypothesis is that "continuous narratives [or sources, yahwistic, elohistic, priestly] which can and must be understood each by itself are woven together in a double or threefold cord" by redactors,[9] whose primary aim was to harmonize the three accounts into an "improvised unity."[10]

---

[8] J. Wellhausen, *Prolegomena to the History of Ancient Israel*, translated from the 1883 edition (New York: Meridian Books, 1957) 342; and *Die Composition des Hexateuchs und der Historischen Bücher des Alten Testament*, 3rd ed. (Berlin: Georg Reimer, 1899) 81.

[9] Wellhausen, *Prolegomena*, 295-96.

[10] Wellhausen, *Composition* 331, 333. Wellhausen (*Prolegomena*, 345-47) summarized at least six stages of growth to the Sinai Complex in its development from being the "history book" of the yahwistic source to the "law book" of the priestly source. He writes that Sinai is first the seat of the deity and the location of revelation. Israel did not travel to Sinai at this original stage of the tradition, nor was law associated with it. Instead, legislation was a forty-year process of professional activity by Moses at Kadesh. Second, Israel was described as journeying to Sinai since it "came to be thought more seemly that the Israelites should undertake the journey

The Documentary Hypothesis allowed Wellhausen to account for the "monstrous growth" of law in the Sinai Complex by locating it within the priestly source. However, what had turned the Sinai Complex into a true "labyrinth of stories" was, according to Wellhausen, the work of redactors.[11] They were the ones responsible for the present lack of unity in the narratives, with their numerous repetitions and contradictions which disrupted the inherent logic within the individual sources. Wellhausen held to this assumption so strongly that he concluded that the combination of the legislation and the repetitions within the narratives had resulted in a "most depressing and unimaginable redaction," which required a source-critical solution.[12]

The central problem of Wellhausen's source-critical hypothesis for the present study is not so much that the canonical Sinai Complex is not interpreted in order to focus on sources, but that the assessment of redactors as passive tradents implies that the canonical text might very well be incoherent, since the primary aim of the "improved unity" is not to create a unique message, but to preserve the parallel sources themselves. Thus it would appear that the "uninterpretable" quality of the canonical Sinai Complex is really a necessary prerequisite for Wellhausen, which allows him to sort out the repetitious parallel sources at another level within the text. And it is precisely at this point where the source-critical method runs into problems, since there are occasions when Wellhausen must attribute a more active and creative role to redactors in establishing the canonical text. For example, he concludes that the position of Exodus 25-31 before Exodus 34 can only be interpreted at the level of redaction because redactors had so successfully reorganized the text.[13] But this raises an uneasy question: If redactors have juxtaposed these two law codes for their own purposes, might other seemingly "uninterpretable" repetitions or contradictions also be part of a redactional design?

to Jehovah." Third, Sinai was dramatized under a "poetic impulse," so that it became the "scene of the solemn inauguration of the historical relation between Jehovah and Israel." Fourth, drama led to covenant, which eventually led to the fifth stage, the legal basis for covenant in the form of Deuteronomy. And finally, the priestly source incorporated the deuteronomic legal version of Sinai into the exodus, so that the law became the great revelatory event for all time.

11 Wellhausen, *Composition*, 82-83, 94-96.

12 Wellhausen, *Composition*, 81.

13 Wellhausen, *Composition*, 97.

B. Gressmann and the Role of Redactors in Literary History

What is only implicit in the source criticism of Wellhausen becomes axiomatic in the subsequent literary history of Gressmann,[14] where redactors were not only judged to be passive tradents, but also tradents of *Sagen*, whose content had long been forgotten.[15] The combination of these factors prompted Gressmann to conclude that the canonical Sinai Complex was an "irreparable chaos," which consisted of a random distribution of forgotten *Sagen*.[16] In view of this situation, Gressmann's starting point for interpretation was to move immediately beyond the "unreadable" canonical text and thus circumvent the "disastrous redaction" by detaching individual stories from their present context, by removing all genealogies, law, sacrificial instructions, and dietary regulations from the text, and finally by actually rearranging the sequence of events within the narratives. In fact, the purpose of a commentary on the Sinai Complex, according to Gressmann, was for the interpreter to make the text readable once again by presenting a "new redaction," which has no correlation to the canonical text.[17]

However, even Gressmann was not always able to circumvent the "disastrous redactor." His conclusion concerning the tablet-motif in Exodus 24, 34 provides an illustration:

> He [the redactor] found two *Sagen* about the law tablets, which we must recognize as parallel narratives of the same event: one from J and the other from E. Instead of working them together as usual, he proceeded another

[14] See H. Gressmann ("Die Aufgaben der alttestamentlichen Forschung," *ZAW* 1 [1924] 1-33 esp. 8, 29) for definition of literary history in contrast to source criticism.

[15] H. Gressmann, *Mose und seine Zeit: Ein Kommentar zu den Mose-Sagen*, FRLANT 1 (Göttingen: Vandenhoeck und Ruprecht, 1913) 191; and *Die Anfänge Israel*, Die Schriften des Alten Testaments 1/2 (Göttingen: Vandenhoeck und Ruprecht, 1914) 12.

[16] Gressmann, *Moses und seine Zeit*, 181; *Die Anfänge Israel*, 12. Gressmann, (*Mose und seine Zeit*, 373-75, 385-86) described at least six stages in the development of *Sagen* within the Sinai Complex. First, he argued that there were simple oral, independent *Sagen*. These *Sagen* could be isolated by asking two questions both of which imply the "incomprehensibility" of the canonical text: which stories do not fit in their present context and which stories are the most obscure. Second, fairy-tale (*Märchen*) motifs were added to the individual *Sagen*. Third, the individual *Sagen* are collected into *Sagenkränzen*—a loose collection of *Sagen* around similar or related themes that is done by narrators. Fourth, the *Sagenkränzen* are written down into *Sagensammlungen*—J and E. Thus J and E are not creative authors for Gressmann, but collectors of tradition. Fifth, J and E are combined. And finally, P is written.

[17] Gressmann, *Die Anfänge Israel*, 16-17.

way. He divided both histories, placed the *Sage* of the
destruction of the tablets between [Exodus 32] and added
the motif of substitution (the reissuing of new tablets) to
the latter account [Exodus 34]. So in a clever manner a
continuous, apparently organic unity has been created
and the seam is still unrecognizable (translation by the
Author).[18]

But at this point Gressmann too leaves us with troubling questions: If the role of the redactor is so influential that the present
unity of the tablet-motif is seamless, then at the very least the
Sinai Complex cannot be the "irreparable chaos" that Gressmann would have us believe, and furthermore, it also raises
doubts about the many unrecognizable seams in the canonical
text that Gressmann has discovered.

C. Von Rad and the Role of Redactors in Tradition History

Von Rad first voices the growing uneasiness of biblical scholars concerning the assumption of literary historians that the canonical text "was a starting point barely worthy of discussion" in
his essay, "The Form-Critical Problem of the Hexateuch."[19]
This work was meant to counter the "disintegrating effect" of
past interpretation, which "led inevitably further and further
away from the final form of the text as we have it," with an alternative tradition-historical hypothesis of the growth of the Hexateuch.[20] Von Rad's aim in this study was to lead interpreters
"back to the final and conclusive form of the Hexateuch by way
of an organically integrated theological process. . . ."[21]
Von Rad's primary means in countering the disintegrating
effects of literary history was to redefine genre. Thus, in contrast to the earlier tendency of literary historians to focus their
study of genre on singular preliterary *Sagen*, von Rad redefined
the term to represent "streams of tradition," which functioned
as creeds within distinct cultic *Sitzen im Leben*.[22] With this redefinition, von Rad concluded that the present form of the Hexateuch was composed of primarily two original genres or cultic

---

[18] Gressmann, *Moses und seine Zeit*, 191.
[19] G. von Rad, "The Form-Critical Problem of the Hexateuch," *The Problem of the
Hexateuch* (London: Oliver and Boyd, 1966) 1.
[20] Von Rad, "Problem of the Hexateuch," 1. For definition of tradition history in
contrast to literary history see G. von Rad, "Literarkritische und überlieferungsgeschichtliche Forschung im Alten Testament," VF 48 (1947) 172-94 esp. 187-88.
[21] Von Rad, "Problem of the Hexateuch," 3.
[22] Von Rad, "Problem of the Hexateuch," 1-3; "Literarkritische und überlieferungsgeschichtliche Forschung," 187-88.

legends: the Settlement Tradition and the Sinai Tradition.[23] The Settlement Tradition was rooted in the Feast of Weeks at Gilgal and it focused on the divine guidance of Israel to the promised land. This confession of *Heilsgeschichte* included four constitutive elements: patriarchal beginnings, oppression in Egypt, deliverance, and the settlement in Canaan.[24] The Sinai Tradition, by contrast, was rooted in the Feast of Booths at Shechem and it focused on theophany and the making of covenant. This confession of the coming of God also included four constitutive elements: preparatory hallowing, the drawing near of the assembly to God, theophany and communication of divine demands, and a concluding sacrifice as a seal of covenant.[25]

Von Rad's redefinition of genre as "streams of tradition" anchored the basic sequence of the Hexateuch in ancient cultic confessions and this meant that the final form of the Hexateuch could no longer be viewed as randomly arranged individual *Sagen*. However, the most significant innovation in the tradition-historical development of the Hexateuch occurred when the Settlement Tradition and the Sinai Tradition became detached from their original cultic *Sitzen im Leben* and were spiritualized during the monarchy period, which allowed the Yahwist to combine them into the present sequence of the Hexateuch.[26] Once the Yahwist had achieved this new literary outline, the writings of the elohistic and priestly authors were "no more than variations upon the massive theme of the Yahwist's conception, despite their admittedly great theological originality."[27]

In spite of von Rad's attempt to distance himself from the literary historians, he still adhered to their view of redactors as being passive tradents. This is evident in his conclusion that the canonical form of the Hexateuch is the result of redactors who "received the testimony to the faith contained in each of the source documents at its own valuation, and held it to be binding."[28] And, according to von Rad, it is this attempt by redactors to preserve tradition that accounts for the lack of unity to the canonical text. This conclusion creates a problem for the pres-

---

[23] Although von Rad clearly focuses on these two traditions, he also makes reference ("Problem of the Hexateuch," 52) to Pedersen's interpretation of Exodus 1-14 as an Exodus Tradition that is based on the passover.

[24] Von Rad, "Problem of the Hexateuch," 3-13, 41-48.

[25] Von Rad, "Problem of the Hexateuch," 13-26, 33-40.

[26] Von Rad, "Problem of the Hexateuch," 48-50.

[27] Von Rad, "Problem of the Hexateuch," 74.

[28] Von Rad, "Problem of the Hexateuch," 77.

ent study. In particular, von Rad's assessment of redactors as being passive tradents raises the suspicion that his repeated concern for the "final and conclusive form of the text" is really aimed at the sequence of events and not at the final literary form of the text. And this suspicion is confirmed when he writes: "The insoluble literary problem [of the Sinai Complex] barely concerns us. . .for it is the internal structure of the tradition which interests us here, the unity of the material as such rather than its literary unity."[29] Thus, although von Rad argued that the Sinai Complex presented a fixed sequence of events, he still does not interpret the canonical text.

However, the "insoluble literary problem" of the Sinai Complex is more important to von Rad than he admits, since it is really a necessary prerequisite for him to sort out the repetitious four-part sequence that provides the "unity of material" for the yahwistic, elohistic, and priestly sources within the Sinai Complex. Von Rad is able to sort out the parallel sources because redactors preserved each tradition, rather than creatively transforming past tradition. In other words, it is the role of redactors as passive tradents that allows von Rad to conclude confidently that "none of the stages in the age-long development of this work has been wholly superseded; something has been preserved of each phase, and its influence has persisted right down to the final form of the Hexateuch."[30] In fact the occurrence of this four-part pattern in the yahwistic source (most important because it is the link between oral cult legend and written literature) allowed von Rad even to reconstruct the oral cultic legend that is absent from the text altogether. Yet there is an internal problem in von Rad's work at this very point. In particular the inability of von Rad to reconstruct clearly the four-part sequence of events in this most important yahwistic source, along with his concession that perhaps the yahwistic account of the Sinai Complex was forced to give way to the elohistic version when the sources were conflated, is a weak link in his tradition-historical solution to the Sinai Complex, and it suggests that redactors might actually play a more creative role in the tradition-historical development of this material than he has

---

[29] Von Rad, "Problem of the Hexateuch," 16. See also M. Noth, (*A History of Pentateuchal Traditions* [Chico: Scholars Press, 1981] 31 n.115) who shares von Rad's assessment at this point when he writes that the Sinai Complex may have already reached such a "complicated compilation within the Pentateuchal tradition that today an intelligible analysis can no longer be successfully undertaken."

[30] Von Rad, "Problem of the Hexateuch," 78.

assumed.[31]

D. A Reassessment of the Role of Redactors in the Formation of the Sinai Complex

Despite the clear differences between source criticism, literary history, and tradition history, the preceding overview underscores three points of agreement among scholars who work in these different methodologies: first, there is a common adherence to the Documentary Hypothesis; second, there is an assumption that redactors are passive tradents whose primary aim was to preserve tradition rather than creative theologians who critically transformed tradition; and third, there is a negative literary judgment concerning the canonical text as being incomprehensible. However, three recent and somewhat independent developments in pentateuchal studies call for a reassessment of the role of redactors in the Sinai Complex, and with it they also present a challenge to the Documentary Hypothesis.

The first development to be noted is the redaction-critical work of Perlitt in his monograph on covenant entitled *Bundestheologie im Alten Testament*. Perlitt directly challenged the prevailing judgment that redactors were passive tradents with his penetrating analysis of the central role that deuteronomistic redactors played in the formation of the Sinai Complex. In the wake of his study it was no longer possible to assume that the aim of redactors in the Sinai Complex was simply to preserve authoritative tradition, since Perlitt clearly demonstrated the theological creativity of the deuteronomistic redactors in transforming a theophany tradition to an occasion of covenant, with the promulgation of law.[32]

The second development is Rendtorff's tradition-historical

---

[31] Von Rad's reconstruction of the tradition-historical development of the Sinai Complex ("The Problem of the Hexateuch," 16-17) presents the following internal problem in logic. He argues that the yahwistic source is the essential link in maintaining continuity between the original cultic legend and the later literary elohistic and priestly sources. The problem that this poses with regard to the Sinai Complex is that the all-important yahwistic source does not clearly reflect the four-part sequence that is essential to the Sinai Complex, so that in the end von Rad is forced to reconstruct the tradition history of the Sinai Complex on the basis of the elohistic source. Thus his conclusion that "all the peculiarities of the individual sources leave us in no doubt that behind the present form of the account there lies one single tradition of a firmly fixed order of events" is called into question by the yahwistic source itself.

[32] L. Perlitt, *Bundestheologie im Alten Testament*, WMANT 36 (Neukirchen-Vluyn: Neukirchener Verlag, 1969) 156-238.

analysis entitled *Das überlieferungsgeschichtliche Problem des Pentateuch*, in which he challenged the Documentary Hypothesis from two directions. First, on the basis of his interpretation of the ancestral history, Rendtorff successfully demonstrated that a creative compiling and arranging of tradition for theological purposes was taking place already at an early literary stage of the tradition (with the Yahwist), and that this process of growth was incompatible with the Documentary Hypothesis.[33] Second, Rendtorff argued that the distinct themes in the Pentateuch (ancestral history, exodus, Sinai, etc.) developed independently and were only later interrelated into the canonical pentateuchal story. This argument, too, was a challenge to the Documentary Hypothesis, with its vision of single, continuous and thematically unified documents (sources) running throughout the Pentateuch/Hexateuch.[34] Rendtorff's challenge to the Documentary Hypothesis in Genesis raises the question of whether the same organic process of theological reflection and "planned theological editing" might not also be operating in the tradition-historical development of the Sinai Complex.

The third development is the rise of a variety of literary criticisms in contemporary biblical studies, whose common denominator is that they require a unified reading of the present form of the text.[35] It should be clear at this point that a demand to interpret the canonical text runs counter to the presupposition of incomprehensibility that is so central to the Documentary Hypothesis. Unfortunately the result of this sharp conflict has been a growing dichotomy in pentateuchal studies between literary critics, who work synchronically and stress the unity of pentateuchal narratives, and tradition historians, who work diachronically and stress the disunity of pentateuchal narratives. Neither approach in my judgment has dealt adequately with the central role of redactors in the formation of the Pentateuch in general and more specifically in the Sinai Complex.

In the following chapters I will attempt to provide a comprehensive redaction-critical interpretation of the Sinai Complex that incorporates aspects of the three innovative developments in pentateuchal studies that have just been noted.

Chapters 2-4 will address the work of Rendtorff and Perlitt by tracing the tradition-historical growth of the Sinai Complex

---

[33] R. Rendtorff, "The 'Yahwist' as Theologian? The Dilemma of Pentateuchal Criticism," *JSOT* 3 (1977) 2-9 = VTSup 28 (1975) 158-66; *Problem des Pentateuch*, 1-81.
[34] Rendtorff, *Problem des Pentateuch*, 80-145.
[35] A major influence in the prominence of literary criticism was J. Muilenburg's call for rhetorical criticism entitled, "Form Criticism and Beyond," *JBL* 88 (1969) 1-18.

through three stages of development, namely a pre-exilic Mountain of God tradition, a late pre-exilic/exilic deuteronomistic redaction, and finally an exilic/early post-exilic priestly redaction.

Rendtorff's thesis that the growth of individual themes (or complexes) in the Pentateuch is a process of "planned theological editing" rather than the interweaving of distinct sources will provide a point of departure for this study. However, the reader will note the significant point of contrast with Rendtorff's thesis in Chapter 4, where it will be argued that priestly tradents provide the final redaction of the Sinai Complex (and the Pentateuch as a whole), rather than deuteronomistic redactors.[36] It should also be noted that Rendtorff's central concern is not with late redactions of the Pentateuch, but with the work of the Yahwist. Unfortunately, the peculiar character of the Sinai Complex, with its late tradition-historical development, precludes a detailed evaluation of Rendtorff's thesis concerning the Yahwist, namely that this work is the result of a collector (*Bearbeiter/Sammler*), who works more within the distinct themes/complexes of the Pentateuch, and does not link them into the pentateuchal story as we have it.[37] The testing of this rather fragmented view of the growth of the Pentateuch would require a more broad based study of the earliest tradition in the Sinai Complex (the Mountain of God tradition) to see whether it was linked with other yahwistic traditions in the Pentateuch. Such research is beyond the scope of the present study, since interpretation will be limited here to the Sinai Complex itself.

Perlitt's redaction-critical work on deuteronomistic tradition in the Sinai Complex will be evaluated in detail within Chapter 3. Although much of Perlitt's work will be followed in the present study, his primary concern with covenant and covenant theology has tended to focus his work almost exclusively on deuteronomistic tradition in the Sinai Complex, and this raises a problem that must be addressed in the present study. The problem is two-sided. On the one hand, Perlitt concedes too great a role to deuteronomistic redactors by attributing the canonical Sinai Complex to their work;[38] on the other hand, he assigns them too minor a role by assuming the Documentary Hypothesis in conjunction with the creative role of the deuteronomistic redactors.[39] This two-sided problem will be addressed in Chap-

---

[36] Rendtorff, *Problem des Pentateuch*, 146-73.
[37] Rendtorff, *Problem des Pentateuch*, 148-58.
[38] Perlitt, *Bundestheologie*, 180 *et passim*.
[39] Perlitt, *Bundestheologie*, 157-60 *et passim*.

ter 2 and in Chapter 4. In Chapter 2 we will reevaluate the character of pre-deuteronomistic tradition and in Chapter 4 we will distinguish a subsequent priestly redaction of the Sinai Complex from the deuteronomistic redaction.

The focus of study will shift in Chapters 5-6 from tradition history to an interpretation of the canonical Sinai Complex. Here the demand of recent literary criticisms to interpret the present form of the text will take center stage. Although I embrace the demand by literary critics to interpret the received text, I hope to demonstrate that a rejection of the assumption of incomprehensibility with regard to the canonical text cannot be replaced by a hermeneutic that demands unified interpretations of pentateuchal narrative. The role of redactors in editing and arranging distinct traditions in order to form the canonical Sinai Complex will be examined through a study of repetition and a type of redaction that I am calling "canon-conscious," which is rooted in the recent work of Childs[40] and Sheppard.[41]

II
THEOLOGY AND SYMBOL IN THE MOUNTAIN SETTING OF THE SINAI COMPLEX

My aim in this study is not simply tradition-historical or literary. It is also theological. By tracing the tradition-historical growth of the Sinai Complex into its canonical form, I hope to explore Israel's emerging theology of divine cultic presence, which is conveyed through the changing imagery of the theophany on the mountain.

The mountain setting is prominent in Exodus 19-24. It is underscored at the outset of the Sinai Complex,[42] and it is referred to frequently throughout: twenty-one times the definite noun for mountain is used alone, with a preposition, or in construct with Elohim;[43] the mountain occurs an additional five times in

[40] B. S. Childs, *Introduction to the Old Testament as Scripture* (Philadelphia: Fortress, 1979) 59-60.
[41] G. T. Sheppard, "Canonization: Hearing the Voice of the Same God through Historically Dissimilar Tradition," *Int* 36 (1982) 21-33.
[42] The mountain setting is repeated in Exod 19:1-3. It occurs in Exod 19:2b to describe Israel's encampment at the base of the mountain and once again in Exod 19:3a to locate Yahweh on the mountain summit.
[43] The mountain is referred to with the definite article (*hāhār*) in Exod 19:23, 20:18, 24:15, 18; with the directive *-āh* (*hāhārāh*) in Exod 24:12; with a range of prepositions which emphasis different spatial locations in relation to the mountain: *bāhār* in Exod 19:12 (twice), 13, 24:18; *negeb hāhār* in Exod 19:2; *min-hāhār* in Exod 19:3, 14; *'al-hāhār* in Exod 19:16; *'el-hāhār* in Exod 24:15; *bĕtaḥtît* or *taḥat hāhār* in Exod 19:17; 24:4; and finally in a series of bound constructions; *kŏl-hāhār* in

construct with Sinai.[44] The emphasis on the mountain setting distinguishes the Sinai Complex from Israel's other itinerary stops,[45] as a geographical midpoint between Egypt and Canaan.[46] However geography does not exhaust the important role of the mountain setting,[47] for it also functions symbolically as a cosmic mountain,[48] which is meant to disclose "the essential

Exod 19:18 and *rōʾš hāhār* in Exod 19:20 (twice); 24:17; and *har hāʾĕlōhîm* in Exod 24:13. This range of occurrences, of course, continues beyond Exodus 19-24 through Exodus 34: *hāhār* in Exod 34:3; *min-hāhār* in Exod 32:1, 15; 34:29; *rōʾš hāhār* in Exod 34:2; *taḥat hāhār* in Exod 32:19; and *bĕkŏl-hāhār* in Exod 34:3.

[44] Mount Sinai is referred to as *har sînay* in Exod 19:18; *ʾal-har sînay* in Exod 19:11, 20, 24:16; *ʾel-har sînay* in Exod 19:23. Further occurrences to Mount Sinai through Exodus 34 are *ʾel-har sînay* in Exod 34:2, 4; *bĕhar-sînay* in Exod 31:18, 34:32; and *mēhar sînay* in Exod 34:29.

[45] In addition to the setting of the mountain, the itinerary notice in Exod 19:1-3a also contrasts to the other itinerary notices by the specificity of the date and by its length. Compare it to the additional notices in Exod 12:37a, 13:20, 14:1, 15:22, 16:1, 17:1a, 19:1-3, Num 10:12, 20:22, 21:10, 22:1. For analysis of the itinerary notices see G. Coats, "The Wilderness Itinerary," *CBQ* 34 (1972) 135-52; F. M. Cross, *Canaanite Myth and Hebrew Epic: Essays in the History of the Religion of Israel* (Cambridge: Harvard University Press, 1973) 309-17, and more recently G. I. Davies, "The Wilderness Itineraries and the Composition of the Pentateuch," *VT* 3 (1983) 1-13.

[46] B. S. Childs (*Exodus*, OTL [Philadelphia: Westminster, 1974] 366) notes the emphasis that is placed on Exod 19:1-3a and concludes that it is the goal of the journey from Egypt. However, compare J. Levenson (*Sinai and Zion: An Entry into the Jewish Bible* [New York: Winston Press, 1985] 23) who argues that Sinai is not the goal of the Exodus, but the midpoint between Egypt and Canaan, and thus represents Yahweh's "unchallengeable mastery over both."

[47] The location of Sinai has been researched extensively without firm results. It has been placed in Kadesh Barnea, in Midian, in the present day Sinai Peninsula. Mount Sinai has been associated with *jebel mūsa* (Mount of Moses) and *jebel qāterîn* (Mount of St. Catherine). For discussion see M. Noth, *The History of Israel*, 2nd ed. (London: Adam and Charles Black, 1960) 128-36 and *Exodus*, OTL (Philadelphia: Westminster, 1962) 155-56; and most recently G. I. Davies, *The Way of the Wilderness: A Geographical Study of the Wilderness Itineraries in the Old Testament*, SOTSMS 5 (London: Cambridge University Press, 1979) 63-69.

[48] See R. Clifford (*The Cosmic Mountain in Canaan and the Old Testament*, HSM 4 [Cambridge: Harvard University Press, 1972]) for discussion of cosmic mountain symbolism in the Hebrew Bible. Compare also R. L. Cohn, *The Shape of Sacred Space: Four Biblical Studies*, AAR Studies in Religion 23 (Chico: Scholars Press, 1981). For earlier literature on sacred mountains in ancient Near Eastern religion see P. Jensen, *Die Kosmologie der Babylonier* (Strasbourg: Trübner, 1890) 195-201; and J. Jeremias, *Der Gottesberg: Ein Beitrag zum Verständnis der biblischen Symbolsprache* (Gütersloh: C. Bertelsmann, 1919) 35-55. For general discussion of mountains as representing sacred space see G. van der Leeuw, *Religion in Essence and Manifestation*, 2nd ed. (Princeton: Princeton University Press, 1986) 52-58, 393-402; M. Eliade, *The Sacred and the Profane: The Nature of Religion* (New York: Harcourt, Brace and Co., 1959) 36-39.

. . . relationship of YHWH to his people."[49]

The symbolic role of the mountain should caution us at the outset not to relegate the setting to background information concerning itinerary, but to investigate how the mountain may in fact be a structuring device within the narrative and how it might be providing a channel for theological discourse concerning divine cultic presence.[50] The opening verses of the Sinai Complex would certainly appear to encourage a study of the symbolic role of the mountain setting, since it is used as the focal point for introducing the main characters, and since it continues to be a central structuring device throughout the Sinai Complex. Note, for example, how Yahweh and Israel are introduced in Exod 19:1-3a as stationary characters, who are carefully juxtaposed to each other at the summit and base of the mountain, while Moses is presented as the one who moves vertically between the two parties as he explores the spatial relationship between them.[51] And note how this interrelationship between characters in the setting of the mountain continues to be a structuring device throughout the Sinai Complex, especially with regard to the movement of Moses. His movement up and down the mountain yields the following scenes: Exod 19:1-8a (Proposal of Covenant); Exod 19:8b-19 (Theophany); Exod 19:20-20:20 (Decalogue); Exod 20:21-24:11 (Book of the Covenant); Exod 24:12-32:35 (Tabernacle); Exod 34:1-35 (Covenant Renewal).[52]

Our overview of the mountain in the Sinai Complex has illustrated its prominence in the narrative, and its symbolic role in creating a world in which the characters interrelate. Three aspects concerning the nature of a symbol must be briefly under-

[49] Levenson, *Sinai and Zion*, 18. See also T. L. Donaldson, *Jesus on the Mountain*, JSNTSup 8 (Sheffield: JSOT Press, 1985) 33.
[50] On the important relationship of temples and cosmic mountains see, for example, Eliade, *Sacred and Profane*, 39-40; R. E. Clements, *God and Temple* (Philadelphia: Fortress Press, 1965) 1-16; Clifford, *Cosmic Mountain*, 20-25; and Sh. Talmon, "har," *TDOT III*, ed. G. J. Botterweck and H. Ringgren (Grand Rapids: Eerdmans, 1978) 427-47.
[51] For discussion on the important role of the mountain in structuring the narrative and providing the context for interrelating the characters see R. Rivard, "Pour une relecture d'Ex 19 et 20. Analysee Sémiotique d'Ex 19, 1-8," *ScEs* 33 (1981) 339. J. Lotman (*The Structure of the Artistic Text*, Michigan Slavic Contributions 7 [Ann Arbor, University of Michigan Press, 1977] 217-18) provides further insight into the structuring role of the mountain and its symbolic significance within the narrative when he writes that "spatial relations [within narrative] turn out to be one of the basic means for comprehending reality," with the result that the "structure of the space of a text becomes a model of the structure of the space of the universe."
[52] Compare this structure to R. Knierim, "The Composition of the Pentateuch," SBLASP 24 (1985) 399-406.

scored, for these particular features of symbol will aid us in seeing the changing character of the mountain setting within the tradition-historical development of the Sinai Complex, and provide insight into the multiple theologies of divine presence that are embedded in the canonical text.

First, symbols are translucent and not transparent.[53] What this means is that symbols demand attention in their own right. In the case of the Sinai Complex this requires that the reader interpret the mountain setting geographically as an itinerary stop in Israel's wilderness travels. However, if the mountain were functioning only geographically it would not be a symbol, it would simply be an object. What makes the mountain setting a symbol in the Sinai Complex is that it also refers to another object, something that is absent (the signified).[54] I will argue that within the Sinai Complex the mountain is a signifier of divine cultic presence.

Second, a study of symbol requires a description of the relationship between the signifier and the thing signified,[55] and this relationship can be of two types: it can be a relationship of resemblance (metaphor) or a relationship of contiguity (metonymy).[56] We will have occasion to explore these two types of relationships in more detail when we describe the changing relationship between the mountain and God in the tradition-historical development of the Sinai Complex. In particular I will argue that in the earliest level of tradition (the Mountain of God tradition), the reader is encouraged to identify the mountain and God, as in a metaphorical relationship of resemblance. We will see however that metaphor gives way to a metonymic relationship of contiguity in the subsequent deuteronomistic and priestly redactions. The result of this change in the relationship between the mountain and God (and thus between the signifier

---

[53] For a discussion of symbol see O. Ducrot and T. Todorov, *Encyclopedic Dictionary of the Sciences of Language* (Baltimore: Johns Hopkins University Press, 1979) 99-105; N. Friedmaan, "Symbol," *Princeton Encyclopedia of Poetry and Poetics*, ed. A. Preminger (Princeton: Princeton University Press, 1974) 833-36; R. Wellek and A. Warren, *Theory of Literature* (New York: Harcourt Brace Jovanovich, 1977) 186-211. For a more extended discussion see T. Todorov, *Theories of Symbol* (Ithaca: Cornell University Press, 1982).

[54] Ducrot and Todorov, *Encyclopedic Dictionary*, 100.

[55] Ducrot and Todorov, *Encyclopedic Dictionary*, 100.

[56] See Wellek and Warren (*Theory of Literature*, 188) who write of religious symbols that they "are based on some intrinsic relation between 'sign' and thing 'signified', metonymic or metaphoric. . . ." See also Ducrot and Todorov, (*Encyclopedic Dictionary*, 102) who use the terms "icon" and "index" to contrast the relations of resemblance (metaphor) and contiguity (metonymy).

and the thing signified) is that instead of representing an identification with God, the mountain comes to symbolize a point of contact between God in heaven and the worshipping community on earth.

Third, symbols only exist for a well defined group of users; they are institutional and sociological.[57] The institutional aspect of symbols will force this study beyond being simply an intrinsic investigation into the narrative world of the Sinai Complex, for it requires that we at least raise the sociological questions concerning what kinds of groups and changing cultic *Sitzen im Leben* are being profiled in the continual reshaping of the mountain setting. Levenson's suggestion that the mountain is an archetype, which allowed for new theological discourse and social change without "rupturing the sense of tradition and continuity of historic identity" is a hypothesis that we must explore in our interpretation of the social implications of the cosmic mountain symbolism.[58]

In summary, my aim in this monograph is to explore the imagery of theophany on the mountain in Exodus 19-24 from two perspectives. First, I intend to probe this imagery tradition-historically. I hope to demonstrate that the development of the Sinai Complex is not source-critical in nature, but primarily a process of creative redaction. And second I want to interpret the imagery of theophany theologically. A study of symbol will provide an avenue for describing the distinct theologies of divine cultic presence that are reflected in the Sinai Complex. These two perspectives complement each other and thus they can be undertaken in tandem in Chapters 2-4, so that a theological interpretation will accompany the redaction-critical study of the Sinai Complex. In these chapters we will see that a range of theologies concerning divine cultic presence are embedded in the Sinai Complex and that these theologies are also reflected in the distinct deuteronomistic and priestly legislations which are presently linked to the revelation on the mountain in Exodus 19-24. Such diversity, however, will introduce another dimension to our study in Chapters 5-6, for it requires that we ask an additional canonical question, namely whether the diverse theologies of divine cultic presence in the Sinai Complex are able to provide any kind of unity to the people of God. This question

---

[57] Ducrot and Todorov, *Encyclopedic Dictionary*, 100. For more extended bibliography concerning the sociological and anthropological aspects to the study of symbol see B. C. Ollenburger, *Zion, the City of the Great King: A Theological Symbol of the Jerusalem Cult*, JSOTSup 41 (Sheffield: JSOT Press, 1987) 19-22.
[58] Levenson, *Sinai and Zion*, 18.

arises from the structure of the canonical Pentateuch itself, which encourages the reader to interpret the Sinai Complex as the one revelation of God on the mountain. The structure of this monograph, with its movement from tradition history to canon, reflects the overall goal of this study to offer a comprehensive interpretation of the Sinai Complex both in its tradition-historical development and in its present canonical form.

Chapter 2

THE MOUNTAIN OF GOD TRADITION
IN EXODUS 19-24

Although this study of Exodus 19-24 is redaction-critical, my focus in this chapter will be tradition-historical. The central question that gives rise to this chapter is: What is the basic contour of the pre-deuteronomistic Sinai Complex that is providing the structure for subsequent editing? This question will be answered in two ways. In the first section the literary shape of the earliest Mountain of God tradition in Exodus 19-24 will be outlined In the second section the theology of divine cultic presence within this earliest tradition will be described.

Two methodological concerns must also be noted at the outset. First, in raising the question of the earliest literary shape of Exodus 19-24 Rendtorff's proposal will be followed, namely that distinct complexes of the Pentateuch be probed separately when tracing their tradition history.[1] Second, Rendtorff's proposal provides a means for reevaluating Perlitt's assessment of pre-deuteronomistic tradition in the Sinai Complex as consisting of sources. My aim is to demonstrate that the pre-deuteronomistic form of Exodus 19-24 does not consist of distinct sources, but is made up of a single tradition.

I
AN OUTLINE OF THE MOUNTAIN
OF GOD TRADITION

The Mountain of God tradition separates into three parts: an introduction, establishing the setting of the cosmic mountain (Exod 19:2b-3a); an account of purification, culminating in a theophany on the mountain (Exod 19:10ab-11a, 12aa, 13b-15a, 16ab-17); and, finally, a concluding sacrificial ritual at the base of the mountain (Exod 24:4ab-5).

[1] Rendtorff, "The 'Yahwist'," 2-9; *Problem des Pentateuch*, 1-28.

A. The Introduction (Exod 19:2b-3a)

The opening itinerary notice in Exod 19:1-3a contains a number of striking repetitions concerning the time of Israel's arrival (Exod 19:1), their approach (*bw'*, Exod 19:1b, 2a), and finally their encampment (*ḥwn*, Exod 19:2ab, b) at the mountain. The function of these repetitions in the present form of the text must give way at this point to tradition-historical questions.[2] Noth underscored the problematic character of Exod 19:1-3a from a tradition-historical point of view and he concluded that the repetition in Exod 19:2b concerning Israel's encampment before the mountain "indicates a fragment from the introductory phrases of one of the older sources which has in other respects fallen out of favor in P."[3] This fragment would continue through Exod 19:3a, where Moses is described as ascending to God. More recently Booij has come to much the same conclusion concerning Exod 19:2b-3a from a somewhat different direction by examining the reference to the unnamed mountain in Exod 19:2b. He writes, "In this introduction *hāhār* evokes a memory of the mountain of God in 18,5 and of Horeb in 17,6."[4] Whatever the connections between Exod 19:2b and past references to the mountain of God in the Book of Exodus may be, the notice of Israel's encampment before the mountain raises the question of whether Exod 19:2b might, indeed, be an introduction to a Mountain of God tradition that continues through Exod 19:3a, where Moses is described as ascending to God. The text reads:

> *wayyiḥan-šām yiśrā'ēl neged hāhār*
> *ûmōšeh 'ālâ 'el-hā'ělōhîm*
> And Israel camped there before the mountain.
> But Moses ascended to God.

Further support for such a conclusion concerning the antiquity of Exod 19:2b-3a arises from the possibility that the reference to God as *hā'ělōhîm* in Exod 19:3a may be a proper name rather than an appellative, and, thus, contrast with the divine name Yahweh in Exod 19:3b, which introduces a divine speech in Exod 19:3b-6.[5] Moreover, the reference to the people in

---

[2] For discussion of the function of these repetitions as spatial form devices in the present form of the text see Chapter 4.

[3] Noth, *Exodus*, 157.

[4] Th. Booij, "Mountain and Theophany in the Sinai Narrative," *Bib* 65 (1984) 17.

[5] O. Eissfeldt, *Die Komposition der Sinai-Erzählung Exodus 19-34*, Sitzungsberichte der Sächsischen Akademie der Wissenschaften zu Leipzig 113/1 (Berlin:

Exod 19:3b as the *bêt ya'ăqōb* and *bĕnê yiśrā'ēl* creates yet an additional contrast to Exod 19:2b-3a, where they are described simply as *yiśrā'ēl*.[6] Thus, Exod 19:2b-3a can be isolated from the itinerary notice that precedes it in Exod 19:1-2a[7] and from the divine discourse that follows it in Exod 19:3b-6.[8] A final criterion for isolating Exod 19:2b-3a as a unit of older tradition is its

Akademie-Verlag, 1966) 14; W. Rudolph, *Der 'Elohist' von Exodus bis Joshua*, BZAW 68 (Berlin: De Gruyter, 1938) 42; Noth, *Exodus*, 153.

[6] Wellhausen, *Composition*, 96; E. Zenger, *Die Sinaitheophanie: Untersuchungen zum jahwistischen und elohistischen Geschichtswerk*, Forschung zur Bibel 3 (Würzburg: Echter-Verlag, 1971) 57. The parallel construction of *bêt ya'ăqōb/bĕnê yiśrā'ēl* in Exod 19:3b is a *hapax legomenon* in this form and it has caught the attention of a number of scholars. Perlitt (*Bundestheologie*, 170) has argued that the parallel form Jacob/Israel only occurs from the sixth century on. H. Cazelles ("Royaume des prêtres et nation consacrée.' Exode [19,6]," *Humanisme et foi chrétienne: Mélanges scientifiques du Centenaire de l'Institut Catholique de Paris* [Paris: Beauchesne, 1975] 542) and again in "Alliance du Sinai, alliance de l'Horeb et renouvellement de l'Alliance," (*Beiträge zur altestamentlichen Theologie* [Fs. W. Zimmerli] ed., R. Donner, R. Hanhart, R. Smend, [Göttingen: Vandenhoeck und Ruprecht, 1977] 78-79) argues for a semantic distinction between *bêt ya'ăqōb/bĕnê yiśrā'ēl*, with the latter term entering the text as a post-deuteronomistic redaction by the priestly school. Whether a semantic distinction lies behind the parallel usage is intriguing, but difficult to confirm. However, the research on *bêt ya'ăqōb/bĕnê yiśrā'ēl* strengthens the conclusion that there is a tradition-historical distinction between Exod 19:2b-3a and Exod 19:3bff.

[7] Although Exod 19:1-2a is most frequently assigned to priestly tradition, Booij ("Mountain and Theophany," 17), may very well be correct when he suggests that priestly redactors might have taken up elements of an already existing tradition in v. 2—particularly the notice of Israel's arrival in the wilderness of Sinai in Exod 19:2ab (*wayyābō'û midbar sînay*). In this case, the Mountain of God tradition would be located in the wilderness of Sinai. The location of a Mountain of God in the wilderness of Sinai would correspond well with the early "March in the South" theophany tradition, where Sinai is not a cosmic mountain, but a southern region from which God would appear (Judg 5:5, Ps 68:9, 18, Deut 33:2). A conclusion concerning Exod 19:2ab as a unit of older tradition would receive support if the summary of Israel's wilderness travels in Number 33 is judged to be an older independent document, since the wilderness of Sinai is also mentioned in Num 33:15-16. For arguments in favor of the antiquity of Numbers 33 see F. M. Cross, *Canaanite Myth and Hebrew Epic*, 308-9.

[8] For further discussion of the divine speech in Exod 19:3b-6 see J. Muilenburg, "The Form and Structure of the Covenantal Formulations," *VT* 9 (1959) 351-57; Noth, *Exodus*, 155-56; Perlitt, *Bundestheologie*, 168; Childs, *Exodus*, 360-61; R. Mosis, "Ex 19,5b.6a: Syntaktischer Aufbau und lexikalische Semantik," *BZ* 22 (1978) 5, n.15.
A. H. McNeile (*The Book of Exodus* [London: Methuen, 1908] 110); S. R. Driver (*The Book of Exodus* [Cambridge: University Press, 1929] 168); and W. Beyerlin (*Origins and History of the Oldest Sinaitic Tradition* [Oxford: Basil Blackwell, 1965] 6) add yet another criterion for separating Exod 19:2b-3a from Exod 19:3b by noting the apparent contradiction in the location of Moses, where he is clearly located on the mountain in Exod 19:3a, but simply addressed by Yahweh from the mountain in Exod 19:3b. The lack of emphasis in clearly locating Moses on the

apparent continuation in Exod 19:10ab, where Moses is given a
series of commands that are meant to prepare the people for
theophany.[9] Evidence for this final criterion requires an examination of the narrative logic and repetitive motifs in Exod 19:2b-
3a, 10ab-11a, 12aa, 13b-15a.

B.   Preparation, Purification and Theophany (Exod 19:10ab-
     11a, 12aa, 13b-15a, 16ab-17)

A number of literary features interrelate Exod 19:2b-3a with
Exod 10ab-11a, 12aa, 13b-15a. First, as Rudolf noted, narrative
logic creates a connection between Exod 19:2b-3a and Exod
19:14 in describing the ascent and descent of Moses.[10] We
might add that the setting of an unnamed cosmic mountain
(hāhār) creates yet an additional link between these passages.
Thus, when Exod 19:2b-3a and Exod 19:14 are interrelated, they
describe Israel's encampment before the mountain (hāhār), the
ascent ('lh) by Moses to God, and his subsequent descent (yrd)
from the mountain (min-hāhār) to the people. Furthermore,
the ritual actions that Moses executes at the base of the mountain in Exod 19:14-15a link this section of narrative with the preceding account in Exod 19:10ab-11a, where Moses received the
commands from God on the mountain.[11] An examination of repetitive motifs in Exod 19:10ab-11a and in Exod 19:14-15a results in the following sequence of commands and their

mountain with God in Exod 19:3b is further reinforced in Exod 19:7a, where Moses
is described as merely approaching (wayyābō') the people.
[9] Zenger, Sinaitheophanie, 57.
[10] Rudolph, Der 'Elohist', 42-44.
[11] Several literary features provide criteria for separating Exod 19:10ab-11a from
its immediate context. First, the introductory heading in Exod 19:10aa to the subsequent commands concerning purification presents a problem. The direct speech
in Exod 19:10ab-11a certainly requires an introductory heading, yet, whether Exod
19:10aa is the original heading to this unit is not clear. One problem is the use of
the divine name Yahweh. However, a more serious problem arises with the repetition of the introductory heading in Exod 19:9aa and in Exod 19:10aa (wayyō'mer
yhwh 'el-mōšeh). This repetition appears to be a "resumptive repetition"—that is,
a repetition which functions to bracket an insertion, thus allowing for the original
narrative to resume. In this case, Exod 19:10aa would not be the original heading
to the subsequent divine commands. For discussion of "resumptive repetition" see
C. Kuhl, "Die 'Wiederaufnahme'—ein literarkritisches Prinzip?" ZAW 64 (1952) 1-
11. Second, Noth (Exodus, 158) summarizes the problem that gives rise to the separation between Exod 19:11a and 11b when he writes that "the occurrence of
Yahweh in the third person [v. 11b] in the middle of a speech of Yahweh [vv. 10ab-
11]...is striking." In view of this literary problem he raises the question of whether
Exod 19:11b might be an explanatory gloss. See also Zenger, Sinaitheophanie, 59-
60.

fulfillment. There are four divine commands in Exod 19:10ab-
11a: Moses must (1) go to the people (*'el-hā'ām*); (2) sanctify
(*qdš*) them for two days (*hayyôm ûmāḥār*);[12] (3) instruct the
people to wash (*kbs*) their clothes (*śmlt*); and (4) command the
people to be ready (*wĕhāyû nĕkōnîm*). Exod 19:14-15a then follows as a series of repetitions, which fulfill the commands given
in Exod 19:10ab-11a: Moses is described as (1') descending from
the mountain to the people (*'el-hā'ām*); (2') sanctifying (*qdš*) the
people; who are then described (3') as washing (*kbs*) their
clothes (*śmlt*); which is followed (4') by Moses commanding
them to "Be ready. . ." (*hĕyû nĕkōnîm*).

Preparation for theophany in the Mountain of God tradition
includes two additional divine commands besides the purification rituals that were already noted in Exod 19:10ab-11a. The
first additional command underscores the sacredness of the
mountain in Exod 19:12aa, when Moses is instructed to set
boundaries for the people: "and you will set boundaries for the
people round about."[13] The second concerns specific instructions in Exod 19:13b about what must be done in response to the
appearance of God on the mountain: "and when the trumpet
sounds (*bimśōk hayyōbēl*) they (*hēmmâ*) will ascend/sacrifice
on the mountain."[14]

An interpretation of this second command in Exod 19:13b is
problematic for two reasons: Who is being commanded to act
with the reference to (*hēmmâ*)? And what are "they" being
commanded to do? The issue is further complicated because
two interpretations are possible for each of these questions.
With regard to the question of who is being addressed, *hēmmâ*
could be a general reference to Israel—that is all the people.
However, Noth has underscored a problem with the third person emphatic *hēmmâ*, and he concluded that it may very well
designate a definite group of people, who are no longer men-

[12] The mention of a third day in the sequence of preparation/theophany in Exod
19:11b, 15ab, 16aa is a later addition to the text. For detailed discussion see Chapter 4. On the expected two-day sequence with the use of *māḥār* see S. J. De Vries,
"The Time Word *māḥār* as a Key to Tradition Development," *ZAW* 78 (1975) 65-
79.

[13] Although the command to create boundaries in Exod 19:12aa continues in the
present form of the text through Exod 19:13a, Exod 19:12ab-13a can be distinguished from Exod 19:12aa, for it actually presents an extended speech of Yahweh
within a speech of Yahweh (Exod 19:10ab-11a, 12aa [12ab-13a], 13b). See also
Zenger, *Sinaitheophanie*, 60; and R. Althann, "A Note on Exodus 19,12ab-13," *Bib*
57 (1976) 242-46.

[14] Noth, *Exodus*, 158.

tioned in the text.[15] Furthermore, distinct interpretations of
what is being required in the command *ya'ălû bāhār* are also
possible. Is this a command to ascend (*ya'ălû* qal) the cosmic
mountain at the close of theophany, or is it a command to make
offerings (*ya'ălû* hiphil) by the cosmic mountain at the close of
the theophany?[16]

A firm conclusion concerning the two possible interpretations cited above is not possible, since, as we shall see, both actions take place in this Mountain of God tradition. Israel does
approach the mountain in Exod 19:17 and a specific group ("the
young men of Israel" *na'ărê bĕnê yiśrā'ēl*) also sacrifices at the
base of the mountain in Exod 24:4ab-5. However, closer examination favors the latter interpretation, since Israel does not actually ascend the mountain in Exod 19:17. Rather, they are simply
led out by Moses to a location at the base of the mountain
(*bĕtahtît hāhār*). In contrast to this, the command to sacrifice is
specifically carried out by a special group in Exod 24:4ab-5,
when we are told that the "young men of Israel" offered sacrifices (*ya'ălû 'ōlōt*).

The preparation for theophany in the Mountain of God tradition can be summarized in the following manner. After Israel's
arrival at the unnamed cosmic mountain is established and
Moses' ascent to God is noted, three commands are given to
Moses: first, he is instructed to purify the people for two days
(Exod 19:10ab-11a); second, the sacred quality of the mountain
is underscored with the command to create proper boundaries
(Exod 19:12aa); and, third, sacrifices are commanded by a particular group at the sound of the trumpet (Exod 19:13b).

The three-part command to Moses at the summit of the
mountain determines the sequence of events at the base of the
mountain, which provides an outline for the subsequent events
within the Mountain of God tradition. As we have noted, the
first action of Moses after his descent is the purification of the
people in Exod 19:14-15a, which is presented as a series of repetitions from Exod 19:10ab-11a. Purification of the people provides the context for the second event at the base of the

---

[15] Noth, (*Exodus*, 158) interprets Exod 19:13b as a divine command, in which a
particular group is instructed to ascend the mountain. He suggests a connection to
Exod 24:1—2, 9-11. Childs (*Exodus*, 343) also acknowledges the problems of Exod
19:13b and suggests the possibility of an interpretative expansion. For review of
past interpretations see Althann ("A Note on Exodus 19,12ab-13," 242-46) who offers yet another solution by interpreting *hēmmâ* as being the conditional particle
"if" on the basis of Ugaritic *hm*.

[16] Koehler-Baumgartner, 705-6.

mountain, namely the appearance of God on the unnamed cosmic mountain in Exod 19:16ab-17. This theophany accentuates the sacredness of the mountain and the need for boundaries between God and the people emphasized in Exod 19:12aa. Finally, the Mountain of God tradition concludes with a sacrificial ritual in Exod 24:4ab-5, which fulfills the command in Exod 19:13b to sacrifice. This pattern between divine commands at the summit of the mountain and their fulfillment at the base of the mountain illustrates how the narrative is structured vertically. Although the structure and sequence of the entire Mountain of God tradition is now before us, the account of theophany still requires a closer tradition-historical analysis.

Scholars have long since agreed that there are contrasting motifs in the description of theophany in Exod 19:16-19. The primary contrast is between storm imagery and volcanic imagery. The storm imagery is focused primarily in Exod 19:16-17, while v 19 or at least part of it is considered to reflect the same motifs. The volcanic imagery is rooted primarily in Exod 19:18, but it can also include v 20. Noth provides a representative example and a point of departure for our present study. He concludes that the volcanic imagery reflects the yahwistic account of theophany in Exod 19:16aa, 18, 20; while the storm imagery reflects the elohistic account of theophany in Exod 19:16ab-17, 19.[17] The volcanic imagery of theophany can be set aside at this point in our investigation of the Mountain of God tradition; we will return to it later within the context of priestly tradition. Our present focus concerns the storm imagery of theophany in Exod 19:16ab-17, 19, for it is here that we are able to trace the outline of the Mountain of God tradition.

In his discussion of the storm theophany in Exod 19:16ab-17, 19, Noth is certainly correct in underscoring the problem of the double introduction to this account in Exod 19:16. The first temporal reference to the third day in Exod 19:16aa (*wayhî*

---

[17] Noth, *Exodus*, 158-59. See also, for example, Beyerlin (*Oldest Sinaitic Traditions*, 8-9) who assigns Exod 19:16ab-17, 19 to an elohistic source and Exod 19:16aa, 18 to the yahwistic source. J. Jeremias (*Theophanie: Die Geschichte einer alttestamentlichen Gattung* WMANT 10 [Neukirchen-Vluyn: Neukirchener, 1965] 103) assigns Exod 19:16-17, 19 to the elohistic source and Exod 19:18 (as well as Exod 34:5-6a) to the yahwistic source. More recently, Zenger (*Sinaitheophanie*, 61) has refined this analysis to conclude that Exod 19:16, 17, 18bb, 19a represents the elohistic source; Exod 19:18aa, ba, 20a the yahwistic source; Exod 19:18ab the combination of the two sources (JE); and Exod 19:19b a deuteronomistic redaction (?). However, compare Zenger's subsequent study (*Israel am Sinai: Analysen und Interpretationen zu Exodus 17-34*, 2nd ed. [Altenberge: Akademische Bibliothek, 1984] 132) where all of Exod 19:19 is assigned to the elohistic source.

bayyôm haššĕlîšî) can be separated from the second temporal
reference to the morning (*bihyōt habbōqer*) not only on the basis of syntax, but, in addition, the three-day chronology conflicts
with the earlier two-day chronology that was mentioned in
Exod 19:10b.[18] Furthermore, Noth is also correct in underscoring the basic unity in imagery of Exod 19:16ab-17, once the initial chronological notice is separated. The description of
theophany in Exod 19:16ab-17 separates into three parts, which
are closely related syntactically and in the progression of events.
The unit begins with a description of theophany in Exod
19:16ab (A), followed by the people's reaction of fear in Exod
19:16b (B), and ending with a description of Moses leading the
people from the camp to the base of the mountain in Exod 19:17
(C):

> (A) Exod 19:16ab
> *bihyōt habbōqer*
> *wayhî qōlōt ûbĕrāqîm*
> *wĕ'ānān kābēd 'al-hāhār*
> *wĕqōl šōpār ḥāzāq mĕ'ōd*
> When it was early morning,
>   there were claps of thunder and bolts of lightning
> and a thick cloud upon the mountain
> and a very loud sound of a trumpet
> (B) Exod 19:16b
> *wayyeḥĕrad kŏl-hā'ām 'ăšer bammaḥăneh*
> And all the people who were in the
> camp trembled
> (C) Exod 19:17
> *wayyōṣē' mōšeh 'et-hā'ām*
> *liqra't hā'ĕlōhîm min-hammaḥăneh*
> *wayyityaṣṣĕbû betaḥtît hāhār*
> And Moses brought out the people
> from the camp to meet God.
> And they were stationed at the base
> of the mountain.

The account of theophany, however, does not continue into
Exod 19:19 as Noth proposes. The specific imagery of Moses
speaking and of Yahweh answering him verbally is not intrinsic
to the imagery of the thunderstorm. Consider the imagery in
Exod 19:16ab-17. The appearance of God in Exod 19:16ab-17

[18] Noth, *Exodus*, 159. The transformation of the preparation and theophany from a
two day to a three day sequence is evident not only in Exod 19:16aa, but also in
Exod 19:11b, 15ab.

begins with thunder (*qōlōt*), hence the link to Exod 19:19 where God answers, *běqôl* (with a voice). Although the singular *qôl* (voice, noise, thunder) often refers specifically to the voice of God (as Exod 19:19 demonstrates), the plural *qōlōt* almost always occurs in the context of a storm, either in conjunction with hail (*brd*), rain (*mṭr*), or lightning (*brq, lpd*), and does not refer to a more specific divine verbal communication.[19] Thus, we must conclude that the plural use of *qōlōt* in Exod 19:16ab in the same context as lightning and a heavy storm cloud ('*ānān kābēd*) simply underscores the imagery of the thunder storm and does not suggest a more specific communication from God;[20] while the singular *běqôl* in Exod 19:19 must be evaluated as an extension of the storm imagery, which points to subsequent theological reflection concerning the quality and character of divine presence as speech. Exod 19:19 will be examined in Chapter 3 within our examination of deuteronomistic tradition.

The additional use of *qôl* in reference to the "very loud sound of the trumpet" (*qōl šōpār*) in the closing line of Exod 19:16ab also does not suggest a more specific divine communication beyond the thunderstorm itself. Rather, the *qōl šōpār* is best interpreted in two ways within the Mountain of God tradition. First, it serves to emphasize the majesty of theophany. Similarly uses of the *qōl šōpār* are evident in the account of David's returning the ark to Jerusalem[21] or again in a Psalm of Zion like Ps 47:6.[22] The second function of the *qōl šōpār* is that the trumpet blast signals the final transition in the Mountain of God tradition from theophany (Exod 19:16ab-17) to sacrifice (Exod 24:4ab-5), just as Moses was originally instructed in Exod 19:13b.[23]

---

[19] The plural *qlt* occurs twelve times. It is used five times in Exodus 9 (Exod 9:23, 28, 29, 33, 34) in conjunction with hail stones (*brd*) to describe the plague. The final occurrence in Exod 9:34 includes a description of thunder (*qlt*), hail (*brd*), and rain (*mṭr*). 1 Sam 12:17, 18 refers twice to thunder (*qlt*) in combination with rain (*mṭr*). Job 28:26 and 38:25 associate thunder (*qlt*) with the storm cloud (*ḥzz*). Exod 20:18 combines thunder (*qlt*) with lightning as in Exod 19:16, but only *lpdm* is used to describe the lightning. Finally, in Ps 93:4 thunder is used alone in the context of the mythological "great waters" (*mym rbym*). For discussion of the singular *ql* as meaning both thunder and voice see Jeremias, *Theophanie*, 108.

[20] For further discussion see Jeremiah, *Theophanie* 108.

[21] 2 Sam 6:15 reads, "So David and all the house of Israel brought up the ark of Yahweh with shouting and with the sound of the trumpet" (*běqôl šōpār*).

[22] Ps 47:6 reads, "God has gone up with a shout; Yahweh with the sound of the trumpet" (*běqôl šōpār*).

[23] See Josh 6:5 where the *yōbēl* is also associated with the *šōpār*, as in Exod 19:13b, 16ab-17.

C. The Sacrificial Ritual (Exod 24:4ab-5)

Steuernagel long ago argued for the antiquity of the sacrificial ritual in Exod 24:4ab-5 because of the prominent role of the "young men of Israel" instead of Moses, who is clearly the central figure in the larger context.[24] Zenger has built on the conclusion of Steuernagel and others[25] by noting that the sacrificial ritual can also be distinguished from its surrounding context both in terms of its setting and its introductory temporal reference: the sacrificial ceremony begins on a new day (*wayyaśkēm babbōqer*) and it depicts the construction of an altar at the base of an unnamed mountain (*taḥat hāhār*).[26] Thus, past scholars have argued on the basis of temporal reference, setting, and primary characters that Exod 24:4ab-5 represents a unit of older tradition that can be distinguished from its present narrative context.

Tradition-historical analysis of Exod 24:4ab-5 is not yet complete at this point, since the three features of this unit of tradition, which distinguished the sacrificial ritual from its present narrative context, also create specific links to different sections of the Mountain of God tradition that have been described thus far. The opening temporal reference as *bōqer*, which underscores that the sacrificial ritual commenced on a new day, is a repetition of Exod 19:16ab, where *bōqer* also marked the inauguration of theophany. The construction of the altar at the base of the unnamed mountain (*taḥat hāhār*) also corresponds with the closing setting of theophany, where Israel was also located at the base of the mountain (*betaḥtît hāhār*). And finally, the description of the "young men of Israel" as offering sacrifices (*ya'ălû 'ōlōt*) completes the narrative logic of the Mountain of God tradition by fulfilling the third command in Exod 19:13b to sacrifice (*ya'ălû*).

D. Conclusion

We have reached a point where we can now address the central question of this section by describing the basic contour and structure of the pre-deuteronomistic Sinai Complex. Already in the earliest level of this tradition the mountain setting is playing

[24] C. Steuernagel, "Der jehovistische Bericht über den Bundesschluss am Sinai," *TSK* 72 (1899) 319-50, esp. 348-49.

[25] See also Beyerlin, *Oldest Sinaitic Traditions*, 39; Driver, *Exodus*, 253; Perlitt, *Bundestheologie*, 196-97; E. W. Nicholson, "The Covenant Ritual in Exodus XXIV 3-8," *VT* 32 (1982) 74-86.

[26] Zenger, *Sinaitheophanie*, 74.

a primary role in the very structure of the narrative. We have seen that once Israel's arrival at the unnamed mountain is established the subsequent narrative is structured in a vertical hierarchy. Characters are clearly separated in the context of the mountain with God at the summit and Israel at the base, while Moses is presented as moving vertically between the two parties. Furthermore, the vertical structure of the narrative is actually symmetrical. The three divine commands given to Moses on the mountain are the instructions for purification (Exod 19:10ab-11a), the need to maintain distance between the sacred mountain and the people (Exod 19:12aa), and the call for sacrifices (Exod 19:13b). These commands provide the structure for actions at the base of the mountain, where Moses purifies the people for theophany (Exod 19:14-15a), where the theophany itself underscores the sacred quality of the mountain (Exod 19:16ab-17), and, finally, where "the young men of Israel" sacrifice (Exod 24:4ab-5). The result of this vertical structure is that the liturgical events that take place at the base of the cosmic mountain acquire the authority of being anchored in divine commands at the summit of the mountain.

Several additional conclusions follow from our study thus far. First, the preceding analysis suggests that the tradition-historical roots of Exodus 19-24 are not made up of distinct sources, but consist of a single account of Israel at the Mountain of God. Second, although this study has been limited to the Sinai Complex, it raises the question of whether the Mountain of God tradition might not be one episode in a larger epic. Third, I have described this earliest tradition within the Sinai Complex as the Mountain of God tradition because of the consistent absence of a more specific name for the cosmic mountain; at this level of tradition the mountain has not yet acquired its canonical designation as Mount Sinai. The character and quality of divine presence that is reflected in this account now requires a more detailed interpretation. I hope to demonstrate in the following section that the imagery of divine presence in the Mountain of God tradition reflects a pre-exilic theology of Zion.

II
MOUNT ZION IN THE MOUNTAIN OF GOD TRADITION

The close association between temples and cosmic mountain imagery in Israel, as well as in the ancient Near East in general, suggests that the description of God on the mountain represents

a cultic theology of divine presence.[27] Thus, the mountain setting is functioning symbolically in the narrative as a signifier of
something that is absent—the signified—which in this case is the
cultic presence of God. My aim in this section is to describe the
character or quality of the divine cultic presence in the Mountain of God tradition by examining the *relationship* that is established between the mountain and God. I hope to demonstrate
two things in this section: first, that the relationship between
the mountain and God is best described as resemblance (metaphor) in contrast to contiguity (metonymy); and, second, that
the metaphorical character of the mountain in the Mountain of
God tradition reflects Zion-Sabaoth theology.

A. The Mountain and Metaphor

When we examine the Mountain of God tradition with an
aim to interpret a theology of divine presence in the temple,
perhaps the most striking image is the presentation of God as
dwelling on the cosmic mountain.[28] Note, for example, how the
divine presence on the mountain is simply presupposed at the
outset of the account (Exod 19:2b-3a), how the identification of
God with the mountain is reinforced in the subsequent description of theophany, where again there is no depiction of a divine
approach to the mountain (Exod 19:16ab-17), and how this identification is carried through in the closing account of sacrifice,
when the mention of the mountain once again presupposes the
presence of God (Exod 24:4ab-5). Two conclusions concerning
the character and quality of divine presence in the Mountain of
God tradition come into focus from this brief overview.

The first conclusion concerns the symbolic character of the
mountain within the Mountain of God tradition. The imagery of
God as dwelling on the mountain encourages an *identification*
between God and the mountain, or perhaps better a relationship of *resemblance*.[29] Thus the mountain is best characterized
as being a metaphor for the divine cultic presence in the Moun-

---

[27] Talmon (*"har"*, 444) summarizes well the close relationship between temples
and cosmic mountain imagery when he writes that "mountains appear as the preferred sites for theophanies. . .and as places where God establishes his covenant
with individuals. . .as well as with his people. . . . In consequence of this development 'sanctuary' and 'mountain' become conceptually identical." See also Clifford,
Cosmic Mountain, 1-33 *et passim*.

[28] See, for example, Beyerlin, *Oldest Sinaitic Traditions*, 6-11.

[29] For discussion of resemblance see Ducrot and Todorov, *Encyclopedic Dictionary*, 102; and P. Ricoeur (*The Rule of Metaphor: Multidisciplinary Studies of the
Creation of Meaning in Language*, University of Toronto Romance Series 37 [To-
ronto: University of Toronto Press, 1977] 173-215).

tain of God tradition, because whenever we read it "we have two thoughts of different things active together and supported by a single word or phrase, whose meaning is a resultant of their interaction."[30] In the Mountain of God tradition the two thoughts concern the mountain as a signifier and the presence of God dwelling upon it as the signified. In fact, the "Introduction" of the Mountain of God tradition in Exod 19:2a-3b creates an inseparable relationship of resemblance by making the mountain (hāhār) and God (hā'ĕlōhîm) a word pair:[31]

> wayyiḥan-šām yiśrā'ēl neged hāhār
> ûmōšeh 'ālâ 'el-hā'ĕlōhîm
> And Israel camped there before the mountain.
> But Moses ascended to God
> (19:2b-31)

This metaphorical identification between God and the mountain need not necessarily be reductionistic. We must recall that the very nature of the symbol is rooted in the fact that there is a radical difference between the signifier and the signified, which is underscored in the notion of absence that is associated with the signified.[32] This insight is also reinforced when we note that the nature of metaphor is to obscure even while it makes an identification.[33] This quality is reflected in the narrative. Note, for example, how the identification of God with the mountain introduces a sacred quality to the setting which requires that proper boundaries be maintained. Even with these qualifications, the metaphorical function of the mountain blurs a

---

[30] I. A. Richards, *The Philosophy of Rhetoric* (Oxford: Oxford University Press, 1936) 94. For additional literature on metaphor in general and evaluations of Richard's "interanimation" theory of metaphor in particular see Ricoeur, *The Rule of Metaphor*, 76-83; and J. M. Soskice, *Metaphor and Religious Language* (Oxford: Clarendon Press, 1985) 43-53.

[31] The LXX illustrates the close association between God and the mountain that is being encouraged in the Mountain of God tradition by actually repeating the mountain in Exod 19:3a: *kai mousēs anebē eis to oros tou theou*, "And Moses ascended the mountain of God."

[32] See Ducrot and Todorov, *Encyclopedic Dictionary*, 99-103. For further discussion of metaphor as a literary figure of similarity or identity see Wellek and Warren, *Theory of Literature*, 186-211.

[33] For discussion of metaphor as obscuring that which it reveals see S. J. Brown (*The World of Imagery: Metaphor and Kindred Imagery* [New York: Russel & Russel, 1966] 48-59). On pp. 49-50 Brown summarizes well this quality of metaphor: "This obscurity arises principally from the fact that in metaphor two notions are, as it were, superimposed, an adventitious and imported image coming vividly before our mental vision, while the notion which is the real subject of the discourse momentarily fades into the background, and is seen only through the image."

clear separation between God in heaven and the people on earth, and promotes instead a more unified conception of the sacred and the profane around the symbol of the mountain.

The second conclusion concerning the quality of divine presence in the Mountain of God tradition is an extension of the first conclusion, namely that the presentation of God on the mountain is *static*. At no time is there a description of a divine approach (*bw'*) or descent (*yrd*) on the mountain from heaven in order for God to meet Moses or Israel. The absence of any motifs of divine mobility reinforces both the imagery of God as dwelling on the mountain, and the unified conception of the sacred and the profane around the symbol of the mountain. The metaphorical identification of the mountain with God in combination with the static presentation of God as dwelling on it suggest that the divine presence on the mountain is permanent.

We can illustrate both the quality of divine presence that is being represented in the Mountain of God tradition and the metaphorical function of the mountain by the following diagram.

MOUNT ZION

HEAVEN

(God dwells permanently on the mountain)

SUMMIT OF THE MOUNTAIN

(Moses as mediator)

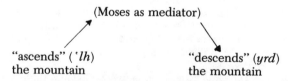

"ascends" (*'lh*)   "descends" (*yrd*)
the mountain   the mountain

BASE OF THE MOUNTAIN

(The people of Israel)

Notice in this diagram how there is an overlapping identification between the mountain and the presence of God because of the static imagery of God as dwelling on the mountain summit.

B. The Mountain and Zion

The imagery of God in the Mountain of God tradition reflects a conception of divine presence that corresponds most closely to pre-exilic Zion-Sabaoth theology.[34] The static presentation of God as dwelling on the cosmic mountain mirrors pre-exilic Zion tradition, where Yahweh was confessed as being continually present in the Jerusalem temple, because it was the place where Yahweh dwelt (*yšb*).[35] Solomon's initial prayer for the temple in 1 Kgs 8:13 illustrates the significant role of the verb "to dwell" (*yšb*) as indicating the permanent presence of God in the temple.[36]

> *bānôh bānîtî bêt zĕbul lāk*
> *mākôn lĕšibtĕkā 'ôlāmîm*
> I have built you an exalted house,
> a place for you to dwell in for ever.

In addition to the static imagery of God as dwelling on the mountain, the role of metaphor in the Mountain of God tradition, with its inherent concept of unity between God and the mountain, also corresponds to Zion-Sabaoth theology.[37] In reflecting on the concept of unity within Zion, Mettinger writes that it has nothing to do with "analogical typology, according to which the earthly sanctuary is a copy of its heavenly counterpart," nor, he continues, can the sanctuary be seen as the place where heaven and earth are held together as "two opposed

---

[34] The literature on Zion is vast. For bibliography and a brief overview see T. N. D. Mettinger, *The Dethronement of Sabaoth: Studies in the Shem and Kabod Theologies* ConBOT 18 (Lund: CWK Gleerup, 1982) 19-37; S. Terrien, *The Elusive Presence: The Heart of Biblical Theology*, Religious Perspectives 26 (New York: Harper and Row, 1978) 161-213 esp. 186 ff; or J. J. M. Roberts, "Zion in the Theology of the Davidic-Solomonic Empire," *Studies in the Period of David and Solomon and Other Essays: Papers Read at the International Symposium for Biblical Studies, Tokyo, 5-7 December, 1979* (Winona Lake: Eisenbrauns, 1982) 93-108. For more extensive discussion see G. Wanke, *Die Ziontheologie der Korachiten in ihrem traditionsgeschichtlichen Zusammenhang*, BZAW 97 (Berlin: de Gruyter, 1966); K. Rupprecht, *Der Temple von Jerusalem*, BZAW 144 (Berlin: de Gruyter, 1976); or Ollenburger, *Zion, the City of the Great King*.

[35] See, for example, Mettinger (*The Dethronement of Sabaoth*, 28) who concludes that *yšb* "is the key expression recurring in significant contexts to express the presence of God in the Temple and on Zion."

[36] For interpretation of 1 Kgs 8:12-13 see M. Görg, "Die Gattung des sogenannten Tempelweihspruches (1 Kg 8, 12f.)," *UF* 6 (1974) 55-63; O. Loretz, "Der Torso eines kanaanäische israelitischen Tempelweihspruches in 1 Kg 8, 12-13," *UF* 6 (1974) 478-80.

[37] See M. Metzger, "Himmlische und irdische Wohnstatt Jahwes," *UF* 2 (1970) 139-58; J. Maier, *Von Kultus zur Gnosis: Studien zur Vor- und Frühgeschichte der "jüdischen Gnosis"*, Religionswissenschaftliche Studien 1 (Salzburg: Kairos, 1964) 101-10; Mettinger, *The Dethronement of Sabaoth*, 29-32.

poles in a field of tension."[38] Rather, the concept of unity so central to Zion is that the temple is the location where spatial dimensions are transcended—where heaven and earth become one in the sacred space of the sanctuary. Thus, within the symbol of Zion no distinction is made between a heavenly and an earthly temple, nor among God's presence in the temple, on the cosmic mountain, or in heaven. Instead, the sanctuary functions metaphorically in creating an identification or a point of overlap between the very different spheres of the sacred and the profane, with the result that, as Metzger argues, they are merely different aspects of the same reality.[39] In Ps 11:4, then, the poet is able to confess simultaneously that Yahweh is in his holy temple, while his throne is in heaven. And in Ps 48:2-3, the Jerusalem temple is at the same time in Zaphon, in the far north.

As we have seen, this concept of unity within Zion is also reflected in the Mountain of God tradition by the way in which God is identified with the mountain. Although the sacred quality of the mountain is underscored in this account by the need for the people to be purified and by the need for proper boundaries between the sacred and the profane, there is not a clear distinction between God in heaven and the people on earth, or between Yahweh and the mountain. Instead, as in Zion, the mountain setting within the Mountain of God tradition represents the location where spatial dimensions are transcended; it is both the place where God dwells and the place where Israel is able to meet God.

C. Conclusion

We have reached a point where we can summarize our study of the Mountain of God tradition.

First, our initial tradition-historical investigation has underscored the central role that the mountain is playing in structuring the pre-deuteronomistic Sinai Complex. The mountain both accentuates the setting of the Sinai Complex, and influences the very structure of the narrative. The result of the structuring role of the mountain is that characters are clearly defined vertically in the narrative, with Yahweh at the summit, Israel at the base of the mountain, while Moses mediates between the parties.

Second, we have also seen that the mountain functions as a metaphor in symbolizing the character of divine cultic pres-

---

[38] Mettinger, *The Dethronement of Sabaoth*, 29-32.
[39] Metzger, "Himmlische und irdische Wohnstatt Jahwes," 149.

ence. In particular, the imagery of God as dwelling on the mountain encourages an identification between God and the mountain that is best interpreted as a static and permanent presence. Furthermore, this permanent presence of God is made known to Israel both through auditory and visual motifs, so that the people hear the claps of thunder and the trumpet blasts, and see the lightning in the heavy storm cloud on the mountain.

Third, I have argued that the imagery of divine presence in the Mountain of God tradition corresponds most closely to Zion. This conclusion implies that the Mountain of God tradition is pre-exilic,[40] and might even reflect cultic practice in the Jerusalem temple.[41] The preparations for a theophany on the morrow (*māḥār*),[42] the specific imagery of theophany,[43] along with the concluding sacrifices by the "young men of Israel"[44] certainly lend themselves to such an interpretation.

The aim of this study however is not to reconstruct the cultic *Sitz im Leben* of the Mountain of God tradition. Instead, we will conclude this chapter by returning to the question that inaugurated our study, for we are now in a position to answer it. The basic contour of the pre-deuteronomistic Sinai Complex is a Mountain of God tradition which reflects a theology of Zion. In having answered our question, we must immediately take note that Zion does not become the canonical account of Israel's encounter with God at the mountain. Rather, the Mountain of God tradition is qualified by two subsequent redactions: one within deuteronomistic tradition, and the other within priestly tradition. My aim in the following chapters is to describe how Zion gives way to Horeb and Sinai—the two canonical accounts of divine presence in Torah.

[40] However, by stating that the imagery in this account (of God dwelling on the cosmic mountain) is pre-exilic, we should also note that it has departed from the *Gattung* of the oldest theophany tradition, where the report of the approach of God was followed by the reaction of nature. See Cross, *Canaanite Myth and Hebrew Epic*, 164; and Jeremias, *Theophanie*, 107, 111.
[41] This conclusion corresponds to a central component in the definition of a symbol: it is always institutional and exists for a well defined group of users. See Ducrot and Todorov, *Encyclopedic Dictionary*, 100.
[42] De Vries, "The Time Word *māḥār* as a Key to Tradition Development," 73-79.
[43] Beyerlin, *Oldest Sinaitic Traditions*, 151-70.
[44] Nicholson, "The Covenant Ritual in Exodus XXIV 3-8," 81.

Chapter 3

THE DEUTERONOMISTIC REDACTION
OF EXODUS 19-24

The focus of study in this chapter will shift from the Mountain of God tradition to the deuteronomistic redaction in Exodus 19-24.[1] Even with this change in focus, the Mountain of God tradition will continue to play an influential role in our study for two reasons. First, it provides the basic structure to the Sinai Complex. Second, its theology of divine presence provides a point of departure for deuteronomistic redactors critically to evaluate Zion.

I
AN OUTLINE OF THE DEUTERONOMISTIC
REDACTION

The influence of deuteronomistic redactors in the formation of the Sinai Complex has received increasing attention in recent scholarship. Perhaps, the most influential study is Perlitt's investigation into the origin and development of *Bundestheologie im*

---

[1] Choosing the correct terminology to describe the deuteronomic/istic redaction within the Pentateuch presents a problem in view of the complexity of terms that are presently employed to describe various stages within the growth of deuteronomic tradition in other sections of the Hebrew Bible. For example, Perlitt (*Bundestheologie*, 2) distinguishes among Dt (Deut 5-28); Dtr (Deut 1-4, Jos 23 [a redactor in the spirit of Dt]); DtrG (Deut 1-2 Kgs 25 [the historical school]); Dtn (the Book of Deuteronomy). Perlitt's work has been expanded upon by Zenger (*Sinaitheophanie*, 164-165) who would distinguish two deuteronomistic redactions. Complexities increase, as C. T. Begg ("The Destruction of the Calf [Exod 32,20/Deut 9,12]," *Das Deuteronomium. Entstehung, Gestalt und Botschaft*, BETL 68 [Leuven: Leuven University Press, 1985] 248-51) has pointed out. He notes an 'American' School; which advocates a two-strata model of deuteronomistic redactions (a pre-exilic dtr[1], and an exilic dtr[2]), and a 'German' (Göttingen) School, which advocates a three-strata model (exilic DtrH, DtrP, DtrN). For additional discussion see also A. D. H. Mayes, *The Story of Israel between Settlement and Exile: A Redactional Study of the Deuteronomistic History* (London: SCM Press, 1983) esp. 1-21. I have chosen to use the term deuteronomistic because I will argue in the second section of this chapter that the redaction of Exodus 19-24 most likely corresponds to what has been described as the first deuteronomistic redaction (dtr[1]).

Alten Testament. Although Perlitt's analysis of covenant spans
the entire corpus of the Hebrew Bible, it is his tradition-historical discussion of Exodus 19-24 that is of particular concern here,
for it provides a starting point for the present study. The central question that motivates Perlitt's investigation is: How did
the Sinai Complex become the center for legal material when its
emphasis was originally on theophany and ritual?[2] In answering
this question, he concludes that the transformation is the result
of deuteronomistic redactors, who introduced the theme of covenant into the Sinai Complex in order to give a new interpretation to the older material.[3] The influence of deuteronomistic
redactors is most clearly evident, according to Perlitt, at three
points in Exodus 19-24: at the beginning, where Israel's arrival
at the mountain is reshaped into a covenant form with the addition of Exod 19:3b-8;[4] during the theophany, where the presence of God on the mountain culminates in divinely spoken law
(Exod 20:1-17);[5] and, finally, at the end, where the sacrificial ritual is reinterpreted as a Covenant-Closing Ceremony (Exod
24:3-8).[6] Subsequent scholars have followed the lead of Perlitt,
and they have even expanded the role of deuteronomistic redactors in Exodus 19-24 to the point where a redaction by this
school is considered to be responsible for the present shape of
the material.[7]

The three points of transformation in the Sinai Complex that
are underscored by Perlitt correspond to the three-part sequence of the Mountain of God tradition. The sequence consists
of an Introduction, a Preparation and Purification for, and Description of, Theophany, and a Sacrificial Ritual. These three
events will also provide the framework for outlining the deuteronomistic redaction of Exodus 19-24. A word of caution, however, is necessary. The prominence that has been attributed to
deuteronomistic redactors in Exodus 19-24 must be critically

---

[2] Perlitt *Bundestheologie*, 159-60.
[3] Perlitt *Bundestheologie*, 181.
[4] Perlitt *Bundestheologie*, 168-81.
[5] Perlitt *Bundestheologie*, 77-102 esp. 91-93.
[6] Perlitt *Bundestheologie*, 191-99.
[7] See, among others, Zenger *Sinaitheophanie*, 100-08, 164-164; E. W. Nicholson,
Exodus and Sinai in History and Tradition (Richmond: John Knox Press, 1973) 53-
84; "The Covenant Ritual in Exodus XXIV 3-8," 74-86; "The Decalogue as the Direct Address of God," *VT* 27 (1982) 422-33; *God and His People: Covenant and
Theology in the Old Testament* (Oxford: Clarendon, 1986); E. Ruprecht, "Exodus
24,9-11 als Beispiel lebendiger Erzähltradition aus der Zeit des babylonischen
Exil," *Werden und Wirken des Alten Testaments*, Fs. C. Westermann (Neukirchen-
Vluyn: Neukirchener Verlag, 1978) 139-73.

evaluated, since the influence of priestly redactors has rarely been distinguished from that of deuteronomistic redactors.

A. *Introduction (Exod 19:3b-5ba, 6b-8a)*

Exod 19:3b-5ba, 6b-8a is an insertion, which places an extended speech by Yahweh and a response by Israel into the introduction of the Mountain of God tradition (Exod 19:2b-3a). Past researchers have argued that this pericope is not integrated well into its present narrative context;[8] that its style departs from the surrounding narrative;[9] and that the language of this unit is deuteronomistic.[10]

Because of a consensus among scholars concerning the unique style of the unit and its lack of integration into the larger narrative context, the majority of past research on this insertion has tended to be form-critical. The present study of Exod 19:3b-5ba, 6b-8a will also begin form-critically. My goal, however, will be to move beyond a form-critical analysis to a redaction-critical interpretation, which will take into account the larger context of the Mountain of God tradition.

Exod 19:3b-5ba, 6b-8a has most frequently been characterized as "a covenantal *Gattung*."[11] However, we might more accurately characterize this pericope as a Proposal of Covenant.

---

[8] See already Wellhausen (*Composition*, 91) where he writes that "namentlich scheint der Anfang v. 3-9 mehr order weniger seine Composition zu sein. . . ." And more recently D. J. McCarthy, *Treaty and Covenant: A Study in Form in the Ancient Oriental Documents and in the Old Testament*, AnBib 21, 2nd ed. (Rome: Pontifical Biblical Institute, 1978) 264.

[9] McCarthy, *Treaty and Covenant*, 269, 272-73.

[10] See Perlitt *Bundestheologie*, 168-99; Zenger *Sinaitheophanie*, 164ff *et passim*; Nicholson, "The Covenant Ritual in Exodus XXIV 3-8," 74-86; H. Haag, "Das 'Buch des Bundes' (Ex 24,7)," *Das Buch des Bundes: Aufsätze zur Bible und zu ihrer Welt*, ed. B. Lang (Düsseldorf: Patmos, 1980) 226-33= *Wort Gottes in der Zeit*, Fs. K. Herrmann Schelke, ed. H. Feld (Düsseldorf: Patmos, 1973) 22-30. Some of the more striking linguistic connections between this pericope and deuteronomistic tradition include the following: the call for Israel to "see" a past event (Exod 19:4; 20:22b, compare Deut 4:3,9; 10:21; 11:7); the metaphor of "eagles' wings" (Exod 19:4, compare Deut 32:9-11); the recurring motif of the "words of Yahweh" (Exod 19:6b, 7; 20:1; 24:3-4aa,7, compare Deut 4:12; 5:5, 22 *et passim*); the form of the offer of covenant, "if you obey by voice" (*'im-šamôaʿ tišmĕʿû [lĕ] bĕqōlî*) (Exod 19:5a, compare Deut 11:13; 15:5; 28:1); and the promise to Israel that they would be Yahweh's "personal possession" (*sĕgullâ*) (Exod 19:5ab, compare Deut 7:6; 14:2; 26:18).

[11] See already A. Dillmann (*Die Bücher Exodus und Leviticus*, Exegetishes Handbuch zum Alten Testament [Leipzig: S Hirzel 1880] 194) who describes vv. 3-6 as "der classische Ausspruch des AT. über Wesen und Ziel des theokratischen Bundes. . . ." For more recent discussion of the syntax of this pericope as a covenantal *Gattung* see Muilenburg, "Covenantal Formulations," 151-57.

In introducing this form-critical designation, Knutson concluded that "the proposal to enter a covenant is quite different from post-covenantal exhortations to keep the covenant as Exod 19:4-6a is often interpreted."[12] A form-critical examination of Exod 19:3b-5ba, 6b-8a confirms Knutson's conclusion.

We can isolate the formal features of Exod 19:3b-5ba, 6b-8a into the following six parts:[13]

> (1) "A Commissioning of Moses"
>   Yahweh called to him from the mountain,
>   saying,
>   Thus you will say to the house of Jacob
>   and convey to the people of Israel.
>   (Exod 19:3b)
>   These are the words which you will speak
>   to the people of Israel.
>   (Exod 19:6b)
> (2) "A Call for Israel to 'see' a Past Act of Yahweh"
>   You saw what I did to the Egyptians,
>   now I bore you on eagles' wings,
>   and brought you to me.
>   (Exod 19:4)
> (3) "An Offer of Covenant"
>   Now if you indeed obey my voice
>   and keep my covenant,
>   (Exod 19:5a)
> (4) "A Promise of Reward"
>   you will be my personal possession
>   from all nations.
>   (Exod 19:5ba)
> (5) "The Proclamation of the 'Words of Yahweh' by
>   Moses"
>   So Moses came
>   and he called the elders of Israel.
>   Then he placed before them all these words
>   which
>   Yahweh had commanded him.
>   (Exod 19:7)
> (6) "The Acceptance of the 'Words of Yahweh' by the
>   People"

[12] J.B. Knutson, "Literary Genres in PRU IV," *Ras Shamra Parallels II*, AnOR 50 (Rome: Pontificum Institutum Biblicum, 1975) 194.

[13] For other divisions of this pericope see, for example, Childs, *Exodus*, 366; Perlitt *Bundestheologie*, 167-75; D. Patrick, "The Covenant Code Source," *VT* 27 (1977) 148-149; and H. Wildberger, *Jahwes Eigentumsvolk: Eine Studie zur Traditionsgeschichte und Theologie des Erwählungsgedankens* (Zürich: Zwingli Verlag) 14-15.

> And all the people answered together,
> saying,
> All that Yahweh has spoken we will do.
> (Exod 19:8a).

Past form-critical discussion of this unit has focused on the "Offer of Covenant" in Exod 19:5a and the "Promise of Reward" in Exod 19:5ba. Taking it as a covenantal *Gattung*, scholars have judged that the emphasis of the pericope rests on the "Offer of Covenant." If the point of emphasis is on the "Offer of Covenant," then the "Promise of Reward" within the covenantal *Gattung* would have to outline the obligations that arise from the acceptance of the covenant conditions—both the promise of reward for obedience and the threat of punishment for disobedience.[14] The problem with this interpretation, as Knutson has rightly pointed out, is that there are no obligations implied in this text.[15] Instead, the "Offer of Covenant" can be accepted or rejected without punishment or reward, since it merely stresses the benefits to Israel in accepting a future agreement with Yahweh. Thus, the pericope can be more appropriately categorized form-critically as a Proposal of Covenant with the emphasis on the "Promise of Reward" in Exod 19:5ba,[16] in contrast to the covenantal *Gattung* where the emphasis rests on the conditions.[17]

The Proposal of Covenant still requires a redaction-critical

---

[14] Muilenburg "Covenantal Formulations," 354-55) concludes that there are two parts to the covenant condition: a conditional statement, and the subsequent promise of reward for obedience and the threat of punishment for disobedience.

[15] Knutson, "Literary Genres in PRU IV," 193.

[16] Knutson's (Literary Genres in PRU IV," 192) work is based primarily on a comparison of this pericope to the letter of Suppiluliuma to Niqmadu, which has been compared to Exod 19:3b-8 as evidence that both are treaty forms containing at least an Historical Prologue (v. 4) and a Statement of Substance (vv. 5-6a). Knutson concludes that "in both the Akkadian proposal of bond and vv. 4-6. . .the agreement is not yet written." Thus, in each text the emphasis is on the benefits to the weaker party in accepting a future agreement with the stronger party. Patrick ("The Covenant Code Source," 148-49) supports this conclusion from an analysis of syntax. He points out that the syntax of Exod 19:5a, 5ba also does not fit the covenantal Gattung. Although it is formulated as a conditional statement, "The Offer of Covenant" in Exod 19:5a (protasis) actually outlines the requirements that are necessary if Israel chooses to take on the qualities described in the Promise of Reward in Exod 19:5ba (apodosis), with the result that the emphasis is on promise.

[17] See also Perlitt (*Bundestheologie*, 1669, 179) who interprets vv. 5b-6a as the center of Exod 19:3b-8, which, he concludes, emphasizes the future promises. The emphasis on promise in the Proposal of Covenant is similar in many respects to Wildberger's (*Jahwes Eigentumsvolk*, 16) form-critical definition of this unit as *Erwählungsproklamation* (a Proclamation of Election).

interpretation. Exod 19:3b-5ba, 6b-8a consists primarily of a
speech by Yahweh that now follows the original introduction in
the Mountain of God tradition, where Israel, Moses, and God
were placed in the context of the mountain (Exod 19:2b-3a).
The speech begins when Yahweh calls (*qr'*) to Moses "from the
mountain" (*min-hāhār*, Exod 19:3b), which presupposes and reinforces the setting that was established in Exod 19:2b-3a
Yahweh opens this speech by summarizing Israel's past history
in order to illustrate how divine guidance had brought the people this far (Exod 19:4). Then the focus changes from the past to
the present with an "Offer of Covenant" (Exod 19:5a), which
culminates in a future "Promise of Reward" that Israel will be
Yahweh's own "personal possession" (Exod 19:5ba).[18] The Proposal of Covenant ends with the summary statement by Yahweh
to Moses that "these are the words (*'ēlleh haddĕbārîm*) which
you will speak to the children of Israel" (Exod 19:6b). Exod
19:7-8a then narrates the approach (*bw'*) of Moses to the people
(Exod 19:7a), his communication of the Proposal of Covenant to
the elders concerning "all these words (*kŏl-haddĕbārîm
hā'ēlleh*) which Yahweh commanded" (Exod 19:7b), and Israel's
unanimous acceptance (*wayya'ănû kŏl-hā'ām yaḥdāw*) of the
divine Proposal of Covenant (Exod 19:8a), with the following
words: "All which Yahweh spoke, we will do" (*kōl 'ăšer-dibber
yhwh na'ăśeh*).[19]

Several comments are in order concerning the function of
the Proposal of Covenant in relation to the Mountain of God
tradition. First, the Proposal of Covenant is not simply an independent unit of tradition that is presently distinct from its
surrounding narrative context. Rather, it is a redaction which
presupposes the mountain setting within the Mountain of God
tradition. Note, for example, how the opening speech of
Yahweh in Exod 19:3b-5ba, 6b-8a lacks any setting at all, unless
it is interpreted as a speech of Yahweh "from the mountain,"
which is specifically mentioned in Exod 19:2b-3a. In addition,
the close tie between the deuteronomistic Proposal of Covenant
and the Mountain of God tradition is also evident in tracing the
movement of Moses. His approach (*bw'*) to the people in Exod
19:7 must also be read in combination with the earlier description of his ascent (*'lh*) in Exod 19:3a.[20]

---

[18] See Muilenburg ("Covenantal Formulations," 352-53) for further discussion of
the temporal transitions in this speech from past to future.

[19] See Perlitt (*Bundestheologie*, 168) and McCarthy (*Treaty and Covenant*, 155 n.6)
for additional literary evaluations of the structure of this unit.

[20] Zenger (*Sinaitheophanie*, 57) argued that the preposition *'ēlāyw* in Exod 19:3ba

Second, if we take our analysis of context a step further in evaluating the role of the mountain setting within the narrative then the interrelation of the deuteronomistic Proposal of Covenant and the "Introduction" in the Mountain of God tradition becomes even clearer. The deuteronomistic redaction not only presupposes the mountain setting in Exod 19:2b-3a, it actually accentuates the important role of the mountain setting by creating a symmetry to the events surrounding the Proposal of Covenant. The symmetry of the pericope presupposes the ascent (*lh*) of Moses in the Mountain of God tradition (Exod 19:3a) as a counter-balance to his subsequent "approach" (*bw'*) to the people (Exod 19:7aa), and it is developed further within the deuteronomistic redaction by the repetition of the verb "to call" (*qr'*, Exod 19:3ba, 7ab) and by the repetition of the divine Proposal of Covenant (Exod 19:3bb-5ba, 6b) as recounted speech by Moses at the base of the mountain (Exod 19:7b). This symmetrical structure can be illustrated as follows:

Moses is on the mountain with Yahweh in Exod 19:3-5ba, 6b, which separates into three parts.

(1)   Moses ascends (*lh*) to God (3a)
(2)   Yahweh calls (*qr'*) to Moses (3ba)
(3)   Yahweh delivers a Proposal of Covenant for Israel (3bb-5ba, 6b)

Moses is at the base of the mountain with Israel in Exod 19:7-8a, which follows the same three-part pattern.

(1')   Moses descends (*bw'*) to the people (7aa)
(2')   Moses calls (*qr'*) to the elders (7ab)
(3')   Moses repeats the Proposal of Covenant (7b)
(4)   The people accept the Proposal of Covenant (8a)

This outline illustrates how the deuteronomistic Proposal of Covenant is a redactional insertion, which presupposes and builds upon the vertical structure of the mountain setting that was central to the Mountain of God tradition. In accentuating the mountain setting, the deuteronomistic redaction has also transformed the Mountain of God tradition in a number of ways. The following three conclusions highlight the transformation in structure that the deuteronomistic Proposal of Covenant introduces into the Mountain of God tradition.

The first transformation is that speech is accentuated. The

provides yet an additional connection between the Proposal of Covenant and Exod 19:2b-3a.

words (děbārîm) of either Yahweh or of the people are a recurring motif throughout the deuteronomistic Proposal of Covenant (Exod 19:6b, 7, 8a), while verbs of speech become one
central organizing device within the redaction. The result is
that the expanded introduction now completes a full cycle in
the process of communication with a beginning, middle, and
end: it begins with the divine Proposal of Covenant to Moses
(Speech of Yahweh: qr' in v 3b; 'mr in vv 3b, 4; ngd in v 4); the
middle is reached when Moses conveys the Proposal of Covenant to Israel (qr' in v 7); and it ends when the people respond
favorably ('nh in v 8a; 'mr in v 8a). Here we see that with the
addition of the Proposal of Covenant, Israel's encounter with
God at the mountain is becoming primarily an auditory
experience.

   Zenger has suggested that the verbs of speech give the pericope a sense of "indefiniteness" (Unbestimmtheit).[21] He may, indeed, be correct, for a certain indefiniteness concerning the
location of Moses within the mountain setting does appear to be
a second transformation in the structure of the Mountain of God
tradition. After the speech of Yahweh on the summit of the
mountain, Moses is not described as descending (yrd) to the
people. Instead he merely brings (bw' hiphil) the words of
Yahweh to the people in Exod 19:7. Furthermore, this de-em-
phasis on a clearly defined vertical hierarchy in describing the
movement of Moses on the mountain is carried over into the
new transition to theophany in Exod 19:8b where his next trip
to the summit is simply characterized as a return (šwb) of the
words of the people to Yahweh. Thus, not only has speech (particularly divine words [haddĕbārîm]) become central to the Sinai Complex with the addition of the Proposal of Covenant, but
the presentation of Moses is being transformed at the same time
to emphasize further the presence of God as speech. Moses
functions here less as a mediator who maintains distance and
clear boundaries between Yahweh and Israel, and more as a
prophet or teacher who simply brings the word of Yahweh to
the people. This prophetic role of Moses is reinforced in Exod
19:4 when he is initially addressed by Yahweh with the commissioning formula "Thus you will say to. . ." (kōh tō'mar lĕ. . .).[22]

   A third transformation in structure to the Mountain of God
tradition is that the Proposal of Covenant adds an entire cycle to
the narrative. Previously the ascent of Moses led directly into

---

[21] Zenger Sinaitheophanie, 59.
[22] Muilenburg, "Covenantal Formulations," 354; Wildberger Jahwes Eigentumsvolk, 15.

preparation for theophany.[23] Now, with the addition of the Proposal of Covenant, the initial ascent of Moses has acquired a completely new function. The proposal and acceptance of covenant in the first cycle now becomes the prerequisite for theophany in a second cycle. This second cycle is inaugurated when Moses returns (*šwb*) the words of the people to Yahweh (Exod 19:8b), which provides the context for a change of theme from covenant to theophany in the next divine speech (Exod 19:9a). Thus, from the point of view of cycles or episodes within the Sinai Complex, Perlitt is certainly correct when he concludes that the Proposal of Covenant is not so much an addition as it is a whole new introduction that is being placed at the outset of the Sinai Complex.[24] The new introduction imports the theme of covenant into the Mountain of God tradition and underscores the auditory presence of God through speech.

B. *Preparation, Purification and Theophany (Exod 19:8b-9a, 19; 20:1-20)*

The second episode in the deuteronomistic redaction includes Exod 19:8b-9a, 19; 20:1-20. This material separates into three parts. Exod 19:8b-9a introduces the theme of theophany. Exod 19:19; 20:1-17 provides the deuteronomistic reinterpretation of theophany as divine speech (Exod 19:19), which culminates in law (Exod 20:1-17). And Exod 20:18-20 describes the reaction of the people to the appearance of God, and their choice of Moses as the one to speak for God. A more detailed interpretation of these three units will illustrate how this material is a "planned theological editing" by deuteronomistic redactors, which is meant to transform the mountain setting of the Mountain of God tradition into Mount Horeb, the mountain of theophany in Deuteronomy.

1. *The Announcement of Theophany (Exod 19:8b-9a)*

The point of emphasis in Exod 19:8b-9a is a speech by

---

[23] See McCarthy (*Treaty and Covenant*, 245-46) for a discussion of the problems of narrative sequence that he detects with the addition of this unit.
[24] Perlitt *Bundestheologie*, 180. The apparent introductory function of the Proposal of Covenant has been noted by a number of interpreters. See J. J. P. Valeton, "Das Worth *berit* in den jehovistischen und deuteronomistichen Stücken des Hexateuchs, sowie in den verwandten historischen Büchern," *ZAW* 12 (1892) 224-60; W. Rudolf, "Der Aufbau von Exodus 19-34," *Werden und Wesen des Alten Testaments*, BZAW 66 (Berlin: Töpelmann, 1935) 41; von Rad, "Problem of the Hexateuch," 40; Noth, *Exodus*, 154; Beyerlin, *Oldest Sinaitic Traditions*, 180-81, 192; Childs, *Exodus*, 360; Nicholson, "The Covenant Ritual in Exodus XXIV 3-8," 83.

Yahweh to Moses in v 9a. This is the second speech by Yahweh
in the deuteronomistic redaction. The first speech was the Proposal of Covenant. In this second speech there is a change of
theme from covenant to theophany.[25] Past scholars have judged
this change of theme to be too abrupt for Exod 19:9a to be related intrinsically to the preceding Proposal of Covenant.[26] My
aim in this section is to reevaluate this conclusion. An examination of two central motifs in Exod 19:8b-9a, namely the "words
of the people" and the approach of God for theophany, will illustrate the important role of this speech in relation to the preceding deuteronomistic Proposal of Covenant.

An initial point of contact between the Proposal of Covenant
and the Announcement of Theophany is the motif of the words
(děbārîm) which occurs both in Exod 19:7-8a and in Exod 19:8b
with a slightly different function in each case: in Exodus 19:7-8a
Moses conveyed the "words" of Yahweh to the people, while in
Exod 19:8b the reader is told that Moses returned "words of the
people" to Yahweh.[27] This repetition provides a spatial transition in setting, which once again locates Moses with Yahweh

[25] On the change of theme in Exod 19:9a see, among others, Beyerlin, *Oldest Sinaitic Traditions*, 6; Perlitt *Bundestheologie*, 168.
[26] For arguments in favor of identifying Exod 19:9a as older tradition see Zenger
Sinaitheophanie, 59. For assessments of Exod 19:9a as later tradition see F. L.
Hossfeld, *Der Dekalog: Seine späten Fassungen, die originale Komposition und
seine Vorstufen* OBO 45 (Göttingen: Vandenhoeck und Ruprecht, 1982) 190; H-.
C. Schmitt, "Redaktion des Pentateuch im Geiste der Prophetie," *VT* 32 (1982)
188.
[27] The near repetition in Exod 19:8b ("And Moses returned [šwb] the words of the
people to Yahweh") and in Exod 19:9b ("And Moses reported [ngd] the words of
the people to Yahweh") has resulted in four additional arguments concerning the
ending of this pericope: (1) Noth (*Exodus*, 154) sought to eliminate the repetition
and therefore concluded that the pericope ended after Exod 19:9a. Thus, for Noth,
Exod 19:9b was a gloss to introduce a new speech by Yahweh in Exod 19:10;
(2) Zenger (*Sinaitheophanie*, 59) interpreted the repetition as a concluding device
like Gen 23:17, 20, and therefore, he argued that the pericope ended after Exod
19:9b; (3) Ruprecht ("Exodus 24, 9-11 als Beispiel lebendiger Erzähltradition," 155)
and Hossfeld (*Dekalog*, 189) interpret the repetition in Exod 19:9b as "Resumptive" (see chap. 2, n.11), but they end the pericope after Exod 19:8; (4) Cazelles
("Alliance du Sinai, Alliance de l'Horeb et Rénouvellement de l'Alliance," 76-77)
argues that Exod 19:9b rather than Exod 19:8b is the original ending, preferring
the verb *ngd* in Exod 19:8b to *šwb* in Exod 19:9b. Thus, for Cazelles, Exod 19:8b-
9a is a secondary expansion.
    Context argues against an interpretation of Exod 19:9a as concluding the unit,
since this speech of Yahweh introduces a new focus on the appearance of God
which becomes central to the remainder of Exod 19; while problems arise when
Exod 19:9a is interpreted as an insertion and thus distinct from Exod 19:3b-5ba, 6b-
8a, since (as we shall see) the units are linguistically interrelated and reflect similar
Tendenz concerning theophany.

rather than with the people, and thus provides the necessary context for the second speech by Yahweh in Exod 19:9a.

A second point of contact to the Proposal of Covenant is the use of the verb "to approach (*bw*')". This verb was used at the close of the first episode to describe the approach of Moses to the people (Exod 19:7) and it now reappears to describe the impending approach of Yahweh to the mountain (Exod 19:9a). This repetition provides an additional link between the Proposal of Covenant and the second divine speech in Exod 19:8b-9a, and further insight into two central features of divine presence for the deuteronomistic tradents. The first thing to be noted is that, in contrast to the Mountain of God tradition, Yahweh does not dwell on the mountain, but is a God who must "approach" (*bw*') it in order to be present for theophany. The second feature is that Moses is becoming idealized as the one who mirrors the movement (*bw*') of God, and, thus, is able reliably to convey the divine words.

In summary, although there is a transition from covenant to theophany in Exod 19:8b-9a, there is also a close interrelation between the two initial speeches of God. The interdependence of the Proposal of Covenant and the announcement of theophany is based on the repetition of specific motifs (i.e., *dĕbārîm*, *bw*'), and includes a developing theological perspective concerning the character of divine presence and the role of Moses as the representative of God. The second speech provides the reader with three important insights concerning theophany: that the presence of God on the mountain requires a divine approach (*bw*'); that the purpose for theophany is for the people to hear (*šm*') divine speech; and that theophany will authenticate Moses as one who speaks with God, which will result in the people trusting (*'mn*) in him forever.

2. *Theophany as Divine Speech (Exod 19:19; 20:1-17)*

The interrelation of Exod 19:8b-9a and Exod 19:19; 20:1-20 is also very explicit. In particular, the deuteronomistic reinterpretation of theophany in Exod 19:19; 20:1-7 fulfills the prediction in Exod 19:9a that Israel would hear (*šm*') divine speech addressed to Moses. An examination of the description of theophany in the Mountain of God tradition (Exod 19:16ab-17) and in the deuteronomistic redaction (Exod 19:19) will underscore the interdependence between these two texts (and thus confirm the redactional nature of Exod 19:19), and will also highlight how the deuteronomistic redaction is a theological extension of the Mountain of God tradition, which has redefined theophany as an experience of speech, which culminates in the revelation of law (Exod 20:1-17).

The contrasts between the imagery of the Mountain of God tradition with its description of the thunder (*qōlōt*) and lightning (*bĕrāqîm*) on the mountain in Exod 19:16ab, and the more specific description of God's presence as speech to Moses (*bĕqôl*) in Exod 19:19 have already been noted in Chapter 2. However, consider more closely the syntax between these two verses:

Exod 19:16ab   *wayhî qōlōt ûbĕrāqîm*
                     wĕ'ānān kābēd 'al-hāhār
                     wĕqōl šōpār ḥāzāq
                     There were claps of thunder and bolts
                     of lightning
                     and a thick cloud upon the mountain
                     and a very loud sound of a trumpet.
Exod 19:19   *wayhî qôl haššōpār hôlēk wĕḥāzēq mĕ'ōd*
                     mōšeh yĕdabbēr
                     wĕhā'ĕlōhîm ya'ănennû bĕqôl
                     As the sound of the trumpet was growing louder
                     Moses was speaking
                     and God was answering in a voice.

Three things stand out when we compare these verses. First, only the auditory motifs of divine presence in the final line of Exod 19:16ab are repeated in Exod 19:19. The result of this selective repetition is that theophany in Exod 19:19 is an experience of divine speech. Second, the syntax of the closing line in the Mountain of God tradition has changed in the deuteronomistic redaction to include participles (*hôlēk wĕḥāzēq mĕ'ōd*). The function of these participles, as *casus adverbialis*, reinforces our first conclusion, for they are meant to describe "more particularly the manner or attendant circumstances. . .under which an action or state has taken place, or is taking place. . . ."[28] As was noted, the more specific "attendant circumstances" of theophany being described in Exod 19:19 are that the indefinite sound of thunder (*qōlōt*) on the mountain is, in fact, divine speech (*bĕqôl*). A third change in syntax between Exod 19:16ab and the opening line of Exod 19:19 is that the *qōl šōpār*, which signaled the divine presence in the Mountain of God tradition, has become definite (*qôl haššōpār*). This subtle shift in syntax suggests that for deuteronomistic redactors the

28 *GKC* § 144h.

divine speech on the mountain has become specific with the promulgation of the Decalogue in Exod 20:1-17, which now functions as the culmination of theophany. Two additional features within the deuteronomistic redaction reinforce this interpretation. The iterative aspect of the verbs in Exod 19:19— "speaking" and "answering"—indicates an ongoing conversation between Yahweh and Moses,[29] which is continued in Exod 20:1 where the speech of God is also underscored.[30] The overall effect of the deuteronomistic redaction is that what had been an appearance of God within the thunderstorm in the Mountain of God tradition now becomes the revelation of Torah. Such a reinterpretation of the cultic presence of God as Torah has a precedent in prophetic literature where the *qôl šōpār* is also interpreted as a warning sign for Israel to hear Torah.[31]

3. *The Fear of the People and Their Choice of Moses (Exod 20:18-20)*

Exod 19:18-20 concludes the account of theophany in the deuteronomistic redaction by describing the reaction of the people to the speech of God.[32] These three verses combine to

[29] On the iterative use of the imperfect see *GKC* § 107f.

[30] Exod 20:1 repeats two motifs that have been prominent in this redaction: the emphasis on divine speech (*waydabbēr*) and the repetition of "all these words" (*kŏl-haddĕbārîm hā'ēlleh*). On the redactional character of Exod 20:1 see Zenger *Sinaitheophanie*, 64, *et passim*.

[31] See especially Jer 6:16-17, 19. Ezek 33:4, 5 also combines the warning of the *qôl šōpār* with the image of the prophet as a watchman. See also Isa 18:3 where Israel is called to hear (*šm'*) the *qôl šōpār*.

[32] Zenger (*Sinaitheophanie*, 66-67) has argued that Exod 20:20 is a separate unit of tradition from Exod 20:18-19 because the reference to God as Elohim in Exod 20:20 is definite (*hā'ĕlōhîm*) in contrast to the indefinite use in Exod 20:19 (*'ĕlōhîm*). A distinction in traditions on the basis of the definite and indefinite form of Elohim is difficult to maintain in Exodus 19-20 and the present analysis of this material has not used this contrast as a key to tradition history. The definite *hā'ĕlōhîm* occurs in Exod 19:3a, 17a, 19b; 20:20, 21 and the indefinite *'ĕlōhîm* in Exod 20:1, 19. Thus Elohim is definite in what appears to be an older tradition of theophany in Exod 19:17a and in the conversation between Moses and God in Exod 19:19b, which appears to be a subsequent theological reinterpretation of theophany as divine speech. Yet, the more immediate introduction to the Decalogue in Exod 20:1, which also interprets the law as a direct address by God, is indefinite. This shifting back and forth between the definite and indefinite use of Elohim in two texts (Exod 19:19; 20:1), which reflect the same *Tendenz* concerning theophany, argues against making a distinction in tradition between Exod 20:19 and 20. Furthermore, the arguments for interpreting Exod 20:19-20 as a unity are also supported by the larger context. Exod 20:19-20 completes the purpose of theophany that was stated in Exod 19:9a and even repeats specific motifs from this text (e.g. the emphasis on divine speech, *šm'*, the description of God as "approaching" [*bw'*] for theophany, the choice of Moses as the one to speak for God).

complete the narrative logic of the second episode by fulfilling
the additional purpose of theophany outlined in Exod 19:9a—
that Israel would have faith in Moses and trust him forever. The
first verse, Exod 20:18, stresses that the people have, indeed,
heard the voice of God. Note here how the emphasis on auditory motifs during theophany gives rise to the contradictory description of Israel as "seeing" (rō'îm) the thunder and the
"sound of a trumpet," in addition to the lightning and smoke on
the mountain.[33] The second verse, Exod 20:19, describes the authentication of Moses by the people. In this verse the people
choose Moses to speak for them, because of their fear of death
from the terror of divine speech. Finally, once Moses has been
commissioned by the people, he assumes his role as the reliable
interpreter of God's words in Exod 20:20, when he conveys the
previous speech of Yahweh in Exod 19:9a to the people by repeating the technical language of divine approach (bw'),[34] he
then instructs the people about the meaning of this central
event: that the fear of God is, in fact, the proper response to the
divine words.

In summary we have seen how the divine speech to Moses in
Exod 19:9a provides the central themes of the episode: the approach of God on the mountain, the auditory presence of God,
and Israel's faith in Moses. In fact, the remainder of the second
episode is so dependent on Yahweh's speech to Moses in Exod
19:9a that the subsequent material simply functions as a fulfillment of this speech: Exod 19:19; 20:1-17 clarifies just how theophany is actually an experience of speech, while Exod 19:18-20
narrates the peoples confirmation of Moses as Yahweh's
representative.

4. *Mount Horeb and the Mountain Setting in the Deuteronomistic Redaction*

Interpretation of the second episode in the deuteronomistic
redaction has underscored how the mountain has become a setting for divine speech, and how theophany itself has been redefined as divine speech which authenticates Moses as the one
who speaks for God. This transformation in the mountain setting corresponds to Mount Horeb, the mountain of theophany in
the Book of Deuteronomy. Specific themes associated with Ho-

---

[33] The contradictory imagery of the people "seeing" the voice of God in Exod
20:18a is carried over into Exod 20:22, where the people are told that they had just
"seen" the voice of God from heaven.

[34] For discussion of bw' as technical language of theophany see Mann, *Divine Presence*, 252-253.

reb in the Book of Deuteronomy provide initial points of contact with the deuteronomistic redaction. For example, a quick reading of Deuteronomy reveals that Horeb is the place where Yahweh appeared in the fire, spoke the Decalogue directly to the people, and made covenant with them (Deut 4:10, 15; 5:2; 28:69); where the people gathered before God to hear divine speech (Deut 4:10); and, where Moses was commissioned as the ideal prophet (Deut 18:16).

A more detailed probe into the two central accounts of theophany within the Book of Deuteronomy (Deut 4:1-40 and 5:1-6:3) brings to light even closer ties between Mount Horeb and the mountain setting in the deuteronomistic redaction of Exodus 19-24. Consider the account of the promulgation of the Decalogue at Horeb in Deut 5:1-6:3.[35] Although there is a dual focus on visual (fire, *mittôk hā 'ēš*) and auditory (divine speech, *dbr*) motifs at the outset of this account, the emphasis in this story is clearly on auditory motifs.[36] Theophany in Deut 5:1-6:3 is an experience of divine speech, which culminates in the Decalogue, and it is this experience of the "words of Yahweh" that is underscored by Moses at the close of the event in Deut 5:22.

The recounting of theophany in Deut 4:11-13 even more pointedly emphasizes the close links between the presence of God on Mount Horeb and the deuteronomistic redaction in Exod 19:8b-9a, 19; 20:1-17. Even though this account begins with visual imagery of fire (Deut 4:11), within two verses the visual motifs have given way completely to the auditory motifs of speech, when the content of theophany is summarized as the "ten words" (Deut 4:13). In fact, the transitional verse in this account of theophany—Deut 4:12—actually employs the same contradictory imagery as Exod 20:18 in order to emphasize that the presence of God was not visual but auditory, when the people are described as "seeing" the "voice" of God: "(you) did not

---

[35] It is beyond the scope of this study to review in detail current research on the synoptic tradition of the Decalogue in Exod 20:2-17 and Deut 5:6-21. However, recent scholarship, which has proposed that Deut 5:6-21 is both tradition-historically prior to Exod 20:2-17 and the point of origin for the law code, provides strong evidence for interpreting the Decalogue in Exodus 19-24 as a deuteronomistic redaction. Concerning the priority of Deut 5:6-21 over Exod 20:2-17 see Perlitt *Bundestheologie*, 90-92; Zenger *Sinaitheophanie*, 164; and Nicholson, "The Decalogue as the Direct Address of God," 423. Concerning the origin of the Decalogue within deuteronomic tradition see most recently, Hossfeld, *Dekalog*, 159, 161-62, 283-84.

[36] See N. Lohfink (*Höre, Israel!: Auslegung von Texten aus den Buch Deuteronomium*, Die Welt der Bibel 18 [Düsseldorf: Patmos, 1965] 104) for further discussion of the description of theophany as a divine voice from the midst of fire.

see a form—only a voice" (*ûtĕmûnâ 'ĕnĕkem rō̄ 'îm zûlātî qôl*).[37]
And, finally, the disassociation of Yahweh from the mountain, by
means of the imagery of a divine approach (Exod 19:8a; 20:20),
also corresponds with Mount Horeb in Deuteronomy, where
Yahweh is said to dwell in heaven and not on the cosmic
mountain.[38]

The points of contact between the deuteronomistic redaction in Exodus 19-24 and the theophany at Mount Horeb in
Deuteronomy 4-5 continue in the presentations of Moses and of
the people. As in the deuteronomistic redaction, Moses is commissioned by God (Deut 4:14, compare Exod 19:9a)[39] and chosen
by the people (Deut 5:27, compare Exod 20:19) to mediate divine speech. Furthermore, the vision of Israel in Exod 20:20, as
people who rightly fear the words of Yahweh, corresponds to
deuteronomistic parenesis. Note especially Deut 5:28-29, where
the reader is made privy to wishful thinking by Yahweh immediately after the revelation of the Decalogue, when he states to
Moses the ideal scenario for Israel—that they would always fear
divine speech and obey deuteronomistic law.

The interpretation of the second episode in the deuteronomistic redaction can be summarized in the following manner.
We have seen that the account of theophany presupposes the
description of the thunderstorm in the Mountain of God tradition (Exod 19:16ab-17). However, deuteronomistic redactors
have also reinterpreted the cultic presence of God in a number
of ways. Exod 19:9a underscored that God does not dwell on
the mountain, but must approach the mountain in order to be
present, and that the two purposes of God's presence are for

[object Object][37] Deut 4:12 is problematic. G. Braulik (*Die Mittel deuteronomischer Rhetorik—
erhoben aus Deuteronomium 4, 1-40*, AnBib 68 [Rome: Pontifical Biblical Institute,
1978] 31, 34 n.85) argues for antithetical parallelism between the lines:
qôl dĕbārîm 'attem šōmĕ'îm
ûtĕmûnâ 'ĕnĕkem rō'îm (zûlātî qôl)
He then argues that *zûlātî qôl* (at the close of the second line) is a caesura, which
does not refer to "seeing" (*rō'îm*), but to "hearing" (*šōmĕ'îm*) in the previous line.
In this way Braulik avoids a zeugmatic construction. However, Exod 20:18 suggests that the zeugmatic construction in describing the presence of God actually
corresponds to deuteronomistic *Tendenz*, with its emphasis on divine speech.
Thus, I would read *zûlātî qôl* with *rō'îm*. For a similar *Tendenz* see also Exod
20:22b; Deut 4:9; 5:24.
[38] Nicholson, "The Decalogue as the Direct Address of God," 424-27.
[39] On the interrelation of Exod 19:9a with deuteronomistic parenesis see S.
Mittmann (*Deuteronomium 1,1-6,3: Literarkritisch und traditionsgeschichtlich
Untersucht*, BZAW 139 [Berlin: de Gruyter, 1975] 146), who concludes that the
point of Exod 19:9a is the *ad majorem gloriam Mosis* from a deuteronomistic point
of view. See also Noth, *Exodus*, 158.

Israel to hear divine speech and to trust Moses. Exod 19:19 and 20:1-17 build upon the first purpose of theophany, by reinterpreting the visual and auditory motifs of the thunderstorm (Exod 19:16ab-17) as a solely auditory experience in which God promulgates the Decalogue to Moses (Exod 19:19; 20:1-17). Exod 20:18-20 completes the second purpose of theophany by showing how the people's fear of divine speech resulted in the authentication of Moses as the one to speak for God. We also saw how the imagery of divine presence, the idealization of Moses, and the reaction of the people in Exod 19:8b-9a, 19; 20:1-20 all correspond to the interpretation of theophany at Mount Horeb in Deuteronomy 4-5. These points of similarity suggests that the redaction is deuteronomistic, and that Mount Zion in the Mountain of God tradition is being transformed by the deuteronomistic redactors into Mount Horeb.

C. The Sacrificial Ritual (Exod 20:21-23:33; 24:3-4aa, 7)

The third episode of the deuteronomistic redaction continues to build on the outline of events in the Mountain of God tradition. Thus, the sacrificial ritual in Exod 24:4ab-5, which concluded the account of theophany in the Mountain of God tradition, remains a central event. It is, however, significantly expanded with the addition of law (Exod 20:23-23:33, the Book of the Covenant), which is framed by narrative (Exod 20:21-22; 24:3-4aa, 7). With the addition of this material, the succinct account of the sacrificial ritual within the Mountain of God tradition is expanded into three parts: the episode begins when Moses enters the presence of God alone in Exod 20:21-22; then the Book of Covenant is revealed to Moses in Exod 20:23-23:33; then the episode closes with a Covenant-Closing Ceremony in Exod 24:3-4aa, 7. Furthermore, two themes are central to this redaction, and they will provide focus for interpretation. The first theme concerns the authoritative role of Moses as the commissioned teacher of deuteronomistic law. This theme is a development from the second episode, where one of the central purposes of theophany was for Israel to trust Moses forever, as the one who speaks with God. The second prominent theme in the third episode is covenant. This theme is a continuation of the Proposal of Covenant in the first episode. The development of these two central themes requires interpretation, for their interrelation in the third episode brings closure to the deuteronomistic redaction of Exodus 19-24.

1. *Moses and the Law*

Moses is central to the third episode of the deuteronomistic redaction. He alone receives the additional revelation of the Book of the Covenant to become the authoritative teacher of law. An interpretation of his character will provide insight into the *Tendenz* of the deuteronomistic redactors of Exodus 19-24, and also illustrate further the similarity between this redaction and the account of theophany at Mount Horeb in the Book of Deuteronomy. Three aspects in the characterization of Moses are particularly important: first, he receives the private revelation of deuteronomic law; second, he bridges the chasm between God in heaven and Israel on earth; and, third, even though he conveys divine speech from heaven, the idealization of him is anti-hierarchical.

First, Moses is set apart in the deuteronomistic redaction because he receives a private revelation of the Book of Covenant. Exod 20:21 marks the beginning of the third episode, and it prepares the reader for the central role that Moses will play, by contrasting his "approach" (*ngš*) into the thick darkness of God's presence, to the people, who are described as "standing afar off" (*mērāḥōq*) from the mountain. This spatial transition in setting is reminiscent of Exod 19:8b (the introduction to the second episode in the deuteronomistic redaction), for it once again locates Moses with Yahweh rather than with the people, which provides the context for divine speech. However, in the third episode, the divine discourse is not a prediction of a public theophany to the people of Israel in the form of the Decalogue (Exod 19:9a, 19; 20:1-17). Rather, it is the completion of theophany as a private revelation to Moses in the form of the Book of the Covenant (Exod 20:23-23:33). Within the plot structure of the deuteronomistic redaction, the primary reason given for this special role of Moses is the fear of the people. It was their fear of divine speech and choice of Moses at the close of the second episode that has propelled him into his special role in the third episode. In this way, the central focus on theophany as divine law in the second episode is carried over into the third episode, but only indirectly through Moses.

Thus, we see that there is a development within the deuteronomistic redaction from a public revelation of the Decalogue to a private revelation of the Book of the Covenant, which Moses must now promulgate for God. The result of this development is that Moses acquires authority in the deuteronomistic redaction, which mirrors his role in Deuteronomy. The accounts of theophany at Mount Horeb also progress from a public revela-

tion of the Decalogue (Deut 4:11-13; 5:1-22) to the private revelation of additional deuteronomic law to Moses (Deut 4:36-40;
5:28ff.), because of the people's fear of divine speech (Deut 5:23-
28).

Second, Moses is idealized because he bridges the chasm between God in heaven and Israel on earth. Exod 20:22b explains
why revelation must be indirect through Moses. The verse
reads: "You (Israel) have seen that it was from heaven that I
spoke with you" (*'attem rĕ'îtem kî min-haššāmayim dibbartî
'immākem*). Exod 20:22b indicates that in addition to the fear of
the people, there is also a spatial or structural reason why Moses
must assume a more central role in channeling divine speech to
Israel. God is in heaven rather than on the cosmic mountain.
The breakdown of any identification between God and the cosmic mountain in this verse, with the "relocation" of divine
speech to heaven underscores the vast chasm between God and
Israel, and accentuates the need for a commissioned teacher like
Moses to promulgate God's law.[40]

The motifs that describe Moses in Exodus 19-24 are also central to the account of theophany at Mount Horeb in Deuteronomy 4-5. In fact, the authority of Moses at Mount Horeb is
stated most forcefully, when it is combined with a confession of
the transcendence of God in Deut 4:36-40, as is the case in the
deuteronomistic redaction of Exodus 19-24. In Deut 4:36-40,
the speech of God is also clearly located in heaven. Furthermore, the confession that God dwells in heaven has the comple-
mentary effect of adding authority to the teaching of Moses on
earth. This authority is reflected in the closing warning of Moses
in Deut 4:39-40, where he states that Israel must remember,
first, that Yahweh is the only God in heaven above or on the
earth below; and, second, that the commandments which he
(Moses) presents to them are in fact the statutes of Yahweh.
Here we see clearly that Moses is the commissioned teacher of
deuteronomic law.[41] This imagery (of Moses authoritatively

---

[40] See Mettinger (*The Dethronement of Yahweh Sabaoth*, 41-42 *et passim*) for discussion of the "relocation" of God to heaven in deuteronomistic tradition.

[41] The role of Moses as a commissioned teacher of deuteronomic law is underscored
in a number of ways throughout the Book of the Deuteronomy. The overall structure of the Book as four speeches by Moses underscores his authority (Deut 1:1-
4:43; 4:44-28:68; 28:69-35:52; 33:1-29, see Lohfink [*Höre, Israel!*, 15-16]). In addition the Leitwort *lmd* "to teach" in describing Moses throughout Deut 4:1-40
(Deut 4:1, 5, 11, 14) underscores his authoritative role as the commissioned teacher
of deuteronomic law. For more general discussion on the role of Moses as a law-
giver in deuteronomic tradition see E. Nielsen, "Moses and the Law," *VT* 32 (1982)
87-98.

conveying deuteronomic law from heaven) is actually acted out
in the third episode of the deuteronomistic redaction, when
Moses promulgates the Book of the Covenant, which he alone
has received from God in heaven.[42]

Third, even though Moses is idealized as the commissioned
teacher of deuteronomic law, the presentation of his special role
is anti-hierarchical. The verbs associated with his movement on
the mountain illustrate this point. Although the verb *ngš* in
Exod 20:21 provides the necessary transition between the second and third episodes to locate Moses with Yahweh rather than
with the people, it de-emphasizes a clearly defined vertical hierarchy in describing the movement of Moses on the mountain.
This has been the *Tendenz* of the deuteronomistic redactors
throughout Exodus 19-24. The descent of Moses at the close of
the first episode was indicated by the verb *bw'* in Exod 19:7, and
the ascent of Moses was marked by the verb *šwb* at the outset of
the second episode in Exod 19:8b. In fact, the avoidance of a
vertical hierarchy in describing the movement of Moses on the
mountain is carried through to the end of this episode, when the
descent of Moses to the people is indicated in Exod 24:3 once
again with the verb *bw'*. This overview of the verbs of transition within the deuteronomistic redaction underscores how the
specific verbs of ascent (*'lh*) and descent (*yrd*) in the Mountain
of God tradition are consistently avoided.

The *Tendenz* of the deuteronomistic redactors to avoid verbs
that express a clear vertical hierarchy affects the imagery of the
mountain setting. The reader is drawn into the question of
whether it is a mountain at all that Moses is descending and ascending when he "approaches" the people or "draws near" to
God. This ambiguity is carried over into the presentation of
Moses. Although he is clearly set apart from the people and idealized as the one who speaks with God, Moses does not function
in the deuteronomistic redaction as a mediator who maintains
distance and clear boundaries between Yahweh and Israel.
Rather, he is idealized as a prophet or teacher, who simply
brings the word of Yahweh to the people.[43] Furthermore, there

---

[42] The literary character of the speeches in Deuteronomy as recounting speech
anchors the authority of Moses in Exodus 19-24 (see R. Polzin, *Moses and the
Deuteronomist. A Literary Study of the Deuteronomic History* [New York: Seabury, 1980] 25-72).

[43] See Nielsen ("Moses and the Law," 98) who also concludes that "the notion of a
Moses as a law-giver was established through the Dtr. traditions." Furthermore,
Nielsen describes the presentation of Moses in deuteronomistic tradition as that of
a *nābî'* (prophet).

is a charismatic quality to the idealization of Moses, which reinforces an anti-hierarchical *Tendenz* within the redaction. This
quality was clearly stated in the divine commissioning of Moses
in Exod 19:9a. There the reader was told that it is not enough
for Moses to be commissioned by God; ultimately it is the people
who must confirm his special role by hearing divine speech in
his words. We saw how the important role of the people in con-
firming the status of Moses actually became the point of focus at
the close of the second episode and set the stage for the private
revelation to Moses in the third episode.

In summary, Moses is idealized throughout the deuteronomistic redaction and especially in the third episode. He alone
receives the revelation of the Book of the Covenant. As the
commissioned teacher of deuteronomic law, he bridges the gap
between God and Israel. And his special role is that of a leader
who is charismatic and anti-hierarchical in speaking for God.
This portrait of Moses reflects his similar role at Mount Horeb in
Deuteronomy. We have already seen that at Mount Horeb
Moses receives a private revelation after the public revelation of
the Decalogue, and that he bridges the chasm between God in
heaven and Israel on earth. And the special status of Moses at
Mount Horeb is also charismatic and anti-hierarchical. Note, for
example, how the recounting of theophany in Deut 4:9-14
moves easily and rapidly between divine discourse to Moses and
to the people without any shift in setting. The same happens in
Deut 5:22-33, where once again there are a number of changes
in discourse without clear shift in setting as the people hear divine speech and authenticate Moses as the one who speaks for
God. Here, too, the reader is drawn into the question of
whether Horeb is a mountain at all. We must explore this quality of Horeb within the Book of Deuteronomy in more detail in
the follow section. At this point in our study we can conclude
that one purpose for this ambiguity concerning Horeb in the
Book of Deuteronomy is to play down hierarchy in characteriz-
ing Moses as the authoritative teacher of deuteronomic law.

2. *Covenant and Deuteronomic Law*

The second central theme in the third episode is covenant.
Covenant, within the deuteronomistic redaction, concerns the
obligations that must be met if Israel is to be the people of God.
Those obligations are outlined and documented in the Decalogue and in the Book of the Covenant. Covenant, therefore, is
central to the deuteronomistic redaction in general, because it
designates deuteronomic law. It is of particular importance in

the third episode, because with the revelation of deuteronomic law, what had only been a Proposal of Covenant in the first episode can now become a reality. The reality of covenant for Israel is signaled at the end of this episode with a Covenant-Closing Ceremony.[44]

Perlitt provides a point of departure for our study of covenant. He argued that covenant functions as a prelude and a postscript for theophany within the deuteronomistic redaction. He supported this conclusion by noting a variety of repetitions between Exod 19:3b-8 and Exod 24:3-8: "to approach" (*bw'*, Exod 19:7; 24:3); "to call" (*qr'*, Exod 19:7; 24:7); "all the words" of Yahweh (*kŏl-dĕbārîm*, Exod 19:7; 24:3, 7); "covenant" (*bĕrît*, Exod 19:5; 24:7); and the unanimous response of the people to the offer of covenant (*yaḥdāw*, Exod 19:8a; *qôl 'eḥād*, Exod 24:3). Perlitt then took an additional step in his interpretation and concluded that these two units even shared a similar three-part structure: an act of communication (the calling of Moses/reading of the law); the designation of what is communicated ("all the words of Yahweh"/the Book of the Covenant); and the unified response of the people.[45]

Perlitt is certainly correct in noting the interrelationship of these episodes and their redactional function as a prelude and a postscript for theophany. Furthermore, he is also correct in arguing that the effect of the deuteronomistic redaction is that theophany is now framed by covenant. The parallel structure, however, between the first and third episodes exceeds the limits of Perlitt's analysis. His too exclusive focus on narrative did not adequately address the relation of narrative and law in the deuteronomistic redaction. My aim in this section is to illustrate

---

[44] Perlitt (*Bundestheologie*, 171), in writing about the use of covenant throughout the deuteronomistic redaction in general and in Exod 19:5a in particular, concludes that ". . .*berit* hier im dtr Sinne gebraucht: nicht als Beschreibung des Gottesverhältnisses (die erfolgt in v. 5b-6a!), sondern als eine auferlegte Verpflichtung, die eben die Bedingung dieses Verhältnisses umschreibt." For a similar interpretation in a much earlier work see R. Kraetzschmer, (*Die Bundesvorstellungim Alten Testament in ihrer geschichtlichen Entwickelung* (Marburg: N. G. Elwert'sche Verlagsbuchhandlung, 1896) 2 *et passim*) and more recently see E. Kutsch ("Gesetz und Gnade," *ZAW* 79 [1967] 30) where he writes, "nach Ex 19:5b soll Israel Jahwes 'Eigentum(svolk)' sein-damit (!) wird das Verhältnis zwischen Jahwe und Israel umschrieben. Wenn das Bewahren, Beobachten der *berit* Jahwes die Vorbedingung für dieses Verhältnis ist, kann mit der *berit* nicht das Verhältnis selbst gemeint sein." In *Verheissung und Gesetz* BZAW 131 (Berlin: de Gruyter, 1973) 9-11, Kutsch defines *bĕrît* in Exod 19:5a as *Fremdverpflichtung*—obligations which are imposed by another (*Verpflichtung eines anderen*). For review and a similar interpretation of covenant to that outlined above see Nicholson, *God and His People*.

[45] Perlitt *Bundestheologie*, 181, 191-92.

the important relationship of narrative and law through two steps of interpretation. The first step is form-critical. I hope to show that when the Book of the Covenant is included as an integral element in the third episode it shares the same six-part form as the Proposal of Covenant in the first episode. The second step requires a more detailed interpretation of the function of the Book of the Covenant within the deuteronomistic redaction in general and within the third episode in particular.

The important relationship between narrative and law in the third episode is made explicit in Exod 24:7, when the reader is told that after Moses left the presence of God, he read from the *sēper habbĕrît* (The Book of the Covenant).[46] If we include the Book of the Covenant as a component integral to the third episode, then the similarities in form between the Proposal of Covenant and the Covenant-Closing Ceremony can be illustrated in the following manner. Each includes: (1) A Commissioning of Moses (Exod 19:3b/Exod 20:22a); (2) A Call for Israel "to see" a Past Action of Yahweh (Exod 19:4/Exod 20:22b); (3) An Offer of Covenant (Exod 19:5a/Exod 20:23-23:19); (4) A Promise of Reward (Exod 19:5ba/Exod 23:20-33); (5) The Proclamation of the "Words of Yahweh" by Moses (Exod 19:7/Exod 24:3a, 7a); and (6) The Acceptance of the "Words of Yahweh" by the People (Exod 19:8a/Exod 24:3b, 7b). Each of these points of correspondence requires closer interpretation.

The formal similarity of the Commissioning of Moses in Exod 19:3b and 20:22a and of the Call for Israel "to see" a Past Action of Yahweh in Exod 19:4 and 20:22b can be illustrated in the following manner:

Commissioning of Moses

Exod 19:3b   Thus you will say (*kōh tō'mar*)
to the house of Jacob (*bêt ya'ǎqōb*)

---

[46] There has been debate over the identification of the *sēper habbĕrît* in Exod 24:7. The debate is whether the phrase refers to the Decalogue in Exod 20:2-17 or to The Book of the Covenant in Exod 20:23-23:33. See Noth (*Exodus*, 198) for arguments which link Exod 24:7 to the Book of the Covenant. For identification of the *sēper habbĕrît* with the Decalogue see, among others, O. Eissfeldt, *The Old Testament: An Introduction* (New York: Harper and Row, 1965) 212-13; Beyerlin, *Oldest Sinaitic Traditions*, 4-5; and Haag, "Das 'Buch des Bundes' (Ex 24, 7)," 226-33. I would argue that within the overall structure of the redaction both law-codes are included as the legislative basis for covenant, and that both should therefore be interpreted as the intended reference in Exod 24:7 (see Childs [*Exodus*, 506], who comes to much the same conclusion). However, the two law-codes are not of equal value within the presentation of the deuteronomistic redaction. The Decalogue is the culmination of theophany for Israel, while the Book of the Covenant is a private revelation to Moses.

and tell the people of Israel (*bĕnê*
yiśrā'ēl)

Exod 20:22a   Thus you will say (*kōh tō'mar*)
to the people of Israel (*bĕnê yiśrā'ēl*)

Call for "to see" a Past Action of Yahweh

Exod 19:4   You have seen (*'attem rĕ'îtem*) what I did
to the Egyptians. . .

Exod 20:22b   You have seen (*'attem rĕ'îtem*) that I
spoke with you from heaven

The next two points of similarity between the Proposal of
Covenant and the Covenant-Closing Ceremony presuppose that
the Book of Covenant is an integral part of the very structure of
the episode. Thus the law-code itself in Exod 20:23-23:33 corresponds form-critically to the "Offer of Covenant" (Exod
19:5a/Exod 20:23-23:19) and the "Promise of Reward" (Exod
19:5ba/Exod 23:20-33) in the Proposal of Covenant. A closer examination of the Book of the Covenant will illustrate this point.

A thorough tradition-historical investigation of the Book of
the Covenant is beyond the scope of the present study. However, a quick overview of its content is necessary for interpreting its function within the deuteronomistic redaction. The Book
of the Covenant evinces a lengthy independent tradition-historical development prior to its location in Exodus 19-24,[47] as well
as further additions which may have been prompted by its present narrative context.[48] In any case, the legislation within the

---

[47] For example, A. Jepsen (*Untersuchungen zum Bundesbuch*, BWANT III/5 [Stutt-
gart: W. Kohlhammer, 1927] 96-105) describes the development of four legal cor-
pora to the Book of the Covenant: Hebrew laws related to other oriental legal
systems; law that was unique to Israel; ancient Israelite moral tradition; and cultic
laws. H. Cazelles (*Etudes sur le code d'alliance* [Paris: Letouzey et Anè, 1946] 109)
has argued for the influence of redaction within the Book of the Covenant in Exod
21:2, 13-14, 23; 22:21; 23:4-5, in connection with the form "when you. . .," which,
he argued, is used to connect the mishpatim to cultic and religious laws in the
second half of the legislation. See also the earlier work of B. Baentsch, *Das
Bundesbuch: Ex xx 22-xxiii 33* (Halle: Max Niemeyer, 1892) Chapters 1-2; or more
recently S.M. Paul, *Studies in the Book of the Covenant in the Light of Cuneiform
and Biblical Law*, VTSup 18 (Leiden: E.J. Brill, 1970) 106-11.

[48] Childs (*Exodus*, 454), for example, lists a series of redactions (Exod 22:20b, 23;
23:9b) which he describes as "deuteronomic glosses." Another problem that arises
in interpreting the Book of the Covenant within its present narrative context is the
similarity between the cultic ordinances in Exod 23:(13)14-19 and Exod 34:14-26.
For discussion of tradition-historical solutions to the relationship of these units, see,
among others, Beyerlin, *Oldest Sinaitic Traditions*, 82-90; F. E. Wilms, *Das jahwistische Bundesbuch in Exodus 34*, SANT 32 (München: Kösel-Verlag, 1973); and J.
Halbe, *Das Privilegrecht Jahwes Ex 34, 10-26*, FRLANT 114 (Göttingen: Vandenhoeck und Ruprecht, 1975) 391-450.

Book of the Covenant includes codified civil law in casuistic form (Exod 21:1-22:16);[49] religious, cultic, and moral instruction in apodictic form (Exod 20:23, 24-26; 22:17-23:19);[50] and a parenetic conclusion in deuteronomistic style (Exod 23:20-33),[51] which is only loosely connected to the preceding legislation.[52] In spite of the variety of legislation and what must certainly be a complex tradition-historical development, the present form of the Book of the Covenant can be separated into two parts: law (Exod 20:23-23:19) and a parenetic conclusion (Exod 23:20-33), which begins with a general statement of promise (Exod 23:20) and also includes a series of promises that are couched in exhor-

---

[49] For discussion of casuistic law, see F. Michaeli, *Le livre de l'Exode*, CAT 2 (Paris: Delachaux and Niestle, 1974) 194; or Paul, *Studies in the Book of the Covenant*, 112-17.

[50] The material included in Exod 20:23, 24-26; 22:17-23:19 is not itself unified and would appear to reflect at least three distinct traditions: Exod 20:23 is frequently attributed to deuteronomistic redactors along with Exod 20:22 (Noth, *Exodus*, 175; Childs, *Exodus*, 465); Exod 20:24-26 is made up of archaic altar laws (E. Robertson, "The Altar of Earth (Ex 20, 24-26)," *JSS* 1 [1948] 12-21); while Exod 22:17-23:19 is described as "the words" (*děbārîm*) in distinction to the *mišpāṭîm* in Exod 21:1-22:16 (Paul, *Studies in the Book of the Covenant*, 118-24; Childs, *Exodus*, 454-57).

[51] Past research on Exod 23:20-33 has gone in several different directions: (1) Exod 23:20-33 has been interpreted as a covenant blessing on analogy to ancient Near Eastern Treaty Forms. This line of research was inaugurated by von Rad ("Problem of the Hexateuch," 27) when he described a four-part cultic structure to Sinai consisting of exhortation and historical prologue (Exod 19:4-6, 19ff); reading of the law (Exod 20:1-17; 20:22-23:19); promise of blessing (Exod 23:20-33); and sealing of the covenant (Exodus 24). This pattern was further refined by comparative study of ancient Near Eastern Treat Forms. (2) Source critics have interpreted the unit as a combination of E and J with deuteronomic additions on the basis of repetitions like the sending of the messenger or the description of conquest (see, for example, Dillmann, *Exodus*, 251-54; Eissfeldt, *Komposition*, 10, 13-21, or Zenger *Sinaitheophanie*, 213-15). (3) Childs (*Exodus*, 460-61) argues against source-critical solutions for three reasons. He notes that repetition is too frequent throughout the pericope to provide criteria for distinguishing sources; second, he argues that a parenetic style similar to Deuteronomy 7 runs throughout the entire unit; and, finally, he points out that there is no reference to the preceding law within Exod 23:20-33. Thus, Childs (*Exodus*, 461) offers a third avenue of interpretation by concluding that the "passage [is] a sermon which once served a homiletic purpose in Deuteronomistic circles in connection with the occupation of the promised land." This theme, he suggests, provides the reason for its present position as a conclusion to the Book of the Covenant because the land is emphasized in the preceding legislation (Exod 23:14ff).

[52] The loose connection between Exod 23:20-33 and the preceding legislation argues against interpreting this unit as a conclusion to the law-code on analogy to Leviticus 26 and Deuteronomy 27 (see von Rad, "Problem of the Hexateuch," 27; Beyerlin, *Oldest Sinaitic Traditions*, 5). Leviticus 26 and Deuteronomy 27 make explicit reference to the previous legislation, while Exod 23:20-33 makes almost no reference to the preceding law.

tation (Exod 23:25-31).[53] This division between law and
parenetic conclusion in the present form of the Book of the Covenant corresponds form-critically to the Offer of Covenant
(Exod 19:5a) and the Promise of Reward (Exod 19:5ba) in the
Proposal of Covenant. The legislation of the Book of the Covenant in Exod 20:23-23:19 provides the content to the Offer of
Covenant that was absent in the Proposal of Covenant,[54] while
the parenetic conclusion in Exod 23:20-33 repeats and reinforces the initial Promise of Reward.

The final two points of similarity between the Proposal of
Covenant and the Covenant-Closing Ceremony include the
Proclamation of the "Words of Yahweh" by Moses (Exod
19:7/Exod 24:3a, 7a) and the Acceptance of the "Words of
Yahweh" by the People (Exod 19:8a/Exod 24:3b, 7a). Their for-
mal similarity can be illustrated as follows:

> The Proclamation of the "Words of Yahweh" by
> Moses

Exod 19:7 (Moses) called (*wayyiqrā'*) to the elders of
Israel and he placed before them all these
words (*kŏl-
haddĕbbārîm hā'ēlleh*) which Yahweh
commanded

Exod 24:3a Moses read to the people all the words of
Yahweh (*kŏl-dibrê yhwh*) and all the
ordinances

Exod 24:7a (Moses) took the Book of the Covenant
and he called (*wayyiqrā'*) to the people

> The Acceptance of the "Words of Yahweh" by the
> People

Exod 19:8a All the people answered (*wayya'ănû*) together (*yaḥdāw*) and they said,
"All that Yahweh spoke, we will do
(*na'aśeh*)"

---

[53] Yahweh promises Israel in Exod 20:20-33 that their bread and water will be
blessed; that sickness will be turned away, their births healthy, and the days of
Israel full. Furthermore, the terror of Yahweh will go before Israel to confuse their
enemies, who will be given into their hand. Also hornets will precede the people
to drive out the inhabitants, with the result that Yahweh will establish the boundaries of the land for Israel (Exod 23:25-31). However, the condition for these
promises is that the people may make no treaty with any other nation or God (Exod
23:32.

[54] See also Patrick ("The Covenant Code Source," 149) who concludes that "the
laws that follow [Exod 20:22], beginning with the prohibition of images, stand in
place of the conditional clause of Exod xix 5."

Exod 24:3b   All the people answered (*wayya 'an*) with
             one voice (*qôl 'eḥād*) and they said,
             "All the words (*kŏl-haddĕbārîm*) which
             Yahweh spoke, we will do (*na 'aǎseh*)"
Exod 24:7b   They (Israel) said, "All that Yahweh spoke,
             we will do (*na 'ǎseh*) and we will obey
             (*wĕnišma '*)"

The form-critical comparison allows for several conclusions. First, it reinforces Perlitt's conclusion concerning the central role of covenant in the deuteronomistic redaction. Second, it suggests that law and narrative are closely intertwined. And, third, it has demonstrated how the first and third episodes share the same six-part structure. However, the repetitions are not exact, and an examination of three differences between them will both underscore the important role of law in the deuteronomistic redaction, and clarify why the first episode is best designated a Proposal of Covenant, and the third episode a Covenant-Closing Ceremony, in spite of their formal similarities.

The first change to be noted occurs within the Call for Israel "to see" a Past Action of Yahweh. The call for Israel in Exod 19:4 to see Yahweh within the exodus event becomes in Exod 20:22a a call for Israel to see the speech of God from heaven. This change provides insight into a progression within the deuteronomistic redaction. The exodus is the event of salvation that has made possible the Proposal of Covenant in the first episode. However, it is the revelation of the Decalogue, as the initial content of covenant, that allows the story to progress from a Proposal of Covenant to a Covenant-Closing Ceremony in the third episode. This change underscores how theophany has been framed by covenant in the deuteronomistic redaction, as Perlitt has already argued, and how theophany itself is subsumed under the theme of covenant, since the Decalogue is both the culmination of theophany and the content of covenant. Yet, the Decalogue is only one important law-code for the establishment of covenant; the Book of Covenant is also necessary in defining Israel's covenant obligations.

A second change occurs within the Offer of Covenant, and it concerns the absence of law in the first episode and its prominence in the third with the legislation of the Book of the Covenant. The absence of law in the Offer of Covenant provided the basis for designating the opening episode as a Proposal of Covenant, with emphasis on the Promise of Reward. The third episode moves beyond the Proposal of Covenant by presenting

nearly three chapters of detailed covenant obligations within
the Book of the Covenant. Here, the Offer of Covenant (rather
than the Promise of Reward), becomes the point of emphasis.
Thus, beneath the surface similarity of the first and third episodes, there is a progression in narrative logic with regard to the
Offer of Covenant from promise to covenant obligations. This
progression is made possible because of the revelation of deuteronomic law (i.e. the Decalogue and the Book of the Covenant).

A third change occurs within the Proclamation of the
"Words of Yahweh" by Moses and the Acceptance of the
"Words of Yahweh" by the People. These repetitions are central to the deuteronomistic redaction.[55] The shift in emphasis
from promise to covenant conditions is possible within the narrative logic of this redaction because of the pattern of Proclamation and Acceptance, which occurs at the close of the Proposal
of Covenant in Exod 19:7-8a. It is the acceptance by the people
of the initial divine offer of covenant in Exod 19:8a that allows
the text to move beyond a mere Proposal of Covenant to the
covenant conditions themselves. Then, the repetition of this
same pattern at the end of the third episode in Exod 24:3-4aa, 7
brings closure to the entire event.

Two differences between the repetition of Exod 19:7-8a and
Exod 24:3-4aa, 7 underscore Israel's obligations in the final Proclamation and Acceptance. The first difference is that the proclamation of the Book of the Covenant and its acceptance by the
people is repeated both before (Exod 24:3-4aa) and after (Exod
24:7) the sacrificial ritual (Exod 24:4ab-5) in contrast to the single occurrence of the sequence in Exod 19:7-8a. At the very
least, this dual occurrence of the people's acceptance in Exod
24:3-4aa, 7 underscores the important role of the Book of the
Covenant for outlining Israel's covenant obligations. The second difference between the two episodes is that Moses is
presented as actually writing down the words of Yahweh in
Exod 24:4aa after the acceptance by the people (*wayyiktōb
mōšeh 'ēt kŏl-dibrê yhwh*). The writing down of the "words of
Yahweh" along with the acceptance of the people brings closure
to Israel's encounter with God at the mountain, and officially

---

55 See the form-critical work of K. Baltzer (*The Covenant Formulary in the Old
Testament, Jewish, and Early Christian Writings* [Philadelphia: Fortress Press,
1971] 29) where he discusses two "corresponding actions: the declaration of 'all the
words of Yahweh' and the affirmative response of the people." Beyerlin (*Oldest
Sinaitic Traditions*, 15); Childs (*Exodus*, 505) suggest a possible covenant ratifica-
tion form: reading of law, response from the people, sacrifice, and sealing of the
oath. See the criticism by Perlitt *Bundestheologie*, 191-92.

marks the inauguration of Israel's obligations to the written Torah contained within the Decalogue and the Book of the Covenant. The result of the redactional additions of Exod 24:3-4aa, 7
to Exod 24:4ab-5 is that what had been a sacrificial ritual in the
Mountain of God tradition is framed by new material and in the
process transformed into a Covenant-Closing Ceremony.

In summary, we have seen that two themes converge in the
third episode of the deuteronomistic redaction: the authoritative role of Moses as a commissioned teacher and covenant.
Furthermore, we have also seen that the linchpin which holds
these two themes together is deuteronomic law. It is both divine revelation and the content of Israel's covenant obligations.

D. *Conclusion*

At the outset of this chapter the question was raised as to
how the Sinai Complex, whose emphasis was originally on theophany and ritual, came to include legal material. In the preceding redaction-critical analysis I have attempted to outline
how this transformation came about, and that it was the work of
deuteronomistic editors. By way of summary, several conclusions concerning the structure of this redaction are now in
order.

First, the dependence of this redaction on the Mountain of
God tradition is clear. We noted specific links at many points
within the deuteronomistic redaction to older tradition, which
need not be repeated here. On a more general level, we saw
the continuing influence of the three-part sequence of the
Mountain of God tradition and the important role of the mountain setting in providing spatial organization for the subsequent
redaction.

Second, the deuteronomistic redactors have significantly expanded the three-part sequence of the Mountain of God tradition. What had been three scenes within one cycle of
movement by Moses on the mountain (Introduction; Preparation, Purification and Theophany; and Sacrificial Ritual) are expanded into three complete cycles or episodes. The primary
technique by which deuteronomistic redactors have expanded
the Mountain of God tradition has been through framing. Both
the description of theophany and the sacrificial ritual in the
Mountain of God tradition have been framed with expanded introductions and conclusions, which provide the context for law.
For example, the account of theophany in the Mountain of God
tradition is framed by Exod 19:8b-9a [10ab-11a, 12aa, 13b-15a,
16ab-17] and 19:19. Exod 19:8b-9a introduces a new purpose

for theophany, while Exod 19:19 brings the event to a different conclusion. Furthermore, this framing provides the content for law through the revelation of the Decalogue (Exod 20:1-17). The same technique is evident with the sacrificial ritual in the Mountain of God tradition. It, too, is framed with Proclamation and Acceptance of the Book of the Covenant in Exod 24:3-4aa [4ab-5] and 7, which also creates links to the preceding legislation (The Book of the Covenant, Exod 20:33-23:33). In fact, the technique of framing even functions at the level of episodes. The result of the deuteronomistic expansion of the Mountain of God tradition is that Israel's experience of theophany at the mountain, which had been one episode, is now framed by introductory and closing episodes, which introduce the theme of covenant. The three episodes can be summarized in the following manner. The first episode consists of a Proposal of Covenant, with the promise that Israel will be Yahweh's "personal possession." The second episode is a reinterpretation of theophany as divine speech, which now culminates with the public revelation of the Decalogue. And the third episode provides a conclusion to the redaction by transforming the sacrificial ritual into a Covenant-Closing Ceremony, in which the private revelation of the Book of the Covenant is promulgated by Moses and accepted by the people.[56]

Third, the mountain setting is transformed by the deuteronomistic redaction. Yahweh no longer dwells on the mountain; further, the vertical hierarchy of characters in the Mountain of God tradition is redefined. We noticed the latter conclusion particularly in tracing the movement of Moses on the mountain. Although a distinction between Moses and the people is clearly maintained (in fact he appears to be even further idealized within the redaction), there is a consistent pattern throughout the redaction to play down a vertical hierarchy in describing the movement of Moses. Thus, Moses does not ascend and descend the mountain, nor does he function primarily to maintain distance and clear boundaries between the God who dwells on the mountain and the people who are encamped below. Instead, Moses is introduced as a commissioned speaker, who is able to convey reliably the words of Yahweh to the people. In this con-

[56] Our primary focus on Exodus 19-24 precludes a detailed redaction-critical study of the breaking of the covenant and its renewal in Exodus 32-34. However, we would agree with Perlitt (*Bundestheologie*, 203-07) that the motif of the tablets first introduced in Exod 24:12 and carried through Exodus 34 is part of this same deuteronomistic redaction. For analysis of the motif of the tablets in Exodus 32-34 see Chapter 5.

text he is described as "approaching" (*bw'*) the people, as "returning" (*šwb*) the words of the people to Yahweh, or simply as "drawing near" (*ngš*) into the thick darkness of divine presence in order to receive privately the Book of the Covenant. The less precise terms for describing the movement of Moses are possible within the deuteronomistic redaction because of its dependence on the Mountain of God tradition, which had already firmly established the central role of the mountain setting.

The final conclusion is this: the deuteronomistic redaction in Exodus 19-24 is a "planned theological editing," which has transformed Mount Zion in the Mountain of God tradition into Mount Horeb, the mountain of revelation in Deuteronomy. This conclusion provides transition from what has been up to this point primarily an outline of the deuteronomistic redaction in Exodus 19-24 to a more theological investigation concerning the character of divine presence in this material.

II
MOUNT HOREB IN THE DEUTERONOMISTIC REDACTION

Mount Horeb is not specifically mentioned in the deuteronomistic redaction of Exodus 19-24, although *har ḥôrēb* does occur later in Exod 33:6.[57] Nevertheless, the redaction-critical study in the previous section allows for three conclusions which aid us in identifying the mountain setting as representing Mount Horeb. First, we have seen that Mount Horeb is clearly the designation for the mountain of revelation in the Book of Deuteronomy. Second, we have also seen that deuteronomistic tradents encourage the reader to identify Mount Horeb as being the mountain of revelation in Exodus 19-24 by presenting Moses in Deuteronomy as recounting the events of Exodus 19-24 (Deut 4:10, 15; 5:2).[58] The success of the deuteronomistic tradents in making this identification between Mount Horeb and Exodus 19-24 is illustrated in the history of scholarship, where Sinai and Horeb frequently become synonymous terms.[59]

---

[57] See Noth (*Exodus*, 253-54) concerning the deuteronomistic influence in Exod 33:1-6.

[58] See Polzin (*Moses and the Deuteronomist*, 25-72) who describes the speech of Moses in Deuteronomy as being "reported speech" from Exodus.

[59] Sinai and Horeb are rarely distinguished from each other either canonically or tradition-historically. Note, for example how Sinai/Horeb is virtually collapsed into one cosmic mountain in three recent studies on cosmic mountain symbolism within the Hebrew Bible: Levenson, *Sinai and Zion*, 15-19; Cohn, *The Shape of Sacred Space*, 44; Donaldson, *Jesus on the Mountain*, 31-35.

However, this identification is premature, for our concern in this chapter is not with the canonical Pentateuch. Third, we have seen that deuteronomistic tradents have not simply encouraged the reader to identify Mount Horeb as the mountain of revelation in the Book of Deuteronomy, but have also transformed the mountain setting in Exodus 19-24 to correspond with Mount Horeb. On the basis of a variety of similarities in vocabulary, imagery, structure and overall *Tendenz*, I have argued that Mount Horeb is, indeed, the mountain setting in the deuteronomistic redaction of Exodus 19-24.

My aim in this section is to probe the theological significance of Mount Horeb. As a symbol, Mount Horeb represents a cultic theology of divine presence, which functions to evaluate critically Mount Zion in the Mountain of God tradition. This section will separate into four parts in order to map the semantic range of the symbol of Mount Horeb, and to explore the extent of its theological critique of Mount Zion. An examination of the tradition-historical development of Mount Horeb within the Book of Deuteronomy in the first part will provide a starting point for interpreting the theological significance of the mountain setting under the following topics: Divine Presence on Mount Horeb, Moses as Cultic Leader on Mount Horeb, and The Vision of Israel at Mount Horeb.

A. *Mount Horeb within Deuteronomistic Tradition*

Horeb plays a central role in the Book of Deuteronomy as the mountain of revelation for the deuteronomic legislation. The reader is introduced to Horeb in the opening chapter of Deuteronomy (Deut 1:2, 6, 19), and reference to it continues throughout the book (Deut 4:10, 15; 5:2; 9:8; 18:16; 28:69). Nevertheless, a tradition-historical analysis of Horeb within the Book of Deuteronomy raises a problem. The problem is that the use of Horeb is not altogether clear. It shifts somewhat between being a more general location (perhaps a plain) and a specific mountain.[60] This ambiguity is particularly evident in the opening chapter, where Horeb is used twice in an itinerary notice (*mēḥōrēb*, Deut 1:2, 19), while it also designates a specific mountain (*bĕḥōrēb*, Exod 1:6). The ambiguity continues to a certain degree throughout the additional occurrences of the term in so far as a specific reference to *har ḥōrēb* is avoided. This ambiguity has theological significance which must be examined later in this section. However, at this point it raises the question of

---

[60] See Clifford, *Cosmic Mountain*, 121-122.

whether Horeb may have indicated a particular location rather than a specific mountain at an early stage in its tradition-historical development.[61]

Whatever the tradition-historical roots of Horeb may have been, it is clear that it becomes the mountain of theophany within deuteronomistic tradition, and the location for the revelation of law. The word "mountain" is used specifically at a number of points in the Book of Deuteronomy (Deut 1:6; 4:11 (twice); 5:44, 5, 22, 23; 9:5 (twice), 10; 10:4, 10) within the context of Horeb, while the numerous references to Exodus 19-24 through the book encourage the reader to interpret Horeb as the mountain where Israel encountered God and received deuteronomic law.

The tradition-historical development of Mount Horeb within the Book of Deuteronomy can be taken a step further, because the account of theophany at the mountain occurs twice: first in Deut 4:1-40[62] and then again in Deut 5:1-6:3. These accounts of theophany have been judged to be distinct redactions within the Book of Deuteronomy. Deut 5:1-6:3 is judged to be part of a first deuteronomistic redaction perhaps at the end of the pre-exilic period; Deut 4:1-40 is considered to be part of a second deuteronomistic redaction that occurs at a later point during the exilic period.[63] Past research has shown how these two accounts

---

[61] See L. Perlitt ("Sinai und Horeb," *Beiträge zur alttestamentlichen Theologie*, Fs. Zimmerli, ed. H. Donner, R. Hanhart, R. Smend [Göttingen: Vandenhoeck und Ruprecht, 1977] 306-10) for a tradition-historical investigation which associates Horeb with a wilderness location.

[62] There is debate over the unity of Deut 4:1-40. See, for example, G. von Rad (*Deuteronomy*, OTL [Philadelphia: Westminster Press, 1966] 48-52) and more recently Mittmann (*Deuteronomium 1,1-6,3*, 115-28) for arguments against the unity of the chapter because, among other things, of the problem of the Numeruswechsel. But compare, Lohfink (*Höre, Israel!*, 92-97); Braulik (*Die Mittel deuteronomischer Rhetorik*, 91-100; and "Literarkritik und archaologische Stratigraphie: zu S. Mittmanns Analyse von Deuteronomium 4,1-40," *Bib* 5 [1978] 351-83); and A. D. H. Mayes (Deuteronomy 4 and the Literary Criticism of Deuteronomy," *JBL* 100 [1980] 25) for arguments in favor of a unified reading of Deut 4:1-40. For a review of this debate and additional bibliography see C. Begg, "The Literary Criticism of Deut 4,1-40: Contributions to a continuing Discussion," *ETL* 56 (1980) 10-55; and most recently D. Knapp, *Deuteronomium 4: Literarische Analyse und Theologische Interpretation*, Göttingen Theologische Arbeiten 35 (Göttingen: Vandenhoeck und Ruprecht, 1986).

[63] See Mayes ("Deuteronomy 4," 48-51) who locates the first deuteronomistic redaction in the late pre-exilic period (this would include Deut 5:1-6:3) and a second deuteronomistic redaction in the exilic period (this would include Deut 4:1-40). However, compare Lohfink (*Höre, Israel!*, 990-91) who would place both redactions in the exilic period. For discussion of the influence of the double redaction of deuteronomistic editors throughout the Deuteronomistic History see Cross, *Ca-*

of theophany reflect an emerging theological perspective concerning divine cultic presence, one that is first presented in
Deut 5:1-6:3 at the end of the monarchy period and then refined in Deut 4:1-40 during the exile. Scholars have also suggested that this tradition-historical development is carried over
into the present form of Deuteronomy by the way in which the
two redactions are juxtaposed. As the later redaction, Deut 4:1-
40 is given precedence in Deuteronomy; it functions both as a
closing exhortation to the first speech of Moses (Deut 1:1-4:40),[64]
and as a theological introduction for interpreting the second
speech of Moses (Deut 4:44-28:68), with its account of the revelation of the Decalogue in Deut 5:1-6:3.[65]

The tradition-historical development of Mount Horeb within
the Book of Deuteronomy provides a framework for evaluating
the deuteronomistic redaction in Exodus 19-24 tradition-historically. The tendency in the most recent scholarship has been to
look for the same two-part redaction in Exodus 19-24 that is evident in the Book of Deuteronomy, particularly with regard to
the incorporation of the two deuteronomic law-codes—the Decalogue and the Book of the Covenant. Zenger, for example, has
argued for two deuteronomistic redactions in the development
of Exodus 19-24, each of which significantly alters the structure
of the material. The first redaction would consist of the Decalogue and the introduction of covenant theology into Exodus 19-
24, while the second would significantly restructure the material
again with the insertion of the Book of the Covenant.[66]

In contrast to the hypothesis outlined above, I have argued
in the previous section that the overall structure of the deuteronomistic redaction in Exodus 19-24 is essentially a single process, which has followed the three-part sequence of the
Mountain of God tradition. Furthermore, I would identify this
redaction with the first redaction in the Book of Deuteronomy,
probably in the late monarchy period. This would mean that
the first deuteronomistic redaction in the Book of Deuteronomy
is "pentateuchal" in nature, that is, the revelation of the Deca-

naanite Myth and Hebrew Epic, 274-89 and R. D. Nelson, *The Double Redaction of
the Deuteronomistic History*, JSOTSup 18 (Sheffield: JSOT Press, 1981). For a brief
overview of scholarship on deuteronomistic tradition see Mayes, *The Story of Israel
between Settlement and Exile*, 1-21.

[64] The relationship between Deuteronomy 1-3 and Deuteronomy 4 has received
extensive study. See, among others, Braulik, "Literarkritik," 357-58; Mayes, "Deuteronomy 4," 31; Polzin, *Moses and the Deuteronomist*, 40-41.

[65] Lohfink, *Höre Israel!*, 91.

[66] Zenger *Sinaitheophanie*, 119ff. See a summary on pp. 164-65. For Zenger, these
redactions would be exilic and post-exilic.

logue at Mount Horeb in Deuteronomy is simultaneously anchored in Exodus 19-24. In that case, the Book of Deuteronomy is not meant to function independently, but as part of a larger epic about Israel's formative encounter with God at the mountain. Support for this conclusion arises from looking at the Decalogue within its context in the deuteronomistic redaction. This revelation is not an end in itself in either Exodus or Deuteronomy. Rather in each context it is meant to lead to the private revelation to Moses of additional deuteronomic law. When viewed as a whole (Exodus 19-Deuteronomy), the point of emphasis in this redaction is the deuteronomic legislation in the Book of Deuteronomy, for it contains most of this private revelation.[67]

The second deuteronomistic redaction is not "pentateuchal" in nature. Rather it is limited primarily to the Book of Deuteronomy (Deut 4:1-40). By this I mean that although this redaction may, in fact, have refined some of the imagery of Mount Horeb in Exodus 19-24, it has not restructured the material in any significant way. The imagery of divine approach, in contrast to a God who dwells on the mountain; the presence of God as speech; the development from a public to a private revelation; and the idealization of Moses as a commissioned teacher of deuteronomic law are all features that are in place in Exodus 19-24 prior to the second deuteronomistic redaction. This is not to say that a more refined redaction-critical analysis would be unable to demonstrate the influence of this latter redaction in Exodus 19-24—as, for example, the explicit reference to "heaven" in Exod 20:22b as the location of divine speech. Nevertheless, additions such as this must be judged as refinements of a structure and overall *Tendenz* that is already in place. Thus, it is more midrashic than redactional in character.[68]

A number of reasons have been provided to account for why a more precise articulation of Horeb became desirable within deuteronomic tradition, which may have given rise to a second

---

[67] For similar discussion concerning the possibility that not only the Sinai Complex, but even the entire Pentateuch served as an introduction to Deuteronomy and the Deuteronomistic History see Mayes, *The Story of Israel Between Settlement and Exile*, 139-49; and Rendtorff, *Problem des Pentateuch*, 167-68.

[68] By midrashic I mean that the reference to "heaven" in Exod 20:22b simply makes *explicit* what is already *implicit* in the overall structure of the deuteronomistic redaction. Thus, even if it is attributed to a second deuteronomistic redaction it would not add significantly to the deuteronomistic redaction already in place in Exodus 19-24. For discussion of such midrashic (or aggadic) forms of interpretation see M. Fishbane, *Biblical Interpretation in Ancient Israel* (Oxford: Clarendon Press, 1985) 281-93.

deuteronomistic redaction during the exilic period: it has been suggested that in the context of the exile there was a need to accentuate the dangers of idolatry, or a need to emphasize the command not to worship other Gods, or a need to state the importance of covenant and law for defining the people of God.[69] I would suggest that another factor which has influenced the more precise articulation of Horeb within the Book of Deuteronomy (Deut 4:1-40) is the rise of a priestly redaction in Exodus 19-24, which has transformed the mountain setting once again in order to incorporate the priestly legislation as being part of the content of God's revelation at the mountain. Within this redaction, priestly tradents present their own theological response to Mount Zion by introducing Mount Sinai (the mountain of revelation for the priestly legislation) as being the mountain of theophany in Exodus 19-24. In the process, they also displace what had been the central role of Horeb in Exodus 19-24, which may have given rise to the second deuteronomistic redaction in Deut 4:1-40.[70] According to this tradition-historical assessment the first deuteronomistic redaction is not the final redaction of Exodus 19-24. Rather, the final redaction is a priestly redaction. A further exploration of this hypothesis must wait for the subsequent chapters.

More could certainly be said concerning the tradition-historical development of Mount Horeb within deuteronomistic tradition. The primary purpose for exploring the tradition history of Mount Horeb has been to provide background for an interpretation of its theological significance. At the very least the tradition-historical development of Israel's encounter with God at the mountain within the Book of Deuteronomy and in Exodus 19-24 allows for three conclusions: first, that the theology of divine cultic presence symbolized in Mount Zion within the Mountain of God tradition presents a problem for deuteronomistic tradents; second, that Mount Horeb is a central symbol within the deuteronomistic response to this problem; and third, that the exile accentuated the problem of divine presence.

B. *Divine Presence on Mount Horeb*

I hope to demonstrate in this section that Mount Horeb symbolizes a different quality of divine cultic presence, which is

---

[69] See, for example, Mayes, "Deuteronomy 4," 48-51.
[70] Compare Perlitt ("Sinai und Horeb," 307-21) who argues just the reverse: that Horeb displaces Sinai in deuteronomistic tradition. However, Perlitt also argues that Sinai returns within priestly tradition.

meant to provide a critique of Mount Zion within the Mountain of God tradition. In particular, we will see that the metaphorical relationship of resemblance between the mountain and God in the Mountain of God tradition (where God was identified as dwelling on the mountain) is replaced by deuteronomistic tradents with a metonymic relationship of contiguity.[71] The shift to metonymy by deuteronomistic redactors no longer allows for the overlap or identification between God and the mountain setting central to the Mountain of God tradition. The result of this is that instead of the mountain symbolizing the dwelling place of God, it becomes the point of contact between God in heaven and the worshipping community on earth both within the deuteronomistic redaction of Exodus 19-24 and in the Book of Deuteronomy. The distinction between Zion and Horeb that I have outlined here can be illustrated by examining two points of contrast between them. The first point of contrast is the image of God dwelling on the mountain in the Mountain of God tradition as compared to the "relocation" of God to heaven in the deuteronomistic redaction of Exodus 19-24 and in the Book of Deuteronomy. The second point of contrast concerns the static imagery of God in the Mountain of God tradition as compared to the mobile imagery of God in the deuteronomistic redaction.

1. *Mount Horeb and the Relocation of God to Heaven*

In the deuteronomistic redaction God is relocated to heaven rather than being identified permanently with the mountain. The result of this separation is that God does not dwell perma-

---

[71] Wellek and Warren (*Theory of Literature*, 194) describe metonymy as poetry of association by contiguity in contrast to metaphor, which is poetry of association by comparison. Hence in metonymy there is not a joining of a plurality of worlds as there is in metaphor, rather there is only a single world of discourse. Brown (*World of Imagery*, 149-53) provides further contrast between metaphor and metonymy, which aids in defining the latter. He notes that metaphor is based on analogy, and that the movement of metaphor is from the concrete to the abstract, with the result that a given idea and figure (a signifier and a signified) intersect in a relationship of identity. In contrast to this, metonymy is a movement from the abstract to the concrete, in which the imported notion (the signified) may be closely linked with the given idea (signifier), but it is never identified with it. The contrast between metaphor and metonymy is developed within linguistics in general by R. Jakobson, "Two Aspects of Language and Two Types of Aphasic Disturbances," *Fundamentals of Language* (The Hague: Mouton, 1956) 55-82. For an analysis of the implications of Jakobson's work within literary criticism see G. Genette, *Figures of Literary Discourse*, (New York: Columbia University Press, 1982) 103-21. For further contrasts between metaphor and metonymy see Ricoeur, *The Rule of Metaphor*, 55-59; and Soskice, *Metaphor and Religious Language*, 57-58.

nently on the mountain, and, when God is present on the mountain, the divine presence must be perceived as speech. An overview of the deuteronomistic redaction in Exodus 19-24 will illustrate this theology of divine presence.

The separation of God from the mountain in the deuteronomistic redaction is made clear through the imagery of a divine "approach" (*bw'*) in Exod 19:9a; 20:20, which severs a permanent identification between God and the mountain. The explicit reference to "heaven" in Exod 20:22a also underscores this point. Once the transcendence of God is firmly established in the deuteronomistic redaction, the emphasis on auditory motifs provides a means of affirming a new vision of the cultic presence of God. The presence of God as speech is made explicit at a number of points. It is stated in the divine announcement of theophany (Exod 19:9a), in the actual description of the event (Exod 19:19; 20:1-17), and in the recounting of theophany by the people (Exod 20:19), by Moses (Exod 20:20) and by God (Exod 20:22a). By relocating God in heaven and by underscoring the need for Yahweh to approach the mountain in order to be present for theophany, deuteronomistic redactors have introduced a distinction between heaven and the cultic presence of God which fragments the concept of unity that was central to Zion and implied in the Mountain of God tradition. According to Mettinger, the rejection of this concept of unity is one of the primary components of the Deuteronomic Name theology.[72] The conclusion by Mettinger that the Deuteronomic Name theology is a central component in the deuteronomistic critique of Zion suggests that in order to interpret in detail the quality of divine presence symbolized by Mount Horeb, we must broaden the scope of our study and also raise the question of the relationship of Mount Horeb to the Deuteronomic Name theology.

The Deuteronomic Name theology designates a theology of divine cultic presence, in which the divine "name" (*šem*) is confessed as being present in the sanctuary.[73] In the Book of Deuteronomy the formulaic confession of the presence of the "name" (*šem*) occurs nine times in two distinct forms (*lĕšakkēn šem*, and *lāśûm šem*),[74] and always within the context of the cult:

---

[72] Mettinger, *The Dethronement of Sabaoth*, 38-79 esp. 46-48.

[73] See G. von Rad, *Studies in Deuteronomy*, Studies in Biblical Theology 9 (Chicago: Henry Regnery Co.; 1953) 37-44; M. Weinfeld, *Deuteronomy and the Deuteronomic School* (Oxford: Clarendon Press, 1972) 191-209. For a recent review of past scholarship see Mettinger, *The Dethronement of Sabaoth*, 41-46.

[74] The aim of the present study is limited in focus in order to underscore an inherent relationship between Mount Horeb and the "place of the name" within the

in Deuteronomy 12 the people are commanded to erect an altar only at the place of the name; in Deuteronomy 14 Moses conveys further cultic instructions concerning tithes—they, too, must be brought yearly before Yahweh to the place of the name; in Deuteronomy 16 the celebration of the Passover is also limited to the place where Yahweh's name dwells; and, finally, in Deuteronomy 26 the offering of first fruits is also directed to the place where the name is present. Although the "place of the name" is undoubtedly a cult center, its specific location is not spelled out in the Book of Deuteronomy. Yet the use of this formula, after the accounts of theophany at Mount Horeb (Deuteronomy 4-5) and always in connection with the cult (Deuteronomy 12, 14, 16, 26), suggests that wherever "the place of the name" is finally located, that location would be Mount Horeb—the place where the cultic presence of Yahweh as speech is anchored in the Book of Deuteronomy.

Von Rad has described the Deuteronomic Name theology as a theological corrective, meant to replace the older idea of Yahweh's presence in the Jerusalem temple.[75] The present study is following von Rad's lead at this point. I would add that Mount Horeb must also be seen as part of the Deuteronomic Name theology, for, as a cosmic mountain, it provides symbolic expression concerning the character and quality of divine cultic presence that is also part of the theological corrective of Mount Zion within deuteronomistic tradition. Mount Horeb (and the

Book of Deuteronomy. A thorough analysis of the Name Formula in Deuteronomic tradition would require that our study be expanded in two directions: contextually and tradition-historically. With regard to context, it would also have to include at least the Deuteronomistic History. Tradition-historically, it would have to include not two, but three forms of the Name Formula within the Book of Deuteronomy: a short form, which does not make reference to the name (*šem*); (*hammāqôm 'ăšer yibḥar YHWH*, Deut 12:14, 18, 26; 14:25; 15:20; 16:7, 15, 16; 17:8, 10; 18:6; 31:11); a longer form, which employs the expression *lĕšakkēn šem* "to establish the name" (*hammāqôm 'ăšer yibḥar YHWH ['ĕlōhêkā bô] lĕšakkēn šĕmô šām*, Deut 12:11; 14:23; 16:2, 6, 11; 26:2); and a longer form, which uses the expression *lāśûm sem* "to put the name" (*hammāqôm 'ăšer yibḥar YHWH 'ĕlōhêkā/kem lāśûm ('et) šĕmô šām*, Deut 12:5, 21; 14:24). For more detailed discussion of the Name Formula within the larger context of ancient Near Eastern literature see S. Dean McBride, *The Deuteronomic Name Theology* (PhD. Thesis, Harvard University, 1969). For a tradition-historical analysis, see, among others, M. Rose, *Der Ausschliesslichkeitanspruch Jahwes: Deuteronomische Schultheologie und die Volksfrömmigkeit in der späten Königszeit*, BWANT 106 (Stuttgart: W. Kohlhammer, 1975) 59-94, and Mettinger, *The Dethronement of Sabaoth*, 38-79 esp. 46-56. For study of the Name Formula within the present context of Deuteronomy see J.G. McConville, *Law and Theology in Deuteronomy*, JSOTSup 33 (Sheffield: JSOT Press, 1984) 21-38.

[75] Von Rad, *Studies in Deuteronomy*, 38-39.

Deuteronomic Name theology) allow for several conclusions concerning the quality of divine cultic presence for deuteronomistic tradents. First, the permanent dwelling of God is separated from the cosmic mountain and located, instead, in heaven. Second, when God approaches the cult, his presence must be perceived as speech. Third, the use of the verb *škn* within the Deuteronomic Name theology to characterize the presence of the divine "name" provides an additional piece of information concerning the quality of divine presence as speech on Mount Horeb. Here we learn that even though the permanent dwelling place of God is in heaven, the "name" or speech of God "is established" on Mount Horeb.[76] And fourth, the emphasis on divine transcendence that runs throughout these conclusions is a qualification of the concept of unity that had been central to Mount Zion. And this lays the groundwork for a shift from metaphor to metonymy in describing the relationship between God and Mount Horeb. The "relocation" of God to heaven, however, is insufficient in itself for Mount Horeb to function metonymically as a symbol of divine cultic presence, since the static imagery of God within the Mountain of God tradition must also be reevaluated.

2. *Mount Horeb and the Mobile Character of God*

A second way in which deuteronomistic tradents have presented a critique of Mount Zion is in the emphasis on divine mobility that is associated with Mount Horeb. In the deuteronomistic redaction of Exodus 19-24 the reader is told explicitly that Yahweh must "approach" (*bw'*) the mountain in order to be present (Exod 19:9a; 20:20).[77] This emphasis on divine mobil-

[76] There is debate over the meaning of the Piel form of škn in the expression *lĕšak-kēn šem*. The translation presented here follows the work of McBride (*The Deuteronomic Name Theology*, 204-10) who has argued that the Qal form of *škn* means "to tent, encamp," and that the Piel form of *škn* is a *Namen setzen* formula best translated as "to establish." However, compare Mettinger (*The Dethronement of Sabaoth*, 56-59) who would disagree with McBride's interpretation primarily for two reasons: methodologically, he argues that McBride has overemphasized the comparative data; and more seriously, he argues that McBride's conclusion with regard to the Qal of *škn* as meaning "to tent, encamp" is "unproven, not to say dead wrong." Thus, the real debate concerning the meaning of the Piel form *škn* in the Deuteronomic Name Formula concerns the Qal form of the word. We must return to this debate in Chapter 4 in order to interpret the Priestly Kabod Theology, where the Qal form of *škn* plays a central role in describing the divine cultic presence.

[77] This conclusion contrasts to Mettinger (*The Dethronement of Sabaoth*, 125) who concludes that "Deuteronomistic theology does not mention how God 'comes' or 'descends'. . . ." Furthermore, note that the use of *bw'* for describing the approach

ity is a necessary correlate if the divine cultic presence is to remain a reality for deuteronomistic tradents, since a static vision of Yahweh in heaven is virtually agnostic.

The function of Mount Horeb in the Book of Deuteronomy complements the imagery of divine mobility in the deuteronomistic redaction of Exodus 19-24 in two ways. First, the use of the verb "to tabernacle" (*škn*) in association with the presence of the divine "name" implies imagery of divine mobility between heaven and the cult.[78] Second, I would suggest that there is also geographical mobility implied in the symbol of Mount Horeb, when it is seen in relation to the Name Formula in the Book of Deuteronomy. By this I mean that the "name" of God at Mount Horeb is not tied permanently to a fixed cultic location as Mount Zion was. This latter conclusion corresponds well to the ambiguity of both Mount Horeb and "the place of the name" throughout the Book of Deuteronomy. However, it runs counter to a broad consensus among scholars that the emphasis on centralization of the cult in Deuteronomy 12 is tied to the Jerusalem temple.[79] Even though Jerusalem is not mentioned in Deuteronomy 12, a strong argument for this conclusion arises from the deuteronomistic redaction of Solomon's dedication of the temple in 1 Kings 8, where the name is repeatedly associated with the Jerusalem temple (1 Kgs 8:20, 29, 33, 35, 41, 42, 43 [twice], 44, 48), and where reference is even made to Horeb (1 Kgs 8:9). Hence the geographical ambiguity of Mount Horeb and the "place of the name" within the Book of

of Yahweh to the mountain with in the deuteronomic redaction of Exodus 19-24 is carried over into Deut 4:1-40, where the verb is repeatedly used to describe Israel's possession of the land as a gift from Yahweh (Deut 4:1, 5, 21, 38). See Braulik (*Die Mittel deuteronomischer Rhetorik*, 95) for discussion of the use of *bw'* in Deut 4:1-40. See McConville (*Law and Theology in Deuteronomy*, 33-35) for discussion of the use of *bw'* in conjunction with *hammāqôm* in the larger context of Deuteronomy. He concludes that "the force of the phraseology" (*bw'* + *māqôm*) "is to stress the agency of Yahweh in Israel's coming into the land." The work of Braulik and McConville underscore how language of divine presence is tied in to the gift of the land in deuteronomic tradition.

[78] So Cross, *Canaanite Myth and Hebrew Epic*, 299; and M. Görg, *Das Zelt der Begegnung: Untersuchung zur Gestalt der Sakralen Zelttraditionen Altisraels*, BBB 27 (Bonn: Peter Hanstein, 1967) 98-124.

[79] See already Wellhausen, *Prolegomena*, 32-33, 492 *et passim*. And more recently J. D. Levenson ("From Temple to Synagogue: 1 Kings 8," *Traditions in Transformation*, ed. B. Halpern and J. D. Levenson [Winona Lake: Eisenbrauns, 1981] 158) who writes "Deuteronomy 12 sounds the great Deuteronomic call for sacrifice in Jerusalem and in Jerusalem alone. . . ." See also R. E. Clements, "Deuteronomy and the Jerusalem Cult Tradition," *VT* 15 (1965) 300-12; and E. W. Nicholson, "The Centralization of the Cult in Deuteronomy," *VT* 13 (1963) 380-89. For a recent review of scholarship see McConvill, *Law and Theology in Deuteronomy*, 21-38.

Deuteronomy must be evaluated in the context of the apparent specificity of the Jerusalem temple in 1 Kings 8.

A thorough redaction-critical investigation of 1 Kings 8 is beyond the scope of this study and perhaps unnecessary for our purposes in evaluating whether the cult centralization in Deuteronomy 12 is permanently tied to the Jerusalem cult.[80] Given the focus of the present study, two features of 1 Kings 8 are of particular importance for interpreting the character of divine mobility within deuteronomistic tradition.

The first point of interest in 1 Kings 8 is the emphasis that Yahweh dwells permanently in heaven and not in the temple. Although Solomon is presented as identifying the presence of God with the Jerusalem temple, deuteronomistic redactors have also gone out of their way to underscore that Yahweh is not restricted to this temple, but actually hears the prayers of the people in heaven (see especially 1 Kgs 8:27, and also vv 34, 36, 39, 43, 45, 49). This imagery suggests that Yahweh is not tied to the Jerusalem cult.

The second point of interest for interpreting the character of divine mobility in deuteronomistic tradition is the use of the "name" in 1 Kings 8. Repeatedly throughout Solomon's prayer the reader learns that the reason why Yahweh hears the prayers of the people at the Jerusalem cult is because his "name" is present there (e.g., v 29). The opening cultic ritual in 1 Kgs 8:1-11 identifies the presence of the "name" as the "tablets of stone" in the Ark of the Covenant, which, the reader is told, represent Horeb (1 Kgs 8:9), and employs imagery of divine mobility in describing the "approach" (*bw'*) of the Ark to the Holy of Holies. These verses underscore the mobile character of the divine presence in the Jerusalem temple with the same language as the deuteronomistic redaction of Exodus 19-24 (Exod 19:9a; 20:20), where *bw'* also describes the divine approach to the mountain. This imagery of divine mobility in association with the Ark suggest that it is not the Jerusalem cult *per se*, but the Ark of the

---

[80] With regard to the influence of deuteronomistic tradents in this chapter, S. J. De Vries (*1 Kings*, Word Biblical Commentary 12 [Waco: Word Books, 1985] 121) writes that "modern criticism is unanimous in attributing the bulk of 1 Kgs 8 to Dtr. . . . [It] is especially crucial in Dtr's overall plan because he here takes advantage of an opportunity to make Solomon the mouthpiece of his theology." The "relocation" of God to heaven, the motif of the divine "name" in the temple, the emphasis on covenant, etc. clearly designate the influence of deuteronomistic tradents in the canonical form of the text. Yet, there is debate with regard to the number of deuteronomistic redactions that are present in the canonical form of the text. For recent discussion see Levenson, "From Temple to Synagogue," 140-66; and Nelson, *The Double Redaction of the Deuteronomistic History*, 69-73.

Covenant with its content of deuteronomic law that is the point of focus for "the place of the name."

The emphasis on deuteronomic law and the imagery of a divine "approach" in 1 Kings 8 suggest that this text may be functioning as the cultic *Sitz im Leben* for the theophany of Yahweh on Mount Horeb. This imagery, however, does not limit the cultic presence of God to the Jerusalem cult. Thus, we can conclude that although there is a centralization of the cult in Deuteronomy, the geographical ambiguity both of Mount Horeb and of "the place of the name" sets the stage for a more mobile understanding of divine cultic presence than was possible with Zion, where the presence of God on the mountain was static, firmly fixed in the Jerusalem temple. In contrast to Zion-Sabaoth theology, the Jerusalem temple could be "the place of the name," but there is nothing inherent to the Deuteronomic Name theology which suggests that it *must* be "the place of the name."[81] This contrast represents a significant difference between Mount Zion and Mount Horeb.

The rejection of the more static view of God as dwelling on the mountain in favor of mobile imagery of God approaching the mountain is an important counterpart to the deuteronomistic emphasis on divine transcendence that has already been described. It is the combination of divine transcendence and divine mobility that allows Mount Horeb to function metonymically as a symbol of divine presence in Exodus 19-24. The result of this combination is that in the deuteronomistic redaction of the Mountain of God tradition, the mountain setting is no longer identified as the place where God dwells. Rather, it represents a relationship of contiguity between the transcendent God and the worshipping community: it is the point of contact which results from Yahweh's "approach" (*bw'*). In particular, the point of contact within the symbol of Horeb is the speech of God that is codified in deuteronomic law. The implication of this particular focus is that the divine presence need not be limited to a particular cult center, but that God is present wherever deuteronomic law is authoritatively proclaimed. For deuteronomistic redactors this can only take place at one cult center, which would appear to be wherever the Ark of the Covenant is located. This location would then be Mount Horeb. With this emphasis on speech and law in worship, one can already see in

---

[81] So also McConville, *Law and Theology in Deuteronomy*, 21-38. Von Rad (*Studies in Deuteronomy*, 38-39) also hints at this when he concludes that the place (*māqôm*) of the name in Deuteronomy need not necessarily be thought of as Jerusalem.

Mount Horeb the cultic roots for worship in the synogogue.[82]

We can summarize the character of divine presence that is symbolized by Mount Horeb in the following diagram:

MOUNT HOREB

HEAVEN

(The permanent dwelling place of God)

↓

God "approaches" (bw')
and the "name" of God "is established" ($škn$)/"is placed" ($śwn$)
on the summit of Mount Horeb
in order to convey Deuteronomic Law to Moses

↓

SUMMIT OF MOUNT HOREB

(Moses as the commissioned teacher of Deuteronomic Law)

↗　　　　　　　　　↖

"draws near" ($ngś$) to　　　"approaches" (bw') the people
God　　　　　　　　with Deuteronomic Law

BASE OF MOUNT HOREB

(The people of Israel)

Yahweh's "personal possession" ($sĕgullâ$)

C. *Moses as Cultic Leader on Mount Horeb*

We have already seen that the presentation of Moses is transformed in the deuteronomistic redaction of the Mountain of God tradition. Moses functions less as a mediator and more as a commissioned prophet or teacher who speaks with God and conveys deuteronomic law to Israel. This idealization of Moses as a cultic leader is a central component within the symbol of Mount Horeb for two reasons. First, the role of Moses as a commissioned teacher complements the emphasis on the presence

---

[82] See Haag ("Das 'Buch des Bundes,' " 30) on the interrelationship of Horeb and the rise of the synagogue. For further discussion concerning the rise of the synagogue see J. Weingreen, *From Bible to Mishna: The Continuity of Tradition* (Manchester, Manchester University Press, 1976) 115-31; Levenson, "From Temple to Synagogue," 143-66. For a more detailed discussion on the cultic transformation that may have taken place under deuteronomic reform see Mettinger, *The Dethronement of Sabaoth*, 67-74.

of God as speech at Mount Horeb. Second, and more importantly, the breakdown of a *metaphorical* identification between God and Mount Horeb in favor of a *metonymic* relationship of contiguity accentuates the need for a commissioned teacher like Moses to bridge the chasm between God and Israel by promulgating God's law. The result is that Moses becomes a metaphor for divine speech within the worshipping community. Two motifs associated with Moses in the deuteronomistic redaction of Exodus 19-24 illustrate how he functions metaphorically in representing divine speech at Mount Horeb.

First, a metaphorical relationship of resemblance is established between God and Moses with regard to their movement on Mount Horeb. In particular, the movement of each is described with the verb "to approach" (*bw'*). An examination of the four instances of this term will illustrate the important role of Moses within the cult. Twice *bw'* describes the "approach" of God to Mount Horeb for theophany, where the emphasis is on divine speech (Exod 19:9a; 20:20); twice *bw'* describes the "approach" of Moses to the people, in contexts where he functions as the one who reliably conveys divine speech (Exod 19:7; 24:3). When the four instances of *bw'* are combined, we see that Moses mirrors the movement of God and that it results in the following idealization of Moses on Mount Horeb: the approach of God for theophany (defined as speech) is transferred to Moses, who becomes the authoritative teacher of deuteronomic law.[83]

Second, a metaphorical relationship of resemblance is also established between God and Moses with regard to the motif of the "name." The motif of the "name" is introduced in the third episode of the deuteronomistic redaction, where its two occurrences frame the legislation of the Book of the Covenant. The motif first occurs in the archaic altar law (Exod 20:[23]24-26) that presently functions as an introduction to the Book of the Covenant.[84] In Exod 20:24 Yahweh promises blessing in every place where the "name" is proclaimed.[85] The motif occurs a second time in the parenetic conclusion to the Book of the Covenant (Exod 23:20-33), which, as we have seen, functions as a concluding promise to the legislation within the Book of the

---

[83] See McConville (*Law and Theology in Deuteronomy*, 33-35) for discussion concerning how the verb *bw'* is extended beyond Moses to the people of Israel.

[84] For interpretation of the altar law see Robertson, "The Altar of Earth (Ex 20, 24-26)," 12-21. For a review of past scholarship and an analysis of Exod 20:23 in relation to vv. 24-26 see Childs *Exodus*, 446, 464-67.

[85] Note also the use of *bw'* in describing the divine approach in Exod 20:24: *bĕkŏl-hammāqôm 'ăšer 'ăzkîr 'et-šĕmî 'ābô' 'ēlêkā*.

Covenant. In Exod 23:21, Yahweh warns Israel not to rebel against his angel or messenger, whom he has sent to lead the people. Israel must listen to his voice, because, we are told, he carries the "name" of God within him. Whatever the prehistory of this text may have been with regard to the angel or messenger of Yahweh, within its present context Moses is the most likely one fulfilling the role.[86] His voice must be obeyed because he is the commissioned teacher, who has received the private revelation of deuteronomic law. Thus, he carries the "name" of God. This role of Moses is not limited to Exodus 19-24, but is embedded in the structure of the Book of Deuteronomy which is presented to the reader as sermons by Moses.[87]

In summary, as a cosmic mountain, Horeb signifies that the cult provides a point of contact (a metonymic relationship of contiguity) between Good in heaven and worshipping community on earth; it also signifies that Moses, as the cultic leader, provides a point of identity (a metaphorical relationship of resemblance) for the divine cultic presence. He not only mirrors the movement of God; he even carries within himself the "name" of God. Our earlier study of Moses in Exodus 19-24 helps us to fill out the deuteronomistic presentation of this cultic leadership on Mount Horeb. The portrait of Moses on Mount Horeb is that of a cultic leader who is charismatic and anti-hierarchical. Not only have deuteronomistic redactors de-emphasized a clearly defined vertical hierarchy in describing the movement of Moses on Mount Horeb, but, they have also underscored that his authority does not rest solely in his divine commission, rather the people must authenticate him by hearing the words of God in his speech. This presentation of Moses within the context of a theology of divine cultic presence as speech raises still further questions about the cultic *Sitz im Leben* of the deuteronomistic redaction in general, and, its relationship to the rise of the synogogue in particular. However, these questions must be left aside, for my aim is not to reconstruct the cultic practice of the Deuteronomic Name theology. Rather, my aim is to probe the symbolic expression of Horeb within deutero-

---

[86] Childs (*Exodus*, 487) may be correct in stating that there is a pre-history to the guiding angel in Exod 23:20-22, which suggests a direct identification with God. The identification of the messenger with Moses in the present context of Exod 19-24, however, cannot be excluded.

[87] Lohfink, (*Höre Israel!*, 15-16) interprets Deut 1:1; 4:44; 28:69; 33:1 as introductions to four speeches by Moses, with Deuteronomy 34 functioning as a closing account of Moses' death. Compare also Polzin, *Moses and the Deuteronomist*, 25-72.

nomistic tradition, and that aim requires that we probe yet a third component central to Mount Horeb.

D. *The Vision of Israel at Mount Horeb*

Mount Horeb also contains a vision of the people of God. One of the prominent characteristics of Israel in the deuteronomistic redaction of Exodus 19-24 and in the Book of Deuteronomy is that they fear the "word of Yahweh." This fear is applauded in Exod 20:20 and in Deut 5:28-29. In the former instance, Moses tells Israel that their fear is meant to keep them from sinning; in the latter text, as we have seen, the reader is made privy to wishful thinking by Yahweh, when he states to Moses the ideal scenario for Israel—that they would always fear divine speech and obey deuteronomic law.

In the opening episode of the deuteronomistic redaction there is an even more central image that is meant to characterize the people of God at Mount Horeb. That image occurs in the "Promise of Reward" within the Proposal of Covenant, when Israel is told that, as the people of God, they will be Yahweh's "personal possession" (*sĕgullâ*, Exod 19:5ba).[88] The use of *sĕgullâ* in the deuteronomistic promise is meant to envision an exclusive relationship between Yahweh and Israel as the ideal for the people of God.[89] This ideal is made explicit by the

---

[88] There is debate whether the term *sĕgullâ* conveys inherent value in its description of Israel (in which case Israel would be described as "a treasure" or "a precious treasure"), or simply describes the quality of the relationship between Yahweh and Israel (in which case Israel would be described as having an exclusive relationship with Yahweh—as God's "private possession" or "personal possession"). See, for example, the following conflicting interpretations and translations. Mosis ("Ex 19,5b-6a: Syntaktischer Aufbau und lexikalische Semantik," 18) writes, "Dennoch hat *sĕgullah* in erster Linie nicht diese kostbarkeit im blick. . . ." J. P. Hyatt (*Exodus*, NCB [London: Oliphants, 1971] 200), Beyerlin (*Oldest Sinaitic Traditions*, 67), and Zenger (*Sinaitheophanie*, 167) agree with Mosis in emphasizing the relational quality of the term by translating *sĕgullâ* as "my own possession." But the translations of Childs (*Exodus*, 341, 367) and Noth (*Exodus*, 157) as "special possession" already begin to imply inherent value in the term. McNiele (*Exodus*, 110) and Driver (*Exodus*, 170) emphasize the inherent quality in the term even more by translating *sĕgullâ* as "peculiar treasure," as does Wildberger (*Jahwes Eigentumsvolk*, 76) "Kostbarer persönlicher Besitz" and Paul (*Studies in the Book of the Covenant*, 30) "treasured possession." Finally see C. F. Keil and F. Delitzsch (*Commentary on the Old Testament I* [Grand Rapids: Eerdmans, 1981 (Reprint of 1862)] 96) who argue that *segulla* does "not denote property in general but valuable property. . . ."

[89] The use of *sĕgullâ* in ancient Near Eastern literature and in nontheological contexts within the Hebrew Bible supports an interpretation of this term in deuteronomistic parenesis as designating an exclusive relationship between Yahweh and Israel. For example M. Greenberg ("Hebrew *segulla*: Akkadian *sikiltu*," *JAOS* 71 [1951] 173) notes that the Akkadian *sikiltum* is an economic term, which translates

syntax of the promise, when the separative use of the preposition *min* is employed in order to distinguish Israel from the other nations (*wihyîtem lî sĕgullâ mikkŏl-ha 'ammîm* "And you will be my personal possession from all people").[90]

The exclusive vision of Israel at Mount Horeb is expanded upon even further in the third episode of the deuteronomistic redaction (Exod 23:20-33). The return to a vision of what the people of God must be in this concluding section to the Book of the Covenant is not an arbitrary move by the deuteronomistic redactors, for, earlier, we saw how this section actually parallels form-critically the "Promise of Reward" in the Proposal of Covenant. In Exod 23:20-33, Israel is promised once again that they will have an exclusive relationship with God, when Yahweh

---

as "private accumulations" or as "a private fund." He illustrates this conclusion from a last will and testament that was found on a Nuzi tablet, which details the division of a man's property between his wife and son. The text reads, "whatever oils and copper which Kirase (the wife) has privately accumulated (*sikiltaša*) are given to her." Greenberg concludes from this that "a woman's *sikiltu* was. . .her own private property"—it is exclusive ownership of property that is not shared. Fur further discussion of the Akkadian *sikiltum* see also M. Held, "A Faithful Lover in an Old Babylonian Dialogue," *JCS* 15 (1961) 11-26 esp. 11-12. For examination of the Ugaritic *sglt* see M. Dahood, "Hebrew-Ugaritic Lexicography III," *Bib* 46 (1965) 313; "The Phoenician Background of Qoheleth," *Bib* 47 (1966) 267; "Hebrew-Ugaritic Lexicography VII," *Bib* 50 (1969) 341. See especially the letter to 'Ammurapi, king of Ugarit, from the Hittite King, in which the former is told, "You are his property" *[s]glth.at* (*PRU* V 60, 12).

The two occurrences of *sĕgullâ* outside of a theological context in the Hebrew Bible also suggest it designates exclusive ownership like the Akkadian *sikiltum* and does not describe something of inherent quality. The first occurrence is 1 Chr 29:3. The occasion of this text is the building of the temple, and the context is a discourse between David and Solomon, in which David emphasizes his commitment to the completion of the temple. David states, "Because of my devotion to the house of my God, my personal possession(s) (*yeš-lî sĕgullâ*), gold and silver, I gave to the house of my God." The second occurrence is Qoh 2:8, where the preacher states, "I gathered for myself silver, gold, the personal possession(s) of kings (*sĕgullat mĕlākîm*), and provinces." In both of these texts *sĕgullâ* might be better translated as "private property." Although *sĕgullâ* is associated with items of inherent value in each text, qualifying terms were required in each case to signify that the "private property" being described is valuable (gold, silver, etc.). For example, in 1 Chr 29:3, David had to specify that the "private property" which he gave to the temple was, in fact, gold and silver. the same is also true for the conclusion of the preacher in Qoh 2:8. He, too, had to specify that his quest for wealth even led to "private property " which was equal to that of kings.

90 On the separative use of *min* see *GKC* § 119w. For an interpretation of *min* in 19:5a see Wildberger *Jahwes Eigentumsvolk*, 76; Mosis, "Ex 19,5b-6a: Syntaktischer Aufbau und lexikalische Semantik," 19. For further discussion on the exclusivity inherent in *sĕgullâ* see H-. J. Kraus, "Das Heilige Volk: Zur alttestamentlichen Bezeichnung 'am qadoš," *Freude Am Evangelium*, Fs. A de Quervain, BEvT 44 (München: Chr. Kaiser, 1966) 52.

pledges to secure the boundaries of their land and to drive out the other nations (Exod 20:27-31). Exod 23:20-33 illustrates in addition how the promise of an exclusive relationship with Yahweh carries with it an implied command for the people of God to be distinct from the nations, for within the context of the promises of Yahweh, Israel is also commanded to be separate from the nations (Exod 23:24, 32-33).[91]

This vision of the people of God, as having an exclusive relationship with Yahweh, is anchored in the revelation at Mount Horeb. Three times in Deuteronomy Israel is called an 'am sĕgullâ (Deut 7:6; 14:2, 26:18),[92] and these three occurrences, according to Deut 28:29, must be interpreted as part of the covenant that Yahweh made with Israel at Horeb.[93] Furthermore, this description of Israel always takes place in the context of election. Deut 7:6 and 14:2 state that Israel has become a "personal possession" of Yahweh because he chose (bḥr) them; while Deut 26:18-19 states that Israel's status as a "personal possession" of Yahweh is the fulfillment of an earlier divine promise of election. The election that is being described at Mount Horeb in the Book of Deuteronomy is particular in focus. It is an exclusive relationship with Yahweh, which mirrors the vision of the people in the deuteronomistic redaction of Exodus 19-24. In fact, Deut 7:6 and 14:2 even share the syntax of the "Promise of Reward" in Exod 19:5ba: in each of these instances the separative use of the preposition min is used to convey that Israel has been elected to be Yahweh's "personal possession. . .from all the people on the face of the earth."

E. Conclusion

We have seen in this section that Mount Horeb is a deuteronomistic symbol of divine cultic presence, functioning within the larger framework of the Deuteronomic Name theology, and

[91] One implication of the exclusive emphasis in deuteronomistic tradition for defining the people of God is that there would not be an emphasis on mission. See O. Bächli (Israel und die Völker: Eine Studie zum Deuteronomium ATANT 41 [Zürich: Zwingli Verlag, 1962] 174-76) for further discussion on the absence of mission in deuteronomistic parenesis.

[92] See also two additional texts, which share the same theological perspective as the instances of sĕgullâ in Deuteronomy. Ps 135:4 emphasizes the election of Israel: "For Yahweh chose (bḥr) Jacob for himself; Israel for his personal possession (sĕgullâ)." Mal 3:17 states that God-fearers will be rewarded by being made Yahweh's "private possession" (sĕgullâ).

[93] Deut 28:69 is a transitional verse in the Book of Deuteronomy between the words of the covenant spoken at Horeb and the words of the covenant spoken in Moab.

that it is meant to provide a critique of Mount Zion within Zion-Sabaoth theology. It represents a qualification of the imagery of God as statically dwelling on the cosmic mountain in favor of a more transcendent view of God as dwelling in heaven and "approaching" the mountain for theophany. I have characterized the presentation of divine cultic presence at Mount Horeb as a shift from metaphor to metonymy. However, while the cultic location is played down in Mount Horeb, Moses, as cultic leader is accentuated. He functions metaphorically in representing the presence of God as speech within the cult. Finally, playing down the cultic location as a central component in a theology of divine presence, gives the people a more prominent role within Mount Horeb. The vision of Israel at Mount Horeb is an exclusive one, of a separate people who hear the voice of God through cultic leaders and consequently fear God.

Chapter 4

THE PRIESTLY REDACTION OF EXODUS 19-24

The focus of study in this chapter will shift from the deuteronomistic redaction to the priestly redaction in Exodus 19-24. As
in the previous chapter, we will see that the Mountain of God
tradition (and the deuteronomistic redaction) will continue to
play an influential role in our study, since the priestly redaction
will also follow the three-part structure of the Mountain of God
tradition, and in the process present its own critique of Zion.

I
AN OUTLINE OF THE PRIESTLY REDACTION

There has been surprisingly little debate about priestly tradition within the Pentateuch in the modern critical study of the
Hebrew Bible.[1] At least since Wellhausen, the most prominent
theory concerning pentateuchal priestly tradition has been that

---

[1] The center of debate in recent years concerning priestly tradition is its date.
The classical view, which is also advocated in this study, is that priestly tradition is
exilic or even later (e.g. Wellhausen). See more recently Ackroyd (*Exile and Restoration*, 85); M. Smith (*Palestinian Parties and Politics that Shaped the Old Testament*, Lectures on the History of Religions 9 [New York: Columbia University
Press, 1971] 101-2), B. A. Levine, "Priestly Writers," *IDBSup* [Nashville: Abingdon,
1976] 683-87), who favor the exilic period; or J.G. Vink ("The Date and Origin of
the Priestly Code in the Old Testament," *OTS* 15 [1969] 1-144), who argues for a
post-exilic compilation. However, there is a growing consensus especially from a
linguistic perspective (but not exclusively) that the "compilation" of priestly tradition is pre-exilic. See, for example, J. Kaufmann ("Probleme der israelitische-jüdischen Religionsgeschichte," *ZAW* 48 [1930] 23-43); M. Haran (*Temples and Temple-
Service in Ancient Israel* [Oxford: Clarendon Press, 1978] 146-47); Z. Zevit ("Converging Lines of Evidence Bearing on the Date of P," *ZAW* 94 [1982] 481-511); A.
Hurvitz ("The Evidence of Language in Dating the Priestly Code," *RB* 81 [1974]
24-56; and *A Linguistic Study of the Relationship Between the Priestly Source and
the Book of Ezekiel*, Cahiers de la Revue Biblique 20 [Paris: J. Gabalda, 1982]); J.
Milgrom (*Cult and Conscience* [Leiden: Brill, 1976], and *Studies in Levitical Terminology* [Berkeley: University of California Press, 1970]); and G. Rendsburg
("Late Biblical Hebrew and the Date of P," *JANESCU* 12 [1980] 65-80). Priestly
material certainly contains cultic, legal, and historical material from Israel's earliest
history; nevertheless, the following redaction-critical studies of Exodus 19-24 points
to the exilic/post-exilic period as the significant period in the compilation of pentateuchal priestly tradition.

it is the latest of three source documents (the yahwistic (J), elohistic (E), and priestly (P) sources), and that it was meant to be
read independently even though it is presently interwoven with
the other sources into an "improvised unity."[2] This Documentary Hypothesis includes assumptions concerning the interpretation of Exodus 19-24 which require closer examination, for
they have influenced past interpretations of Mount Sinai within
the Pentateuch in general, and, more specifically, the interpretation of Mount Sinai within priestly tradition. Two widely held
conclusions require our attention: the first is tradition-historical
in nature, while the second is theological. Wellhausen provides
illustration of both points.

In working within the framework of the Documentary Hypothesis, Wellhausen concluded that the theophany of Yahweh
on Mount Sinai in Exodus 19-24 represented two distinct traditions. He argued that it was an important episode in the pre-
exilic yahwistic source, and also central to the exilic priestly
source.[3] In assessing the literary character of these two sources,
Wellhausen concluded that the two sources contrasted sharply:
narrative predominated in the yahwistic source, while law was
central to the priestly source.[4]

Wellhausen's tradition-historical assessment of Mount Sinai
in the yahwistic and priestly sources laid the groundwork for an
additional conclusion concerning theology. His theological conclusions were based on the stark literary contrasts between the
two sources. The narrative style of the yahwistic source suggested to Wellhausen that:

> Here all is life and movement: as Jehovah Himself, so the
> man of God [Moses], is working in a medium which is
> alive. . . . His work and activity may be told in a narra-
> tive, but the contents of it are more than a system, and
> are not to be reduced to a compendium; it is not done
> and finished off, it is the beginning of a series of infinite
> activities.[5]

The central role of law in the priestly source at the cost of narrative led to the following negative theological assessment:

[2] Wellhausen, *Composition*, 331, 333; *Prolegomena*, 295 *et passim*.

[3] Wellhausen, *Prolegomena*, 342-44.

[4] Wellhausen, *Prolegomena*, 342-44. In *Composition*, 96-97 he outlines the complete priestly source in the Sinai Complex as including Exod 19:1-2a; 24:(14-15a?)
15b-18; 25-31; 34:29-35; 35-Numbers 10.

[5] Wellhausen, *Prolegomena*, 346-47.

In the Priestly code the work of Moses lies before us
clearly defined and rounded off. . . . It is detached from
its originator and from his age: lifeless itself, it has driven
the life out of Moses and out of the people, nay, out of the
very Deity.[6]

Wellhausen certainly has not spoken the final word on priestly
tradition in the Pentateuch, even though his conclusions—that
priestly tradition is an independent source, which is theologically sterile—might very well represent the majority view even
today.[7]

One significant departure from Wellhausen, which provides
a methodological starting point for this chapter, is the proposal
of Cross in *Canaanite Myth and Hebrew Epic* that priestly tradition in the Pentateuch is not a source, which is meant to be read
independently, but a redaction, which presupposes and expands
upon older tradition.[8] A theory of priestly tradition as a redaction rather than as a source has profound tradition-historical and
theological implications for interpreting Exodus 19-24. Tradition-historically it calls into question the limitation of the
priestly school to less than five verses in Exodus 19-24.[9] Theologically, it challenges the negative judgment of priestly tradi-

---

[6] Wellhausen, *Prolegomena*, 347.

[7] See the recent criticism of this consensus by Levenson, *Sinai and Zion*, 2-3.

[8] Cross, *Canaanite Myth and Hebrew Epic*, 293-94. See the similar conclusion by
I. Engnell, *Gamla Testamentet I* (Stockholm: Svenska kyrkans diadonistyrelses
bokförlag, 1945) 209-59. The work of Rendtorff (*Problem des Pentateuch*) is also
important to this study in evaluating priestly tradition. See the recent response to
Rendtorff's work by K. Koch ("P-Kein Redacktor!," *VT* 37 [1987] 446-67). Compare Ackroyd (*Exile and Restoration*, 86 n.13) who raises the question of whether P
might better be described as the "last tradent" (i.e., "the final formulator of the
already existing tradition"), but in the end he favors an independent priestly
source. Hossfeld (*Dekalog*, 163-213) has recently attributed a larger role to a pentateuchal (priestly) redactor in the formation of Exodus 19-24, but this redaction is
interpreted in addition to a Documentary Hypothesis. Along this same line see also
R. E. Friedman (*The Exile and Biblical Narrative*, HSM 22 [Chico: Scholars Press,
1981]; "Sacred History and Theology: The Redaction of Torah," *The Creation of
Sacred Literature*, University of California Publications: Near Eastern Studies 22
[Berkeley: University of California Press, 1981] 25-34; and *Who Wrote the Bible?*
[New York: Summit Books, 1987] 217-45) who also argues for both a priestly source
and a priestly redaction. Finally, see W. Johnstone ("Reactivating the Chronicles
Analogy in Pentateuchal Studies, with Special Reference to the Sinai Pericope in
Exodus," *ZAW* 99 [1987] 16-37) who also calls for a more thorough reevaluation of
the Sinai Complex as the product of redactional activity.

[9] Law so predominated in the priestly source, according to Wellhausen, that he
was willing to concede no more than five verses of narrative (Exod 19:1-2a; 25:15b-
18a) as providing the context for seventy-two chapters of cultic priestly legislation
(Exodus 25-31; 35-40, Leviticus, Numbers 1-10).

tion as being lifeless, and suggests, instead, that, as a redaction, priestly tradition in Exodus 19-24 is an attempt in the exilic period to give new life to Moses, the people, and even the deity.

My aim in this chapter is to describe how priestly redactors superimpose yet another reading of Israel's encounter with God into Exodus 19-24 by introducing Mount Sinai as the setting of theophany. The three-part sequence that was introduced in the Mountain of God tradition and carried through the deuteronomistic redaction will also be followed here. Consequently, we will separate our study of priestly tradition once again into three parts: Introduction; Purification, Preparation and Theophany; and Sacrificial Ritual.

A. Introduction (Exod 19:1-2a, 5bb-6a)

The influence of priestly redactors is evident at two points in the opening episode of Exodus 19-24. In Exod 19:1-2a the setting of theophany is located more precisely as taking place in the wilderness of Sinai. In Exod 19:5bb-6a the "The Promise of Reward" within the deuteronomistic Proposal of Covenant is expanded with the addition of priestly imagery. These additions require closer examination.

1. The Itinerary Notice (Exod 19:1-2a)

Past research on the itinerary notice in Exod 19:1-2a has demonstrated that this unit is part of a larger framework for Israel's journey from Egypt to Canaan, which extends from Exodus through Numbers,[10] and that it is limited to priestly tradition.[11] When working within the framework of the Documentary Hypothesis, past interpreters have frequently ignored the immediate context of Exod 19:1-2a in order to interpret this itinerary notice as an introduction to the account of theophany in Exod 24:15b-18a.[12] However, once priestly tradition is reevaluated as a redaction, the focus of study must change to an interpretation of the itinerary notice (Exod 19:1-2a) in its present context with the Mountain of God tradition (Exod 19:2b-3a).[13] This change in focus confronts the reader

---

[10] See G. W. Coats ("The Wilderness Itinerary," CBQ 34 [1972] 146-47) and Cross (Canaanite Myth and Hebrew Epic, 309-17) for discussion of the itinerary notice as a structuring device in Exodus-Numbers.

[11] For discussion of the itinerary notice within priestly tradition see Beyerlin, Oldest Sinaitic Traditions, 2; Hyatt, Exodus, 200; Clifford, Cosmic Mountain, 109.

[12] See, for example, Noth, Exodus, 155.

[13] See Chapter 2 for arguments in favor of a distinction in traditions between Exod 19:1-2a and Exod 19:2b-3a.

with a series of repetitions in Exod 19:1-3a which require interpretation: two repetitions result from the unexpected sequence
within the itinerary notice itself,[14] while a third repetition occurs when the itinerary notice is read in the larger context of
the Mountain of God tradition. An examination of these repetitions within their present narrative context will provide insight
into the *Tendenz* of the priestly redactors.

The first repetition consists of two temporal clauses in Exod
19:1a, which emphasize the time of Israel's arrival:

> On the third month (*baḥōdeš haššělîšî*) after the people
> of Israel had gone forth out of the land of Egypt
> On this very day (*bayyôm hazzeh*) (Exod 19:1a)

This initial repetition immediately demands the reader's attention, because the two temporal clauses are not harmonized. The
opening temporal clause makes a general reference to the third
month, and this reference is clearly located in the past tense of
narrative time as we would expect: it is the third month "after
the people of Israel had gone forth out of the land of Egypt."[15]
The second temporal clause, however, makes reference to a spe-

---

[14] The present sequence of the text is unexpected, when the itinerary notice in
Exod 19:1-2a is compared to the other itinerary notices in Exod 12:37; 13:20; 14:1;
15:22, 27; 16:1; 17:1a and to the summary of Israel's travels in Numbers 33. In light
of the above texts one would expect Exod 19:1-2a to read:
> Israel journeyed from Rephidim,
> and they came to the wilderness of Sinai
> and they camped in the wilderness
> on the third "month". . .

However, the order has been disrupted so that the text presently reads:
> On the third month. . .
> on this very day
> (they) came to the wilderness of Sinai
> and they journeyed from Rephidim
> and they came to the wilderness of Sinai
> and they camped in the wilderness

A variety of tradition-historical solutions have been presented to account for the
lack of logic in the present text. For example, Wellhausen, (*Composition*, 96) and
Rudolph (*Der 'Elohist'*, 42) concluded that Exod 19:1 was redactional. Gressmann
(*Mose und seine Zeit*, 180 n.3) argued instead that Exod 19:2a was redactional. Eissfeldt (*Komposition*, 12, 24) went in yet another direction by suggesting that Exod
19:1 was P and that Exod 19:2a was L.

[15] Compare Noth (*Exodus*, 155) who argued that *baḥōdeš* in the first temporal
clause was intended to be read as "new moon" and thus designates a specific day.
The problem with this harmonization is that the phrase *baḥōdeš haššělîšî* in the
first temporal clause of Exod 19:1a suggests the more general reference to "month"
(see Gen 7:11; Num 9:11). As Dillmann (*Exodus*, 191) long ago pointed out, we
would expect *bě'eḥād laḥōdeš* for a more specific temporal reference (see Gen 8:5;
Exod 40:2; Num 1:1, 18; 29:11).

cific day in contrast to the more general reference to "the third month," while the use of the nearer demonstrative "on this day," as opposed to the more remote demonstrative, "on that day," also contrasts to the past tense of narrative time that was established with the opening temporal clause.[16] The result of this repetition is that the unexpected second temporal clause catches the reader's attention and becomes the point of emphasis. A further examination of this latter temporal clause within the context of priestly tradition in the Pentateuch illustrates the larger design of priestly redactors in calling attention to *bayyôm hazzeh* as the time of Israel's arrival at the mountain of God. The phrase occurs only four times in the Pentateuch: it marks the first day of the flood (Gen 7:11), Israel's arrival at the wilderness of Sinai (Exod 19:1a), the sanctification of priests (Lev 8:34), and the Day of Atonement (Lev 16:30).[17] This distribution indicates how important the events at the mountain of God are to priestly redactors for the salvation of the people, since the events here are the midpoint between the curse of the flood and the sanctification of the priesthood with the subsequent Day of Atonement.[18]

The second repetition in the itinerary notice consists of the verb "to come" (*bw'*) in conjunction with the "wilderness of Sinai":

> They came (*bw'*) into the wilderness of Sinai
> and they journeyed from Rephidim
> And they came (*bw'*) into the wilderness of Sinai (Exod 19:1b-2a)

This repetition actually stops action momentarily to emphasize the new setting. Such a disruption of plot in order to emphasize setting is a spatial form technique. Spatial form devices are defined as "techniques. . .which. . .subvert the chronological se-

---

[16] Compare here De Vries (*Yesterday, Today and Tomorrow*, 139-51 esp. 142) who concludes that the reference to *bayyôm hazzeh* in the second temporal clause serves only to date the past event that is being referred to in the first temporal clause. I would argue instead that *bayyôm hazzeh* emphasizes the present significance of this event in relation to the reader, perhaps for cultic reasons. For cultic interpretations of these dates see, among others, E. Kutsch, "Der Kalender des Jubiläenbuch und das Alte Testament," *VT* 11 (1961) 43; Noth, *Exodus*, 155; Hyatt, *Exodus*, 200; Cassuto, *Exodus*, 224.

[17] The only other use of *bayyôm hazzeh* in the Hebrew Bible occurs in 1 Kgs 2:26, when Solomon banishes Abiathar the priest.

[18] *bayyôm hazzeh* is often equated with *bĕ'eṣem hayyôm hazzeh*, which is also anchored in priestly tradition. For discussion see De Vries, *Yesterday, Today and Tomorrow*, 139-51.

quence inherent in narrative."[19] When spatial form devices predominate in a narrative, setting and characterization frequently become the central focus of the text instead of plot and chronology. This would certainly appear to be the case in the itinerary notice of the priestly redaction. The purpose for calling attention to the "wilderness of Sinai" becomes clearer when the priestly itinerary in Exod 19:1-2a is interpreted in its larger context with the Mountain of God tradition in Exod 19:2b-3a. The combination of these two traditions creates the third and final repetition with the verb "to camp" in the closing line of the priestly itinerary and the opening line of the Mountain of God tradition:

> and they camped (ḥnh) in the wilderness
> and Israel camped (ḥnh) there before the mountain
> (Exod 19:2a-2b)

This final repetition provides a link between the distinct traditions, and also locates the Mountain of God more specifically in the wilderness of Sinai, with the result that the unnamed cosmic mountain, which Moses ascends in Exod 19:3a, is best interpreted as Mount Sinai.[20] The narrative logic of the three repetitions moves in the following manner: first the time is underscored in the initial repetition, then the general setting of the wilderness of Sinai is established in the second repetition, and finally the reader is brought to the base of the mountain in the third repetition.

2. The Priestly "Promise of Reward" (Exod 19:5bb-6a)

In addition to the more specific location and time of Israel's arrival at the mountain, priestly redactors have expanded the "Promise of Reward" in the deuteronomistic Proposal of Covenant. In the last chapter we saw how the "Promise of Reward"

---

[19] J.R. Smitten and A. Daghistany, *Spatial Form in Narrative* (Ithaca: Cornell University, 1981) 15-16.

[20] The conclusion of Cassuto (*Exodus*, 225) is instructive concerning the effect of this linking on the reader: "Only this is clearly to be inferred from the passages [Exod 19:1-2] that the mountain called in this section Mount Sinai is the same as the one named in chapter iii 'the mountain of God' and Horeb. . . ." Noth (*Exodus*, 155) makes an interesting tradition-historical conclusion at this point when he writes, "The 'wilderness of Sinai' takes its name from the mountain and is a general description of the desert region in the neighbourhood of the mountain." The present study is suggesting just the reverse argument, that the unnamed cosmic mountain in Exod 19:2b acquires a more specific designation as Mount Sinai through the introduction of the "wilderness of Sinai" into the text.

was the point of emphasis, and how this promise contains a vision of Israel as being in an exclusive relationship with Yahweh as God's personal possession. In the present form of the text, the "Promise of Reward" does not end at Exod 19:5ba but actually continues through Exod 19:5bb-6a.

When Exod 19:5ab is combined with Exod 19:5bb-6a, the "Promise of Reward" includes three statements: (1) Exod 19:5ba, the promise that Israel will be Yahweh's "personal possession" (*sĕgullâ*) distinct from the nations (*mikkŏl-hā'ammîm*); (2) Exod 19:5bb, the proclamation of the universal rule of Yahweh (*kî-lî kŏl-hā'āreṣ*); and (3) Exod19:6a, the promise that Israel will be a "kingdom of priests" (*mamleket kōhănîm*) and a "holy nation" (*wĕgôy qādôš*). The relationship of these three lines has posed a problem of interpretation, particularly with regard to the middle line, since the proclamation of Yahweh's universal rule appears to be a "parenthetical remark" which actually disrupts the text.[21] The majority of past interpreters have either harmonized the three lines as a single promise, or read the universal claim of Yahweh's rule in the middle line as the cause for the preceding deuteronomistic promise.[22] Yet, problems arise with both of these solutions, and I would argue instead that the proclamation of Yahweh's universal rule functions as an introduction to the following promise in Exod 19:6a. The syntax of Exod 19:5b-6a provides three reasons in support of this conclusion.

First, the *waw* that begins the final promise in Exod 19:6a (*wĕ'attem tihyû-lî*. . .) is best interpreted in this context as being disjunctive: "but you will be to me. . . ." The disjunctive *waw* syntactically interrelates the promise that Israel will be a "kingdom of priests" and a "holy nation" to the preceding proclamation of Yahweh's universal rule and thus presents a strong argument against separating these two statements.[23]

Second, the inverted word order in the promise of Exod 19:6a (*wĕ'attem tihyû-lî*. . .) reinforces the first point for it suggests that this line is the point of emphasis which is set off by the universal claim of Yahweh rule in Exod 19:5bb, and that it is not

---

[21] Childs, *Exodus*, 367.

[22] See, for example, Wildberger, *Jahwes Eigentumsvolk*, 14, 76; Beer, *Exodus*, 96; Michaeli, *L'Exode*, 165-66; Perlitt, *Bundestheologie*, 72; Zenger, *Sinaitheophanie*, 167.

[23] See *GKC* § 154 concerning the disjunctive use of the *waw copulativum*. See also Beyerlin, *Oldest Sinaitic Traditions*, 75; and Mosis, "Ex 19,5b.6a: Syntaktischer Aufbau und lexikalische Semantik," 14.

an independent sentence which merely finishes the promise.[24]

Third, a problem of logic arises when the proclamation of Yahweh's universal rule is read with the opening promise in Exod 19:5ba. The problem is that the exclusive focus of the deuteronomistic promise cannot be harmonized with the claim of Yahweh's universal rule, which is necessary if the *kî*-clause in Exod 19:5bb (*kî-lî kŏl-hā 'areṣ*) is interpreted as the cause or basis for the promise in Exod 19:5ba.[25] This problem in logic is overcome if the deuteronomistic promise in Exod 19:5ba and the proclamation of Yahweh's universal rule in Exod 19:5bb are not harmonized, but interpreted as distinct units of tradition which are presently juxtaposed to each other.[26] The distinct unit of tradition that is introduced with the proclamation of Yahweh's universal rule in Exod 19:5bb would continue through the promise in Exod 19:6a. The syntactical relationship between the three lines of Exod 19:5b-6a that is being advocated here results in the following translation:[27]

---

[24] Muilenburg, "Covenantal Formulations," 353.

[25] Scholars have presented two arguments in an attempt to harmonize the proclamation of Yahweh's universal rule in Exod 19:5bb as the cause of the exclusive deuteronomistic promise in Exod 19:5ba. One argument tries to harmonize the two lines by suggesting that Exod 19:5bb qualifies Exod 19:5ba (so M. Buber, *Moses* [Oxford: University Press, 1946] 101, and more recently Michaeli, [*L'Exode*, 165]). But if Exod 19:5bb qualifies Exod 19:5ba, then it cannot be the reason for the promise. A second argument is put forward by Wildberger (*Jahwes Eigentumsvolk*, 76), that Exod 19:5bb is not universal in scope, but is actually a geographical reference meant to refer to the West Jordan area. See the response by Perlitt (*Bundestheologie*, 172), who concludes that Exod 19:5ba reflects the universalism of Isa 42:5.

[26] As an introduction to the subsequent promise in Exod 19:6a, the *kî*-clause in Exod 19:5bb would not be causal, but asseverative in function. See Brockelmann (*Hebräische Syntax*) 31(b) on the asseverative use of *kî* in nominal clauses. Compare also B. Bandstra (*The Syntax of Particle Ky in Biblical Hebrew and Ugaritic* [Diss., Yale University, 1982] 132, 218) who interprets the *kî* in Exod 19:5bb as circumstantial, concessional in relation to Exod 19:6a. The meaning of *kî* in this context can be described in even more detail. Koehler-Baumgartner (KB 423) note that the asseverative function of *kî* at the beginning of a nominal sentence is used for "introducing an interpretation." This syntactical function of *kî* corresponds well with the present tradition-historical argument that Exod 19:5bb-6a is a redaction which introduces a new interpretation. For further discussion of the asseverative function of *kî* see Mosis, "Ex 19,5b.6a: Syntaktischer Aufbau und lexikalische Semantik," 16; and J. Muilenburg, "The Linguistic and Rhetorical Usages of the Particle ki in the Old Testament," *HUCA* 32 (1961) 146.

[27] This translation corresponds most closely to the LXX which reads,

   v. 5ba   *esethē moi laos periousios apo pantōn tōn ethnōn*

   v. 5bb   *emē gar estin pasa hē gē*

   v. 6a   *humeis de esethē moi basileion hierateuma kai ethnos hagion*

Note here the inclusion of the disjunctive *de* in Exod 19:6a, which interrelates the final two lines (see Arndt and Gingrich, BAG 170[1]), and the explanatory use of *gar*

v. 5ba You will be my chosen people from all the nations.
v. 5bb Indeed all the earth is mine
v. 6a   but you will be to me a kingdom of priests and a holy nation.

An examination of the imagery in the expanded promise of Exod 19:5bb-6a creates yet additional contrasts to the deuteronomistic promise in Exod 19:5ba, which further supports the preceding analysis of syntax.[28] The metaphors of Israel in Exod 19:6a as being a "kingdom of priests" (*mamleket kōhănîm*) and a "holy nation" (*gôy qādôš*) within the larger context of the world (*kî-lî kŏl-hā 'āreṣ*) are not imagery that arise from deuteronomistic literature.[29] Rather, this imagery finds its

(see BAG 151[2]). the result of these elements of syntax is that the LXX would favor a reading of Exod 19:5ba as an independent sentence from Exod 19:5bb-6a. The LXX contrasts sharply with the MT accentuation, which interrelates Exod 19:5ba with the claim of Yahweh's universal rule in Exod 19:5bb (note the *Munah* and the *Majela* connecting Exod 19:5ba and Exod 19:5bb, and the *Sillug* between Exod 19:5bb and Exod 19:6a).

[28] Compare Noth (*Exodus*, 154, 157); Perlitt (*Bundestheologie*, 174-77; Zenger (*Sinaitheophanie*, 164-65); Hossfeld (*Dekalog*, 185-89) for arguments in favor of a deuteronomistic origin to this promise.

[29] The syntax of Exod 19:6a allows for three initial conclusions, which are presupposed in this interpretation:

(1) The two descriptions of Israel are in a parallel construction, with "priests" (*kōhănîm*) and "holy" (*qādôš*) being attributes of "kingdom" (*mamleket*) and "nation" (*gôy*). See, for example, R. B. Y. Scott, "A Kingdom of Priests (Exodus xix 6)," *OTS* 8 (1950) 219; J. B. Bauer, "Könige und Priester, ein heiliges Volk (Ex 19,6)," *BZ* 2 (1958) 285; W. L. Moran, "A Kingdom of Priests," *The Bible in Current Catholic Thought*, ed. J. L. McKenzie (New York: Herder and Herder, 1962) 7; G. Fohrer, "Priesterliches Königtum', Ex 19,6," *TZ* 19 (1963) 361.

(2) The emphatic "you" (*wĕ'attem*) at the beginning of this promise underscores the "all Israel" focus. See, for example, Muilenburg, "Covenantal Formulations," 353-54; Mosis, "Ex 19,5b.6a: Syntaktischer Aufbau und lexikalische Semantik," 23-24; Scott, "A Kingdom of Priests," 217; Bauer, "Konige und Priester," 283-86; Wildberger, *Jahwes Eigentumsvolk*, 81. For a contrasting interpretation see Beer (*Exodus*, 97) who would read *mamleket kōhănîm* distributively.

(3) The attributes "priests" and "holy" must be interpreted as having adjectival force in their construct relationship with "kingdom" and "nation." Thus, all Israel is being described here as a "kingdom of priests" and a "holy nation." See, for example, Scott, "A Kingdom of Priests," 2109; Childs, *Exodus*, 367; Muilenburg, "Covenantal Formulations," 353; Mosis, "Ex 19,5b.6a: Syntaktischer Aufbau und lexikalische Semantik," 21. This interpretation contrasts to a variety of past attempts to establish a semantic distinction between the two descriptions of Israel. For examples of interpretations which argue for distinct groups behind the two terms see W. Caspari, "Das priesterliche Königreich," *TBl* 8 (1929) 105-10 esp. 107; Beyerlin, *Oldest Sinaitic Traditions*, 71-73; Moran, "A Kingdom of Priests," 17-18; Fohrer, "Priesterliches Königtum," 361; Cazelles, "Royaume des prêtres et nation consacrée' Exode (19,6)," 541-45; J. Coppens, "Exode, XIX, 6: Un Royaume ou une Royauté de Prêtres?," *ETL* 53 (1977) 185-86.

closest parallels in literature like Trito-Isaiah, where the people of Israel are called "priests of Yahweh" (*kōhănê yhwh*) by the other nations (Isa 61:5-6),[30] or Ezekiel, where Yahweh's holiness is described as being made known to all nations through Israel (Ezek 20:41).

The contrast in imagery between deuteronomistic parenesis and the promise in Exod 19:5bb-6a can be illustrated further at two points. The first additional contrast concerns the description of Israel as a *gôy qādôš* ("holy nation") in Exod 19:6a, rather than an *'am qādôš* ("holy people"), which is the preferred term in deuteronomistic parenesis.[31] Von Rad stated the problem with the use of *gôy* ("nation") in Exod 19:6a, when he pointed out that this term only refers to the other nations in deuteronomistic parenesis and never to Israel, who are always described as an *'am* ("people").[32] The second contrast concerns the use of "holy" (*qādôš*) in Exod 19:6a, where it functions as a goal to be sought after. The problem is that the holiness of the people in deuteronomistic parenesis is always a presupposition at the outset, and never a promise or goal to be sought after. Thus, the basis for preaching in the deuteronomistic tradition is because the people are holy, and not because they must become holy.[33] For example, the holiness of Israel in Deut 7:6 is the presupposition for the preceding exhortation in Deut 7:1-5 that the people must be distinct from the surrounding nations.[34] This parenesis corresponds well to the deuteronomistic promise in Exod 19:5ba, which states that Israel will be separate from the nations, but it conflicts with Exod 19:6a where holiness is a promised goal to be sought after. The promise of holiness in Exod 19:6a corresponds more closely to priestly tradition, where holiness is anchored in Yahweh and presented as the goal for

---

[30] H-. J. Hermisson (*Sprache und Ritus im Altisraelitische Kult: Zur 'Spiritualisierung' der Kultbegriffe im Alten Testament*, WMANT 19 [Neukirchen-Vluyn: Neukirchener Verlag, 1965] 101-3) rightly sees the priestly roots of this imagery and its correlation to Isa 61:5-6. However, by assigning the Exodus material to J he has problems accounting for the obvious parallels and is forced to make a distinction between form (Isaiah and Exodus are not similar) and content (Isaiah and Exodus are similar).

[31] See Deut 7:6; 14:2, 21; 26:19; 28:9.

[32] G. von Rad, *Das Gottesvolk im Deuteronomium*, BWANT 47 (Stuttgart: W. Kohlhammer, 1929) 10 n.5.

[33] Kraus, "Das Heilige Volk," 54; Fohrer, "Priestliches Königtum," 362.

[34] Perlitt (*Bundestheologie*, 173-74) appeals to Deut 4:6, 33 to argue that deuteronomistic redactors did in fact refer to Israel as the *gôyim*. However a close look at these texts does not support such a conclusion. In Deut 4:6-8 it is the nations who are speaking, while Deut 4:33 is a rhetorical question, which is also meant to refer to the other nations.

Israel. The priestly legislation repeatedly echoes this
perspective through the frequent command, "You are to be
holy, for I Yahweh your God am holy."[35]

Our analysis of the syntax of the three statements in Exod
19:5b-6a has underscored how the vision of Israel as being
Yahweh's personal possession in Exod 19:5ba is distinct from the
proclamation of Yahweh's universal rule and the divine promise
of holiness in Exod 19:5bb-6a. An interpretation of the imagery
in Exod 19:5bb-6a has further underscored the contrast
between the distinct promises, and it has demonstrated the
close relationship between the promise of holiness in Exod 19:6a
and the call to holiness within the priestly legislation. Thus, it
would appear that priestly redactors have introduced their own
interpretation of promise in Exod 19:5bb-6a, which emphasizes
the holiness of the people as a reward for covenant loyalty.
Furthermore, this promise takes place, according to the priestly
redaction, at a new setting—the mountain in the wilderness of
Sinai.

B. *Preparation, Purification and Theophany (Exod 19:11b, 12ab-13, 15b, 16aa, 18, 20-25)*

The more specific setting of Sinai and the emphasis on holiness in the priestly promise is carried over into the second episode of the priestly redaction at two points. First, priestly
redactors provide more specific information about Israel's preparation for theophany in order to underscore the sacredness and
danger of Mount Sinai, and thus the need for Israel to be pure
(Exod 19:11b, 12ab-13, 15b). And second, they reinterpret the
account of theophany itself (Exod 19:16aa, 18, 20-25) and the
mediatorial role of Moses. The interpretation of priestly tradition in the second episode will follow this division.

1. *The Preparation for Theophany (Exod 19:11b, 12ab-13, 15b)*

In contrast to deuteronomistic redactors, whose method was
to frame the Mountain of God tradition (e.g., Exod 19:8b-9a
[Mountain of God tradition] Exod 19:19. . .) with new material,
priestly redactors engage the Mountain of God tradition more

---

[35] See for example Exod 31:13; Lev 19:2; 20:26; Lev 21:8, 15; 22:9, 15. For further
discussion about the relationship of the promise in Exod 19:5ba-6a to the priestly
legislation see Kraus, "Das Heilige Volk," 59; Fohrer, "Priestliches Königtum," 362;
F. V. Winnet, *The Mosaic Tradition* (Toronto: University of Toronto Press, 1949)
163; Cazelles, "Royaume des prétres et nation consacrée," 542/, and "Alliance du
Sinai," 70, 78-79.

directly at three points (Exod 19:11b, 12ab-13, 15b).[36] These three additions disrupt the syntax of the preparation for theophany in the Mountain of God tradition in order to call attention to the new information.[37] First, Exod 19:11b switches to the third person (in reference to Yahweh) even though it already occurs in the context of divine speech (Exod 19:10-11a [11b]). The result of this addition is that in mid speech Yahweh abstractly refers to himself by name.[38] Second Exod 19:12ab-13a is the interjection of an extended speech by Yahweh within a speech of Yahweh (Exod 19:12aα [12ab-13a] 13b).[39] And third Exod 19:15b provides further information concerning how the people are to prepare for theophany.[40] The new information provided by the priestly redactors can be summarized as follows: they identify the mountain as being Mount Sinai in Exod 19:11b; they underscore its danger as a cosmic mountain in Exod 19:12ab-13;[41] they emphasize the need for ritual purity in Exod 19:15b, and in the process they also add more precise information to the account of Israel's preparation for theophany with regard to the time (third day) and the manner in which theophany will take place (a divine descent in fire on Mount Sinai). A more detailed interpretation of the priestly redactional additions will illustrate these points.

First, the addition of Exod 19:11b builds on the location of the wilderness of Sinai from the opening itinerary notice, for now the reader is explicitly told that the cosmic mountain in the wilderness of Sinai is indeed Mount Sinai ('al-har sînāy). Furthermore, Exod 19:11b changes the two-day chronology for preparation in the Mountain of God tradition to three days and emphasizes it through repetition (kî bayyôm haššēlîšî. . .layyôm haššēlîšî. . .). We should note that the three-day sequence is car-

---

[36] The conclusion here contrasts to Zenger (*Sinaitheophanie*, 59) who argued that there is no connection between the Proposal of Covenant in Exod 19:3b-6 and the motif of sanctification that is introduced in Exod 19:10. See Childs (*Exodus*, 368) who writes that there is a "connection between the promise of becoming a 'holy nation' (*qādôš*) and the demand to purify oneself (*qiddaštām*)."

[37] See also Zenger *Sinaitheophanie*, 67.

[38] See Noth, *Exodus*, 158; and Zenger *Sinaitheophanie*, 59-60.

[39] See Althmann, "A Note on Exod 19:12ab-13a," 242-46; and Zenger *Sinaitheophanie*, 60.

[40] See Noth, *Exodus*, 158.

[41] For discussion of the danger of cosmic mountains as sacred space see Eliade, *The Sacred and the Profane*, 14-16. For discussion of the danger of sacred space in the context of the priestly legislation, see M. Douglas, *Purity and Danger: An Analysis of the Concepts of Pollution and Taboo* (London: Routledge and Kegan Paul, 1978) 7-40. For discussion of sacred space in relation to Mount Sinai see Terrien, *Elusive Presence*, 133 *et passim*.

ried through the priestly redaction of this episode at two other points. When Moses descends the mountain and warns the people "to be ready," priestly redactors once again include reference to the third day (lišlōšet yāmîm) in Exod 19:15b, while they also add a new introduction to the description of theophany in Exod 19:16aa, which underscores that theophany occurred on the third day (wayhî bayyôm haššělîšî).[42] The priestly redaction of Exod 19:11b also makes explicit that Yahweh's presence on Mount Sinai requires his descent (yrd). The descent of Yahweh on Mount Sinai contrasts to the more static imagery of God as dwelling on the mountain in the Mountain of God tradition, and it also contrasts to the deuteronomistic imagery of God as approaching (bw') the mountain for theophany. The contrast between the deuteronomistic and priestly redactions at this point can actually be taken a step further, since these distinct terms also prepare the reader for different images of divine presence. The approach of God in the deuteronomistic redaction (Exod 19:8b-9a) allowed the people to hear God, while the divine descent in Exod 19:11b will provide the context for the people to see God (. . .yērēd yhwh lě'ênê kŏl-hā'ām. . .).

The second addition by priestly redactors in Exod 19:12ab-13a underscores the danger of Mount Sinai as a cosmic mountain, for it expands the succinct command of Exod 19:12aa in the Mountain of God tradition with an elaborate command concerning the need for proper boundaries. In fact, the need for boundaries has become so important to priestly redactors that Yahweh is presented as even providing Moses with the exact words that must be communicated to the people:[43]

> And you will set boundaries for the people round about (Exod 19:12aa)
> saying, (lē'mōr) "Beware of ascending the mountain or of touching its borders. . . . (Exod 19:12ab-13a)

The third addition by priestly redactors in Exod 19:15b underscores the need for the people to be ritually pure in light of

---

[42] In the Mountain of God tradition it would appear that theophany occurred in the early morning on the morrow (mḥr), but in the present form of the text it is extended to the third day. The juxtaposition of distinct temporal clauses is reminiscent of Exod 19:1a. Exod 19:16a reads, wayhî bayyôm haššělîšî bihyōt habbōqer, "and when it was the third day, when it was early morning." Note a similar repetition of temporal clauses in Exod 34:2, which also emphasizes Mount Sinai, this time in the context of Covenant Renewal (wehyeh nākôn labbōqer wě'ālîtā babbōqer 'el-har sînay "Be ready by morning and ascend in the morning to Mount Sinai").

[43] See also Noth, Exodus, 158; and Hyatt, Exodus, 201.

the extreme danger of the divine presence. Thus priestly redactors provide further interpretation of what Moses meant when he commanded the people "to be ready" in Exod 19;15a. With the addition of Exod 19:15b the readers learns that cultic purity requires abstaining from sexual intercourse.[44]

2. *The Description of Theophany (Exod 19:16aa, 18, 20-25)*

Priestly redactors have not only expanded Israel's preparation for theophany in the Mountain of God tradition, they also present their own reinterpretation of theophany in Exod 19:16aa, 18, and of Moses as cultic mediator in Exod 19:20-25.

a.   a.   *Theophany as an Experience of Fire (Exod 19:16aa, 18)*

Priestly redactors do not simply change the time of theophany to an occurrence on the third day with the addition of Exod 19:16aa; they also emphasize in Exod 19:18 that the presence of God on Mount Sinai is a visual experience of fire.

An examination of Exod 19:18 in the larger context of the Mountain of God tradition in Exod 19:16ab-17 illustrates the redactional character of this verse:

(A)   Exod 19:16a   (The description of theophany as thunder (qlt), lightning, etc.)

   (B)   Exod 19:16b   And all the people ($k\breve{o}l$-$h\bar{a}\,\ddot{a}m$) who were in the camp trembled (hrd)

      (C)   Exod 19:17   Moses brought out ($y\d{s}\,$) the people from the camp to meet God. And they were stationed beneath ($b\breve{e}tah\d{t}\hat{\imath}$) the mountain ($hahar$).

      (C')   Exod 19:18a   But Mount Sinai ($w\breve{e}har$ $s\hat{\imath}nay$) was wrapped in smoke because Yahweh descended (yrd) on it in fire. And its smoke ascended ($7h$) like the smoke of a kiln.

   (B')   Exod 19:18b   And the whole mountain ($k\breve{o}l$-$h\bar{a}h\bar{a}r$) trembled (hrd) greatly.

(A')   Exod 19:19   (Deuteronomistic reinterpretation of theophany as speech [ql])

---

[44] See also Childs, *Exodus*, 369; and Cassuto, *Exodus*, 230.

Several conclusions concerning tradition history come into focus from structuring the text in this way. In contrast to the deuteronomistic redaction in Exod 19:19, which repeated the last line of A in order to emphasize that theophany was an experience of speech, the priestly redaction in Exod 19:18 interacts with B (Exod 19:16b) and C (Exod 19:17) of the Mountain of God tradition, in order to create contrast between the people at the base of the mountain (Exod 19:16b-17) and Yahweh at its summit (Exod 19:18). More specifically, Exod 19:18a contrasts the descent (*yrd*) of Yahweh on Mount Sinai (C') to the approach (*yṣ'*) of the people to meet God at the base of the cosmic mountain in Exod 19:17 (C),[45] while Exod 19:18b contrasts the trembling (*ḥrd*) of the mountain (B') to the fear (*ḥrd*) of the people in Exod 19:16b (B).[46]

By inserting Exod 19:18 into the context of the Mountain of God tradition priestly redactors have reinterpreted the older tradition in three ways. First, the description of theophany in Exod 19:18 is concerned solely with visual imagery of fire (*'ēš*) and smoke (*'āšan*). This description contrasts sharply with the deuteronomistic interpretation of this event in Exod 19:19 as an auditory event of divine speech. Second, priestly redactors also make explicit that the sacramental presence of God as fire on the mountain requires a divine descent (*yrd*), which prohibits a permanent identification between God and the mountain. And, third, the priestly interpretation of theophany is given symbolic expression in Mount Sinai,[47] which is personified as trembling as

---

[45] The redactional links between the Mountain of God tradition in Exod 19:17 (C) and the priestly redaction in Exod 19:18b (C') are very precise. They create a series of contrasts within an inverted structure: Exod 19:17 describes (1) the approach of the people (*yṣ'*) and (2) their location at the base (*bĕtaḥtît*) (3) of the mountain (*hāhār*); while Exod 19:18b identifies (3') the mountain as Mount Sinai, then (2') it describes the divine descent (*yrd*) in fire, and concludes (1') by noting that the smoke ascended (*'lh*) above the mountain.

[46] Exod 19:16b (B) and Exod 19:18b (B') use almost exactly the same language (*kŏl-hā'ām/kŏl-hāhār* and *ḥrd*).

[47] The syntax of Exod 19:18 suggests that introduction of Mount Sinai as the location of theophany is the central point in the text. The emphasis on Mount Sinai in Exod 19:18 is so strong that the mountain is actually mentioned three times in the opening sentence. Mount Sinai is first introduced with disjunctive syntax (*wĕhar sînay*), then it is referred to again in *kullô*, and finally a third time in the relative clause with *'ālāyw*. Exod 19:18a literally reads, "But Mount Sinai smoked, all of it, because Yahweh descended on it in fire" (*wĕhar sînay 'āšan kullô mipnê 'ăšer yāred 'ālāyw yhwh hā'ēš*). In addition, Mount Sinai functions as the subject of the three main verbs in Exod 19:18: Mount Sinai smoked (*'šn*); its smoke ascended (*'lh*); and it trembled (*ḥrd*).

a result of the divine descent.[48]

b. *Moses as Cultic Mediator (Exod 19:20-25)*

Priestly redactors also redefine the role of Moses with the addition of Exod 19:20-25.[49] Past scholars have frequently judged this unit to be a "dismal anticlimax" in its present narrative context, because the additional cycle of movement by Moses seems to disrupt the flow of the narrative by interjecting an entire episode into the Sinai Complex at the point when the reader is prepared for the promulgation of the Decalogue by Yahweh.[50] The conclusion of past scholarship that Exod 19:20-25 disrupts the flow of the narrative is most certainly correct. Thus, this unit of

---

[48] The personification of Mount Sinai as trembling underscores its cosmic quality by bringing to mind the personification of other cosmic mountains like Baal's mountain Zaphon. See Clifford *Cosmic Mountain*, 57-65) for description of Zaphon. The use of *ḥrd* in Exod 19:18b also requires two comments. First, Jeremias (*Theophanie*, 102 n.1) and Cross (*Canaanite Myth and Hebrew Epic*, 167) favor the LXX reading at this point over the MT, in which the former has replaced the reference to the "whole mountain" (*kŏl-hāhār*) with a reference to "all the people" (*pas ho laos*). This reading however does not fit Exod 19:18 with its focus on Mount Sinai and it overlooks the personification of Mount Sinai at this point. Thus I have followed the MT text in my interpretation. A second comment concerning *ḥrd* is that it does not describe an earthquake. The verb is used over fifty times in the Hebrew Bible, where it designates fear in people and is never used to describe an object as quaking or shaking. See, for example, 1 Sam 14:15 where *ḥrd* describes the fear of the people in the camp of the Philistines during Jonathan's attack on them. When the earth is also described as shaking in this story, the verb *rgz* is used. The trembling of Mount Sinai in Exod 19:18b is personification. For a similar use of *ḥrd* see Ezek 26:18, where the isles are said to tremble in fear in Ezekiel's death lament over the downfall of Tyre (note also here the use of *ḥrd* with *bhl* [to be disturbed or terrified]). Finally, the reaction of fear by Mount Sinai to the appearance of Yahweh in fire actually participates in some of the oldest theophanic imagery in Israel. See Jeremias (*Theophanie*, 7-16) who concludes that the oldest *Gattung* of theophany includes a report of the approach of Yahweh and a reaction of nature to the divine presence.

[49] The introduction of Aaron, who has not been part of the narrative until this point, has provided the basis for a number of scholars to judge Exod 19:20-25 as a later priestly addition. See, for example, Rudolph, *Der 'Elohist'*, 44. Zenger (*Sinaitheophanie*, 171) limits the priestly addition to Exod 19:21; while Hossfeld (*Dekalog*, 164-71) attributes Exod 19:22, 24 to a priestly redaction. For a more complete bibliography see H. Valentin, *Aaron: Eine Studie zur vor-priesterschriftlichen Aaron-Überlieferung*, OBO 18 (Göttingen: Vandenhoeck und Ruprecht, 1978) 392-93.

[50] Childs, *Exodus*, 368. See Noth (*Exodus*, 153) who describes the "peculiar details" of the narrative context of the Decalogue in that Moses is commanded both to speak with Yahweh in the context of the people and to keep the people away from Yahweh; while the people are also pictured both as being afraid and not wanting to approach the mountain while also needing to be warned repeatedly to stay away from the mountain.

narrative is spatial in form. However, we have already seen that priestly redactors have used spatial form techniques at a number of points in their redaction of Exodus 19-24, and thus the judgment of Exod 19:20-25 as "anticlimactic" may represent a misinterpretation of the important function of this unit within the larger context of the priestly redaction. Closer interpretation of this unit will illustrate how priestly redactors use the disruption in narrative logic in Exod 19:20-25 to shift the presentation of Moses away from the deuteronomistic image of him as a teacher who conveys divine speech, in order to emphasize his role as a priestly mediator, who maintains distance and clear boundaries between Yahweh and the people. Three aspects of Exod 19:20-25 illustrate this point.

First, the imagery and structure of Exod 19:20-25 correspond to central motifs in the priestly redaction. For example, the setting of the events in Exod 19:20-25 is clearly designated as being Mount Sinai (Exod 19:20, 23), Yahweh is present because of a divine descent (*yrd*, Exod 19:20), and, in addition, the structure of the unit emphasizes the vertical hierarchy between characters at Mount Sinai in much the same way as does Exod 19:18. In fact, the disruption in the flow of the narrative at this point would appear to be because of a priestly concern clearly to locate Moses in the setting of Mount Sinai. Note how Moses is described as ascending (*ʿlh*) the mountain in Exod 19:20 and as descending (*yrd*) it again in Exod 19:25. Thus, with the addition of Exod 19:20-25 characters are clearly located in the context of Mount Sinai with Yahweh have descended (*yrd*) to the summit of Mount Sinai (*ʾel-rōʾš hāhār*, Exod 19:20), with Israel a safe distance away at the base of the mountain (Exod 19:23), while Moses moves vertically between them.

Second, there is an inseparable relationship between form and content in Exod 19:20-25. What this means is that the speeches of Yahweh in Exod 19:21-22, 24 provide commentary on the structure of Exod 19:20-25 and its function within the larger narrative context. This point requires illustration. As we have already noted, the ascent of Moses in Exod 19:20 is unexpected, since the reader expects a divine speech to all of the people after Exod 19:19. However, once the flow of the narrative has been disrupted and Moses is clearly located at the summit of Mount Sinai, the new setting allows for two speeches by Yahweh (the first in Exod 19:21-22 and the second in Exod 19:24), which pick up the earlier theme of danger concerning the presence of God and expand it even further. The result of these divine speeches is that in the end only Moses and Aaron are given divine approval to ascend the mountain. Neither the people (Exod 19:21-22) nor even a sanctified priesthood (Exod 19:24) may enter the divine presence on Mount Sinai. Thus, we see that these speeches are a commentary on the structure of Exod 19:20-25, since the insertion of the unit has achieved exactly what the divine speeches demand. By disrupting the flow of the narrative in the deuteronomistic redaction (which had progressed from a conversation between Moses and Yahweh [Exod 19:19] to a culmination in the public promulgation of the Decalogue [Exod 20:1-17]), priestly redactors have successfully embedded the content of the divine commands into the very structure of the narrative, with the result that theophany is limited to a priestly mediator. This point comes into clearer focus by interpreting the revelation of the Decalogue in the context of the priestly redaction.

Third, with the addition of Exod 19:20-25 the revelation of the Decalogue (Exod 20:1-17) is no longer a public experience of theophany, but a Torah that is revealed to Moses alone on Mount Sinai and mediated through him to Israel:[51]

> And Moses descended (*yrd*) to the people
> and he (Moses) said (*'mr*) to them, (Exod 19:25)
> "God spoke all these words saying, . . . (Exod 20:1)

A brief contrast between the priestly redaction and the deuteronomistic redaction will provide a summary conclusion to the preceding interpretation of this episode. Priestly redactors have moved in a strikingly different direction in this episode than the deuteronomistic redactors. They have not simply framed the Mountain of God tradition with new material, but engaged it more directly. As a result, priestly redactors build upon the preparation and the description of theophany in the Mountain of God tradition, while they also reinterpret it. One possible reason why priestly redactors have engaged the Mountain of God tradition more directly is that their interpretation of this event is actually closer in some respects to the older tradition than was the deuteronomistic redaction. Consider the following points. Priestly redactors reaffirm and even build upon the vertical hierarchy of characters that was central to the Mountain of God tradition, but played down in the deuteronomistic redaction, and they also emphasize the role of Moses as priestly mediator. In fact this latter point is so central that in the end Moses even mediates the revelation of the Decalogue.

---

[51] See also Hossfeld, *Dekalog*, 166.

However, in spite of the similarities that were outlined above, the priestly redaction presents a strong critique of the Mountain of God tradition, since the visible presence of God as fire does not presuppose the permanent presence of God on the mountain, but requires a divine descent. Furthermore, the place of this divine presence has now become Mount Sinai for priestly redactors, while the only persons allowed to approach the presence of God at Mount Sinai are Moses and Aaron.

3. *The Priestly Redaction and the Priestly Legislation*

There are a number of connections between the priestly redaction and the priestly legislation, which suggest that the designation of Mount Sinai in Exodus 19-24 is meant to provide a narrative context for the priestly legislation. The central role of Mount Sinai as the setting for theophany in Exodus 19-24 corresponds to the central role of this cosmic mountain throughout the Priestly legislation in Exodus 25-31, 35-40, Leviticus, Numbers 1-10.[52] Furthermore, emphasis on the presence of God as a visible experience of fire is underscored at two points in the priestly legislation—in the account of the sanctification of the cult in Leviticus 8-9 and once again in the account of the Day of Atonement in Leviticus 16.[53] And finally, the limitation to Moses and Aaron as the only ones who are able to approach the presence of God in Exod 19:20-25 provides yet another connection between the priestly redaction of Exodus 19-24 and the sanctification of the cult in Leviticus 8-9, since in the latter account only Moses and Aaron are presented as entering into the presence of God in the Tent of Meeting in Lev 9:23-24.

C.   *The Sacrificial Ritual (Exod 24:1-2, 5, 6, 8, 9-11, 15b-18a)*

The literary structure of Exodus 24 as a whole is often judged to be a confused attempt both to conclude the Book of the Covenant and to introduce the priestly legislation. Consequently, interpretation of this chapter is usually limited to a tradition-historical analysis in which at least two distinct units are described: an initial Covenant-Closing Ceremony, which gives way to a theophany of the Kabod Yahweh in the latter half of the chapter. Scholars generally attribute the distinct units respectively to deuteronomistic and priestly traditions, at which point the process of interpretation ends because the distinct tra-

---

[52] See Lev 7:37-38; 25:1; 26:46; 27:34; and also Num 28:6.
[53] The fire in the altar plays a central role in the public worship in Lev 9:24 and again in Lev 16:12-13 when incense is put on the fire before Yahweh.

ditions are not understood as interrelating with each other in the present form of Exodus 24.[54] My aim in this section is to demonstrate that the influence of priestly redactors is not limited to the latter half of the chapter, but that the priestly redaction extends throughout the chapter and that it is meant to reinterpret the deuteronomistic Covenant-Closing Ceremony as a Sanctification Ceremony of the people, in order to provide an introduction to the priestly legislation. In short, I hope to show how the priestly redaction of Exodus 24 is a "planned theological editing" that is modeled on the Sanctification Ceremony of the priesthood and the first public worship service of Israel in Leviticus 8-9.

The influence of priestly redactors is evident at five different points in Exodus 24: in the introduction to the chapter in Exod 24:1-2; in the description of the sacrifices in Exod 24:5; in the addition of the blood ritual in Exod 24:6, 8; in the vision of God in Exod 24:9-11; and finally, in the description of theophany in Exod 24:15b-18a. Each of these redactional additions requires interpretation. However, at the close of this section, they must be interpreted as a whole in order to illustrate how they are meant to transform the deuteronomistic Covenant-Closing Ceremony into a Sanctification Ceremony of the people.

1. Introduction (Exod 24:1-2)

The command in Exod 24:1-2 for Moses to ascend the mountain alone introduces his mediatorial role into the immediate context of the deuteronomistic Covenant-Closing Ceremony. Contrasts, however, between Exod 24:1a and Exod 24:1b-2 indicate two levels of tradition in this introduction. The text reads:

> And to Moses he said,
> "You, Aaron, Nadab and Abihu, and the seventy elders
> of Israel ascend to Yahweh (Exod 24:1a).
> And you (the participants) will worship from afar
> (merāḥōq)
> Moses will approach (ngš) alone to Yahweh,
> but they will not approach (ngš)
> and the people will not ascend with him (Exod 24:1b-2).

Exod 24:1b-2 interjects qualifications into the initial divine command of Exod 24:1a, which disrupt the narrative by creating a

---

[54] For a general introduction to past scholarship see Childs, *Exodus*, 499-502. For more detailed analysis see Perlitt, *Bundestheologie*, 181-203; and Zenger *Sinaitheophanie*, 72-79.

series of contrasts. For example, in Exod 24:1a Yahweh addresses Moses in the second person and commands all the participants without distinction to ascend the mountain.[55] This command conforms to the vision of God that is described in Exod 24:9-11, where the command in Exod 24:1a is fulfilled and Moses is presented as an equal participant in the worship on the mountain.[56] Thus Exod 24:1a and 9-11 appear to be interrelated as a single unit. Exod 24:1b-2 juxtaposes an additional command to Exod 24:1a, which also shifts to the third person in reference to Moses even though it is meant to be a continuation of divine speech.[57] Here Moses is singled out to approach (*ngš*) God alone, while the others are now commanded to worship from afar (*mērāḥōq*.[58] The emphasis on Moses as mediating between Yahweh and the other participants contrasts both with the command in Exod 24:1a, and with the description of theophany in Exod 24:9-11 as being to all the "nobles."[59]

The contrasts between Exod 24:1a and Exod 24:1b-2 and the distinct imagery of theophany in Exod 24:9-11 (which will be examined subsequently) suggest that Exod 24:1a, 9-11 is an independent account of theophany, which has been brought into its present context as a framework to the Covenant-Closing Ceremony.[60] As an independent tradition, Exod 24:1a, 9-11 described Moses and at least the seventy elders as equal participants in the meal and vision of God on the mountain.[61]

[55] Th. C. Vriezen, "The Exegesis of Exodus xxiv 9-11," *OTS* 17 (1972) 102-3; and Zenger *Sinaitheophanie*, 72-73.

[56] E. W. Nicholson, "The Interpretation of Exodus xxiv 9-11," *VT* 24 (1974) 79.

[57] Ruprecht, "Exodus 24,9-11 als Beispiel lebendiger Erzähltradition," 138.

[58] Ruprecht, "Exodus 24,9-11 als Beispiel lebendiger Erzähltradition," 138. Perlitt (*Bundestheologie*, 184) notes the following opposite pairs, which accentuate the role of Moses in Exod 24:1b-2: Moses versus the people; the contrast between the command for Moses to come alone (*lĕbaddô*) versus the reference to the entire group (*hēm*); and the command to approach (*wĕniggaš*) versus the command not to approach (*lō' yiggāšû*).

[59] See Beyerlin, *Oldest Sinaitic Traditions*, 14; Perlitt, *Bundestheologie*, 184; Vriezen, "Exegesis of Exodus xxiv 9-11," 103.

[60] See already Gressman (*Mose und seine Zeit*, 185) who wrote, "Die behandelte Sage steht ganz für allein; sie hat weder parallelen gefunden noch eine Weiterentwicklung erlebt." See more recently Nicholson, "The Interpretation of Exodus xxiv 9-11," 78, 86; Perlitt, *Bundestheologie*, 184; Vriezen, "Exegesis of Exodus xxiv 9-11," 118-19.

[61] Noth, *History of Pentateuchal Traditions*, 186. See also Perlitt, *Bundestheologie*, 183; E. W. Nicholson, "The Antiquity of the Tradition in Exodus xxiv 9-11," *VT* 25 (1975) 69-79, and "The Interpretation of Exodus xxiv 9-11," 80; W. H. Schmidt, *Exodus, Sinai, und Mose: Erwägungen zu Ex 1-19 und 24*, Erträge der Forschung 191 (Darmstadt: Wissenschaftliche Buchgesellschaft, 1983), 84; Vriezen, "Exegesis of Exodus xxiv 9-11," 110.

The addition of Exod 24:1b-2 indicates how the redactors who incorporated Exod 24:1a, 9-11 into its present context also wished to transform the role of Moses from that of a "noble" with the other leading elders to a priestly mediator.[62] This transformation in the character of Moses reflects priestly *Tendenz* and points to the influence of priestly redactors as those responsible for the present position of this unit. An interpretation of Exod 24:1-2 in its larger narrative context further supports this conclusion.

The emphasis on the mediatorial role of Moses and the need for distance between God and the worshippers in Exod 24:1-2 echoes motifs from the two divine speeches that were addressed to Moses in Exod 19:20-25, when Israel and the priesthood were forbidden to ascend the mountain while Moses was singled out as an acceptable mediator. In Exod 24:1-2 the danger of the cosmic mountain is again underscored, so that in the end only Moses is allowed to approach God. However, the links between Exod 24:1-2 and its larger context are even more precise than the continuation of the motifs that we have just cited. The use of *ngš* to describe the approach of Moses to God in contrast to others who worship from afar (*mērāḥōq*) in Exod 24:1-2 repeats the deuteronomistic introduction to the third episode in Exod 20:21 where Moses is also described as approaching (*ngš*) God in contrast to the people who stood afar off (*mērāḥōq*). Yet the repetition underscores very different uses in the distinct traditions. In the deuteronomistic redaction of Exod 20:21, the "approach" (*ngš*) of Moses to God was the result of the people's fear to hear God; while in the priestly redaction of Exod 24:1-2 it is God (and not the people) who demands that only Moses approach (*ngš*), because of the danger of theophany and the need to maintain distance between God and the worshippers. The command by God in Exod 24:1-2 for Moses and a special group to ascend the mountain also creates a link to Exod 24:9-11, where the fulfillment of this command takes place. Thus, priestly redactors have repeated the introduction to the deuteronomistic redaction of the third episode and framed the Covenant-Closing Ceremony in Exod 24:3-7 with new material in Exod 24:1-2, 9-11, which emphasizes the mediatorial role of Moses, and points the reader beyond the events in Exod 24:3-7.

---

[62] Noth, *History of Pentateuchal Traditions*, 186. A number of scholars have followed Noth at this point. See, among others, Perlitt, *Bundestheologie*, 183; Schmidt, *Exodus, Sinai und Mose*, 84; Nicholson, "The Antiquity of the Tradition in Exodus xxiv 9-11," 74; and "The Origin of the Tradition in Exodus xxiv 9-11," *VT* 26 (1976) 150-53. For a more complete bibliography see Valentin, *Aaron*, 397-402.

Priestly redactors, however, do not simply frame the ceremony
in Exod 24:3-7 with new material, they also reinterpret the sacrificial ritual in Exod 24:4ab-5 with two additions.

2. Sacrifice and Blood Ritual (Exod 24:5, 6, 8)

The priestly additions to the sacrificial ritual in Exod 24:4ab-
5 include the description of the sacrifices in Exod 24:5 and the
blood ritual in Exod 24:6, 8. The description of the sacrifices
that were offered by the "young men of Israel" has presented
problems for interpretation. The problem concerns the absolute construction of *zĕbāḥîm šĕlāmîm* as a description of the second sacrifice.[63] In his study of the history of Israelite sacrifice,
Rendtorff concluded that this construction could not be original,
and that one of the terms must have been added.[64] Our aim is
not to determine the original form of the sacrifice, but simply to
note that the closest parallel to this sacrifice is the *zĕbāḥ šĕlāmîm* or *zibḥê šĕlāmîm* sacrifice, and that this is a distinctively
priestly offering.[65] Thus, if the absolute construction *zĕbāḥîm
šĕlāmîm* must be accounted for redaction-critically as Rendtorff
has argued, then it is best attributed to priestly redactors, for
they would be bringing the sacrificial ritual in Exod 24:5 into
conformity with their own understanding of offering.

Two points further support a conclusion that the *zĕbāḥîm šĕlāmîm* sacrifice is the result of priestly redactors. The first point
concerns redactional technique. Such a direct engagement of
the sacrificial ritual to the degree of actually changing the type
of offering corresponds with the techniques that were noted
earlier in the preparation and description of theophany, where
priestly redactors also directly engaged the Mountain of God
tradition. The second point arises from the larger context of the
priestly legislation. As noted early, my overall aim in this section is to demonstrate that the priestly redaction is modeled on

---

[63] This term only occurs one other place in the Hebrew Bible, in 1 Sam 11:15.

[64] R. Rendtorff (*Studien zur Geschichte des Opfers im Alten Israel*, WMANT 24
[Neukirchen-Vluyn: Neukirchener Verlag, 1967] 41, 98-99, and esp. 150-51) argues
that the ceremony in Exod 24:5 originally included the *ʿōlōt* and the *šĕlāmîm* sacrifices because of the verb *ʿlh* and the sprinkling of the altar in Exod 24:6 (which he
would include in the older account). Zenger (*Sinaitheophanie*, 75, 150) argues instead that the *zĕbāḥîm* sacrifice is original and that it reflects the Throne Audience
of the monarchy in Jerusalem.

[65] See, for example, Exod 29:28; Lev 3:1, 3, 6, 9; 4:10; 7:11-21, 29, 34, 42; 9:18;
10:14. For secondary discussion see Rendtorff, *Geschichte des Opfers*, 149; H.
Schmid, *Das Bundesopfer in Israel: Wesen, Ursprung, und Bedeutung der Alttesta-
mentichen Schelamim* (München: Kösel-Verlag, 1964) 27-38; J. Milgrom, "Sacrifices and Offerings," *IDBSup* (Nashville: Abingdon, 1976) 769.

the Sanctification Ceremony of the priesthood and the first public worship service of Israel in Leviticus 8-9. At this point we might simply underscore that the offering for the people during the first public worship service in Lev 9:18 is the zĕbāḥ šĕlāmîm sacrifice. Thus a priestly redaction of the sacrifice in Exod 24:5 as being the zĕbāḥîm šĕlāmîm offering would bring this event into conformity with the public worship service in Lev 9:18.

There is an additional transformation of the sacrificial ceremony in Exod 24:4ab-5. Exod 24:6 changes the focus of the ceremony from the sacrifices of the "young men of Israel" to a blood ritual, which is performed by Moses.[66] The reader is told that Moses takes the blood from the sacrifice, and places one half of it in small vessels ('aggānōt), while he sprinkles the other half on the altar.[67] The sprinkling of the altar in Exod 24:6 is only the initial stage of this blood ritual. The ceremony is completed in Exod 24:8, when Moses sprinkles the remaining half of the blood on the people after their acceptance of the deuteronomic legislation in Exod 24:7.

This blood ritual has presented problems of interpretation. Past scholars have included it either as part of the original sacrificial ceremony,[68] or as part of a deuteronomistic redaction.[69] But in either case the blood ritual is viewed only in the context of the Book of the Covenant, where it is interpreted as representing the sealing of the covenant between Yahweh and Israel. Kutsch would even translate the "blood of the covenant" (dam habbĕrît) in Exod 24:8 as the "blood of obligation" to correspond with the deuteronomistic interpretation of covenant.[70] However, Mayes underscores a problem with an interpretation of the blood ritual in Exod 24:6, 8 as being deuteronomistic. He writes:

"the blood of the covenant' [in Exod 24:8] is impossible as an expression of deuteronomic or deuteronomistic belief; for with its clearly ritualistic presupposition it stands in

[66] See also Zenger Sinaitheophanie, 75.
[67] 'aggānōt is used only infrequently in the Hebrew Bible. See Cant 7:3; Isa 22:24. Compare also the Ugaritic Myth, Sacher and Shalim and the Gracious Gods;, where a similar vessel is associated with cultic activity (w'l.agn.sb'm "seven times over the vessel" CTA 23:15, 31, 36).
[68] Dillman, Exodus, 156-57; Driver, Exodus, 253; G. Beer, Exodus, KAT 3 (Tübingen: J.C.B. Mohr [Paul Siebeck], 1939) 126-27; Beyerlin, Oldest Sinaitic Traditions, 37-48; Childs, Exodus, 505.
[69] Perlitt, Bundestheologie, 196-98; Zenger Sinaitheophanie, 164-65.
[70] E. Kutsch, "Das sog. 'Bundesblut' in Ex xxiv 8 und Sach ix 11," VT 23 (1973) 25-30, and Verheissung und Gesetz, 86-87.

complete contrast with the deuteronomic emphasis on the words or the law by which Israel's relationship with Yahweh is established.[71]

Several features of Exod 24:6, 8 suggest that the blood ritual is not functioning as a conclusion within deuteronomistic tradition to seal the Covenant-Closing Ceremony, but that it is part of a Sanctification Ceremony within priestly tradition. Syntactically, Exod 24:6, 8 are quite distinct from Exod 24:7. The careful separation of the blood and the sprinkling of it on the altar (Exod 24:6) and on the people (Exod 24:8) is not dependent on the Proclamation and Acceptance of the Book of the Covenant in Exod 24:7. In fact, if anything the blood ritual extends the ceremony beyond the deuteronomistic conclusion.[72] Furthermore, the mediatorial and ritualistic action of Moses in sprinkling blood in Exod 24:6, 8 contrasts sharply with his role as the speaker or teacher of divine law in Exod 24:7. In contrast to the lack of connections to deuteronomistic tradition, we find an exact parallel to this event in priestly tradition, where Moses is actually presented in the same role, when he purifies the priesthood in Lev 8:22-30 by sprinkling blood both on them and on the altar.

The function of the blood ritual in Lev 8:22-30 as a means of purification would suggests that the similar ritual in Exod 24:6, 8 is the result of priestly redactors and that it is meant to function in the same way: as a purification ritual. This parallel provides yet another link between the priestly redaction of Exodus 24

---

[71] A. D. H. Mayes, *Deuteronomy*, NCB (London: Oliphants, 1979) 67. See also J. D. McCarthy, *"berit* in Old Testament History and Theology," *Bib* 53 (1973) 117.

[72] There are a variety of interpretations of this material. Perlitt, (*Bundestheologie*, 196-97) separates the sprinkling of blood on the altar in Exod 24:6 from the sprinkling of blood on the people in Exod 24:8. According to Perlitt, Exod 24:8 stems from a deuteronomistic reinterpretation of sacrifices in Exod 24:4ab-6. Perlitt supports his argument by reconstructing the earlier ritual in Exod 24:5 as including the 'ōlōt and šĕlāmîm sacrifices, which then requires Exod 24:6 because the sprinkling of blood is rooted in the šĕlmamîm sacrifice. Two problems arise with this interpretation: the separation of Exod 24:6, 8 leaves the halving of blood in Exod 24:6 uninterpreted, while the interpretation of Exod 24:8 as deuteronomistic does not correspond with deuteronomistic parenesis. The lack of parallels within deuteronomistic parenesis also calls into question Zenger's interpretation (*Sinaitheophanie*, 74-75, 164-65). Finally, Nicholson's argument ("The Covenant Ritual in Exodus xxiv 3-8," 81) that context requires Exod 24:6 to be original to the sacrifices in Exod 24:5 because of the combination 'ōlōt and šĕlāmîm sacrifices is called into question when one notes that the same combination of 'ōlōt and šĕlāmîm sacrifices in Exod 32:6 does not include a blood ritual.

and the Sanctification Ceremony of the priests and initial public worship service of Israel in Leviticus 8-9.

3. *The* Visio Dei *(Exod 24:9-11)*

Earlier we noted how priestly redactors in Exodus 24 incorporated an independent tradition of theophany in Exod 24:1a, 9-11 as a framework to the deuteronomistic Covenant-Closing Ceremony, while they also accentuated the mediatorial role of Moses by adding Exod 24:1b-2. The description of theophany in Exod 24:9-11 now requires interpretation. Although past scholars have frequently interpreted Exod 24:9-11 as a covenant-closing meal,[73] a closer look at the imagery of this unit suggests that it describes a worship service on the cosmic mountain before the heavenly temple of God. Two aspects of the text illustrate this point: the vision of God in Exod 24:10-11a and the description of the meal in Exod 24:11b. An examination of the imagery and the function of Exod 24:9-11 within the larger context of Exodus 19-24 will clarify how priestly redactors use this pericope as an introduction to the priestly legislation in Exodus 25-31.

Exod 24:10-11a is an account of a very direct and immediate vision of "the God of Israel" by the group of worshippers who were commanded in Exod 24:1a to accompany Moses part way up the mountain.[74] This vision of God employs cosmic mountain imagery in association with the temple. In particular, the im-

---

[73] See, for example, Noth, *Exodus*, 19; Beyerlin, *Oldest Sinaitic Traditions*, 33, 37; McCarthy, *Treaty and Covenant*, 162; Vriezen, "Exegesis of Exodus xxiv," 104-5; R. Smend, "Essen und Trinken—ein Stück Weltlichkeit des Alten Testaments," *Beiträge zur Alttestamentlichen Theologie*, Fs. W. Zimmerli (Göttingen: Vandenhoeck und Ruprecht, 1977) 455-56.

[74] Several features of the description of God in Exod 24:10-11a emphasize the immediateness of this theophany as a direct vision of God (*Visio Dei*). First, as Perlitt, (*Bundestheologie*, 184) has noted, the perception of the participants is emphasized by repetition, which frames the description of theophany: "they saw (*wayyir'û*) Elohe Israel" (Exod 24:10a); and "they saw (*wayyeḥĕzû*) God" (Exod 24:11ba). Second, the use of the technical term for prophetic clairvoyance, "to see" (*ḥzh*) in Exod 24:11ba further underscores the directness of the *Visio Dei*. On the use of this verb see also Amos 1:1; Isa 1:1; Mic 1:1. Third, the specific notice that the leaders of Israel were not struck down accentuates their close proximity to God. See Ruprecht ("Exodus 24:9-11 als Beispiel lebendiger Erzähltradition," 141) who argues for disjunctive syntax in Exod 24:11ba, "He (God) did not lay his hand on the leaders of Israel, although they saw God." Finally, the directness of the vision is also underscored when comparison between the sapphire stone and heaven are made without *tertium comparationis*. Ruprecht, "Exodus 24,9-11 als Beispiel lebendiger Erzähltradition," 143, 145) builds on the work of H. Hensel (*Die Sinaitheophanie und die Rechtstraditionen in Israel* [Diss. Theol. Heidelberg, 1971] 68-72) to conclude that the lack of a *tertium comparationis* emphasizes the

agery of sapphire stone (*libnat hassapîr*) as the pavement under the feet of God corresponds to the precious stone, lapis lazuli, that was central to the cult of Babylon, where the blue color of lapis lazuli referred to the pinnacle of the temple tower.[75] The temple tower participated in cosmic mountain imagery because it was considered to be the place where the deity dwelt, and thus it provided a link between heaven and earth.[76] Thus, lapis lazuli in the pinnacle of the temple actually provided a glimpse of the deity within the heavenly temple, and Exod 24:10-11a is participating in this same symbolism. The leaders of Israel have a direct and immediate vision of God enthroned in the heavenly temple. We should note that the account of theophany in Exod 24:10-11a has departed from the cosmic mountain imagery of Exodus 19 by introducing more specifically the temple imagery that was associated with sapphire. However, before we interpret the function of this shift in imagery within the larger context of Exodus 19-24, the second part of Exod 24:9-11 requires interpretation.[77]

The vision of God in Exod 24:9-11 concludes with a meal in Exod 24:11b. Although many past scholars have interpreted this meal as yet another account of covenant-closing, we should note that covenant is not mentioned in this account,[78] nor does

transcendence of God. He also notes that this is typical in Ezekiel (Ezek 1:26, 8:2; 10:1). For further discussion see also Terrien, *Elusive Presence*, 134-35.

[75] Exod 24:10b reads, "under his feet as it were a pavement of sapphire stone, like the very heaven for purity (*ṭhr*)." *ṭhr* (purity) might also be translated as "clearness" to underscore the direct vision of those on the mountain. For a translation of purity see KB 348. For Ugaritic parallels see C. H. Gordon, *Ugaritic Textbook*, AnOr 38 (Rome: Pontificium Institutum Biblicum, 1965) Glossary #1032. See Ruprecht, "Exodus 24,9-11 als Beispiel lebendiger Erzähltradition," 146-51) for discussion of lapis lazuli within Babylonian religion and its function within Exod 24:9-11. The parallels, however, do not necessarily lead to Ruprecht's conclusion "dass die Erzählung von Ex 24,9-11 in dieser Gestalt nur aus exilischer Zeit stammen kann." See the criticism of Schmidt, *Exodus, Sinai und Mose*, 85 n.114.

[76] For discussion of the relationship between temples and cosmic mountain imagery see R. E. Clements, *God and Temple* (Philadelphia: Fortress, 1965), 1-16 *et passim*. For more specific discussion of this relationship through the symbolism of the Ziqqurat see Clifford, *Cosmic Mountain*, 1-8, 20-25 *et passim*; A Parrot, *Ziqurats et Tour de Babel* (Paris: Machel, 1949) 202-17. Finally for discussion of the relationship of temple and cosmic mountain imagery in the larger context of phenomenology of religion see M. Eliade, *The Sacred and the Profane: The Nature of Religion* (New York: Harcourt, Brace and Co., 1959) 36-40.

[77] The description of Baal's temple in *CTA* 4 also provides parallels to Exod 24:9-11, both in the imagery of the vision—the heavenly temple is described with the terms *ṭhr* ("clarity of stones" *CTA* 4 v 81-82; 95-97) and *lbnt* ("pavement" *CTA* 4 v 73; vi 35)—and in the description of a meal before the deity.

[78] See Perlitt, *Bundestheologie*, 186.

God participate in the meal (as is the case in other covenant ceremonies which include a meal).[79] Instead the eating and drinking take place on the cosmic mountain in the presence of God. Biblical parallels of people eating "before God" usually portray a festival of public worship, which also appears to be the case in Exod 24:9-11.[80] Isa 25:6 is a particularly striking example, for it actually describes such a festival with food on the cosmic mountain before Yahweh Sabaoth.

In summary, as an independent tradition of theophany, Exod 24:1a, 9-11 is a description of the appearance of God to the leaders of Israel, who see "the God of Israel" enthroned in his temple at the summit of the cosmic mountain. Their vision of God culminates in a festival of worship.

Two conclusions are possible at this point concerning the function of Exod 24:9-11 in the larger narrative context of Exodus 19-24. First, the sacredness and danger of the cosmic mountain in Exod 24:9-11 corresponds to the imagery of Mount Sinai in Exod 19:18. Yet, as we noted, Exod 24:9-11 stresses the connection between the temple and the cosmic mountain that was previously absent. This shift in focus prepares the reader for the revelation of the priestly legislation, since the vision of the heavenly temple foreshadows the ascent of Moses to the summit of Mount Sinai, where he will receive a copy (*tabnît*, Exod 25:9) of the temple and its cult in Exodus 25-31.[81] Second, Exod 24:9-11 provides an even larger link to the priestly legislation, for the festival of worship foreshadows a similar festival before the tabernacle in Leviticus 9. The parallels between these two accounts include the description of the festival of worship, the appearance of God, and perhaps most strikingly the same characters (Moses, the elders, Aaron, Nadab and Abihu). The result of this repetition is that the priestly legislation is introduced in Exod 24:9-11 and concluded in Leviticus 9 with public worship.[82] There is also thematic development within this repetition. In particular the construction of the cult in Leviticus 9 will provide a safe channel for the presence of God so that "all the people" will be able to approach God in Lev 9:24 in contrast to

[79] See, for example, the covenant meals in Gen 26:26-30; 31:43-53 where God is a participant.

[80] See, for example, Dt 12:7, 18; 14:23, 26; 15:20; 27:7; Ezek 44:3; 1 Chr 29:22. See also Ruprecht, "Exodus 24,9-11 als Beispiel lebendiger Erzähltradition," 140 n.3; and Nicholson, "The Interpretation of Exodus xxiv 9-11," 93-94.

[81] See Clifford, *Cosmic Mountain*, 123.

[82] See also C. Westermann, "Die Herrlichkeit Gottes in der Priesterschrift," *Wort-Gebot-Glaube*, Fs. W. Eichrodt, Beiträge zur Theologie des Alten Testaments (Zürich: Zwingli, 1970) 237-38; and Hossfeld, *Dekalog*, 203-4.

the limitation of public worship to the leaders of Israel in Exod 24:9-11.

4. *The Kabod Yahweh*

Priestly redactors conclude the third episode with Exod 24:12-18. This final pericope provides the immediate context for the initial revelation of the priestly legislation in Exodus 25-31. The central event in Exod 24:12-18 (and perhaps the central event in the entire priestly redaction of Exodus 19-24) is the description of theophany on Mount Sinai in Exod 24:15b-18a. A detailed interpretation of the imagery in this account of theophany must wait until the following section, when we explore the significance of Mount Sinai as representing a priestly theology of divine presence. The function of this unit in the context of Exodus 24 does require interpretation at this point for it completes the inner logic of the priestly redaction of Exodus 19-24, and brings to completion the modeling of Exodus 24 on Leviticus 8-9.

Priestly redactors have combined the description of theophany on Mount Sinai in Exod 24:15b-18a with a distinct unit of tradition in Exod 24:12-15a, 18b which introduces the motif of the tablets into the Sinai Complex.[83] The motif of the tablets provides a link between the account of theophany in Exodus 19-24 and the events of Covenant Renewal in Exodus 32-34. This link is important for interpreting the overall structure of the Sinai Complex and we will explore its significance in Chapter 5. What is important at this point in our study is the way in which priestly redactors have linked the account of theophany in Exod 24:15b-18a with Exod 24:12-15a, 18b through the repetition of the verb "to ascend" (*'lh*) in Exod 24:12a, 13b, 15a, 18a. The

---

[83] The introduction of Joshua, Aaron, and Hur connects Exod 24:12-15a with Exod 17:8-16 where the same characters appear. On the tradition-history of Exod 17:8-16 see Noth, (*Exodus*, 173-79); for discussion of Exod 17:8-16 in the context of the mountain of God see Schmid, (*Mose*, 62-64); on the heroic qualities of Moses in this unit see G. W. Coats ("Moses versus Amalek. Aetiology and Legend in Exod. XVII 8-16," *VTSup* 28 [1975] 29-41). Source-critical solutions to Exod 24:12-15a vary: it has been assigned to E (Wellhausen) and J (Noth). Most recently, Zenger (*Sinaitheophanie*, 217) assigned Exod 24:12 to JE and Exod 24:13-14 to P. Exod 24:12-15a appears to have been an introduction to Exodus 32 prior to the incorporation of the priestly legislation since Aaron appears in Exod 32:1, Joshua in Exod 32:17, and the motif of the tablets in Exod 32:15-16. Whatever the tradition-historical roots of Exod 24:12-15a might be, the motif of the tablets suggests that it was already functioning within deuteronomistic tradition, where it served as a transition from the revelation of the law and the establishment of covenant in Exodus 19-24 to the breaking of the covenant and Covenant Renewal in Exodus 32-34.

repetition of this motif results in the following structure. After Moses is commanded to ascend the mountain alone in Exod 24:12a, his journey to the top of Mount Sinai separates into three stages.[84] First, Moses is with the other participants on the mountain in Exod 24:13-14, which ties this unit to the vision of God in Exod 24:9-11 even though the names of the characters have changed. Second, Moses is described as ascending only part way up the mountain for a six-day period of preparation in Exod 24:15-16a before completing his ascent. Third, on the seventh day the Kabod Yahweh appears to the people on the top of Mount Sinai and Moses completes his ascent to the summit of the mountain in Exod 24:16b-18. This structure underscores even further the vast distance between Yahweh and the people at Mount Sinai and the very essential role of a priestly mediator to bridge this gap. Furthermore, the function of Moses as the priestly mediator who is able to enter into the very presence of God on Mount Sinai completes the logic of the priestly redaction, since it allows for the revelation of the priestly legislation in Exodus 25-31.

The structure of Exod 24:12-18 requires yet an additional analysis, because the sequence of action in the ascent of Moses also completes the modeling of Exodus 24 on Leviticus 8-9. The overall similarity in structure between these two central priestly texts can be illustrated in the following manner. Each account moves through a five-part sequence which begins with purification and culminates in the appearance of the Kabod Yahweh. The similar sequence begins with a blood ritual for the purpose of purgation (the people are sanctified with blood in Exod 24:6, 8; the priests are purified with blood in Lev 8:22-30). The blood ritual is followed by a meal before God which takes place in the context of public worship (Moses, Aaron, Nadab, Abihu, and the seventy elders participate in the meal in Exod 24:9-11; the priests feast before God in Lev 8:31-32). After the meal there is a period of consecration prior to the actual approach of the priestly mediator into the very presence of God (Moses prepares for six days on Mount Sinai in Exod 24:15-16a; the priests prepare for seven days before the door of the Tent of Meeting in Lev 8:33-36). Once consecrated the priestly mediator ap-

[84] The ascent of Moses in three stages (Exod 24:13-14, 15-16a, 16b-18) has been carried through to the account of his descent in Exod 32:15-19, where Moses first descends the mountain with the "two tablets of testimony" (šny lḥt h'dt Exod 32:15-16); second, Moses and Joshua hear noise in the camp (Exod 32:17-18), and finally Moses is described as reaching the camp and seeing the golden calf, at which time he destroys the tablets (Exod 32:19).

proaches the very presence of God (Moses enters the summit of
Mount Sinai to receive plans for the Tent of Meeting in Exod
24:16b-18; Moses and Aaron approach God in the Tent of Meeting in Lev 9:23a). Finally, each text culminates with a theophany of the Kabod Yahweh before all the people (the Kabod
Yahweh appears on Mount Sinai in Exod 24:17, and at the altar
before the Tent of Meeting in Lev 9:23b-24).

D. *Conclusion*

At the outset of this chapter I posed the question of whether
priestly tradition in the Sinai Complex might not be better described as a redaction, which presupposes and expands upon
older tradition, rather than as an independent source. In the
preceding analysis I have attempted to outline the nature and
scope of priestly tradition in Exodus 19-24 as a redaction, and I
have argued that it is meant to provide a narrative context for
priestly legislation. In support of this final point we have repeatedly seen a correspondence between the *Tendenz* of this redaction and the priestly legislation in general and more specifically
a number of close connections to the sanctification of the priests
and the first public worship service of Israel in Leviticus 8-9. By
way of summary several conclusions concerning the character
and structure of the priestly redaction are now in order.

First, as was the case in the deuteronomistic redaction, the
priestly redaction has followed the three-part sequence of the
Mountain of God tradition, while at the same time it has restructured the narrative and introduced new motifs into the account
of theophany at the mountain. The three-part sequence and the
major motifs of the priestly redaction can be illustrated in the
following manner. In the first episode, the priestly redaction
provided a more specific setting for theophany in the wilderness
of Sinai, while it also introduced the promise of holiness for
Israel. The second episode built on both the new setting and
the motif of holiness. In this episode the preparation for theophany is expanded to accentuate the danger of Mount Sinai and
the need for Israel to be pure; at the same time theophany itself
is reinterpreted as a visual experience of fire when Yahweh descends upon Mount Sinai. The priestly redaction concludes with
a transformation of the deuteronomic Covenant-Closing Ceremony into a Sanctification Ceremony, which culminates in a
theophany of the Kabod Yahweh. This final theophany on
Mount Sinai is the central point of the priestly redaction, for it
provides the immediate context for the revelation of the priestly
legislation in Exodus 25-31.

Second, several conclusions concerning the technique of the priestly redactors and the structure of the priestly redaction are possible at this point. Priestly redactors have moved in a strikingly different direction from the deuteronomistic redactors. They have not simply framed the Mountain of God tradition with new material. Rather they engage the Mountain of God tradition more directly and thus build upon it at many specific points. The three additions to the preparation for theophany in Exod 19:11b, 12ab-13, 15b are a striking example of this as is the transformation of the sacrifices in Exod 24:5. A common technique of the priestly redactors has been to disrupt the flow of the narrative in order to provide more specific information about the narrated events in Exodus 19-24. This technique began at the outset of the priestly redaction with the itinerary notice in Exod 19:1-2a, when repetition became the organizing device instead of plot or chronology. The disruption of narrative plot continued with the addition of the promise in Exod 19:5bb-6a, the several additions to the account of preparation for theophany in Exod 19:11b, 12ab-13, 15b, and perhaps most notably with the insertion of Exod 19:20-25 when the entire account of theophany came to an abrupt halt. This technique is best characterized as a spatial form device (a narrative technique which emphasizes character and setting over plot and chronology), since in every case the disruption of the flow of the narrative has provided the context for priestly redactors to emphasize either the setting of theophany as being Mount Sinai, or the location of characters in the context of the mountain.

Third, the mountain setting has also been transformed by priestly redactors. This conclusion actually builds upon the previous point concerning redactional technique, since spatial form devices within the priestly redaction have also affected the overall structure of the Exodus 19-24. This conclusion suggests that although the priestly redaction and the Mountain of God tradition may function within the same stream of tradition, they certainly are not the same. In particular, the disruption of chronology and plot has repeatedly provided the occasion for priestly redactors to underscore the vast distance between Yahweh and Israel at Mount Sinai by reaffirming the clearly defined vertical hierarchy between characters that was evident in the Mountain of God tradition. In addition, priestly redactors expand the hierarchical structure even further by underscoring that Yahweh does not dwell on Mount Sinai, but must descend in order to be present at the summit of the mountain. The priestly portrayal of Moses reinforces their reinterpretation of the mountain setting. He is clearly located within the priestly redaction either at the summit of Mount Sinai with Yahweh or at the base of the mountain with Israel. Consequently, his movement on Mount Sinai shifts his function to underscore his role as a mediator who maintains distance and clear boundaries between the sacred and the profane.

In summary our study suggests that the priestly redaction in Exodus 19-24 is a "planned theological editing," which has transformed Mount Zion in the Mountain of God tradition into Mount Sinai, the mountain of revelation in priestly tradition. The quality of divine presence that is symbolized in Mount Sinai now requires a more thorough interpretation.

II
MOUNT SINAI IN PRIESTLY TRADITION

The important role of Mount Sinai within priestly tradition has long since been noted by biblical scholars, and the preceding redaction-critical study of Exodus 19-24 has in a certain respect simply confirmed this consensus. It has underscored the priestly concern about Mount Sinai as the location of theophany at a number of points: in the itinerary notice of Exod 19:1-2a; in the priestly reinterpretation of theophany in Exod 19:11b, 18, 20, 23; in the appearance of the Kabod Yahweh in Exod 24:16a; and throughout the priestly legislation itself (e.g. Exod 31:18). However, the preceding redaction-critical study of Exodus 19-24 also challenges the past consensus concerning Mount Sinai within pentateuchal tradition. In particular, the interpretation of Mount Sinai as an innovation by priestly redactors moves against a general consensus among past scholars that Mount Sinai is anchored in pre-exilic tradition (either within an independent cult legend or in the yahwistic source).[85] This past consensus has tended to provide the basis for a theological interpretation of Mount Sinai as the mountain of law or covenant, which was often viewed as functioning in opposition to Mount Zion, the mountain of the temple.[86] However, the present proposal that Mount Sinai is anchored tradition-historically in priestly tradition raises new questions concerning its theological significance. My aim in this section is to probe the theological significance of Mount Sinai in priestly tradition, and in the pro-

[85] For an interpretation of Sinai as being rooted in a cult legend see von Rad, "Problem of the Hextateuch," 1-25, and within the yahwistic source see Wellhausen, *Prolegomena*, 343-45; or more recently Terrien, *Elusive Presence*, 131-36.
[86] See, for example, the recent study of Donaldson, *Jesus on the Mountain*.

cess to reevaluate Wellhausen's conclusion (noted at the outset of this chapter) that the priestly account of Israel at Mount Sinai is theologically "lifeless." I hope to demonstrate that, as symbol, Mount Sinai represents a distinctive priestly cultic theology of divine presence which contrasts to Mount Horeb in deutero-nomistic tradition and also functions critically to evaluate Mount Zion in the Mountain of God tradition. This section will separate into four parts in order to interpret the theology of divine presence symbolized by Mount Sinai. A more detailed examination of the tradition-historical development of Mount Sinai in priestly tradition in the first part will provide a starting point for interpreting the theological significance of the mountain setting in the priestly redaction of Exodus 19-24 under the following topics: Divine Presence on Mount Sinai, Moses as Cultic Leader on Mount Sinai, and The Vision of Israel at Mount Sinai.

A. *Mount Sinai within Priestly Tradition*

The preceding redaction-critical study suggests that the distribution of Mount Sinai in Exodus 19-24 is not the result of two distinct traditions (a yahwistic and priestly source), but that its central role in the Sinai Complex is priestly and tradition-historically the latest addition to this material. On the basis of this work I am arguing that Mount Sinai must not be interpreted as pre-exilic tradition which stands in opposition to Mount Zion (as for example, a contrast between law and temple), but that it is an innovation by priestly tradents, which symbolizes the ex-ilic/post-exilic tabernacle and thus qualifies the pre-exilic temple theology of Mount Zion.[87] The results of the redaction-critical work in Exodus 19-24 must be placed in the larger

---

[87] A more exact date for the priestly redaction is difficult to determine and it would require a more detailed examination of the relationship between narrative and law within pentateuchal priestly tradition. For example, if the redaction of priestly legislation into the Pentateuch corresponds to the canonization of this material (and thus signifies the *terminus ad quem* of priestly legislation), then the priestly redaction would have to be post-exilic, since contrasts between the Passover Papyrus of the Elephantine Papryi (see *ANET* 491-92) and the canonical form of the priestly legislation suggest that the latter material was still in formation in 419 B.C.E. (For discussion of these contrasts see, among others, H. Cazelles, "La mission d'Esdras," *VT* 4 [1954] 113-40 esp. 126; P. Grelot, "Le Paprys Pascal d'Elephantine et la probleme du Pentateuque," *VT* 5 [1955] 250-65 and "La dernière etape de la rédaction sacredotale," *VT* 6 [1956] 176-98). However, it is conceivable that the priestly legislation would have gone through a period of revision even after it was redacted into the Pentateuch, in which case the priestly redaction could be as early as the exilic period.

framework of a tradition-historical investigation of Sinai within the entire Hebrew Bible.

The point of departure for our present tradition-historical investigation will be two problems the distribution of Mount Sinai in the Hebrew Bible has posed for past interpreters who have argued that it is rooted in pre-exilic tradition. The first problem concerns the references to Mount Sinai within the Pentateuch. The majority of references to Mount Sinai are confined to the immediate context of the priestly legislation (Exodus-Leviticus-Numbers, 29 of 36 occurrences). The second problem concerns the references to Mount Sinai outside the Pentateuch, where it is absent altogether from pre-exilic literature. Reference to Mount Sinai occurs for the first time in post-exilic literature when it is included within the prayer of Ezra during Covenant Renewal (Neh 9:13). These two problems raise the following question: If Mount Sinai is a prominent pre-exilic tradition, then why is it so strangely absent from Israel's *Heilsgeschichte* until the time of Ezra in the post-exilic period? A fresh look at the distribution of Mount Sinai in the Hebrew Bible will provide a framework for answering this question. The thirty-six references to Sinai in the Hebrew Bible separate into three different contexts: the "March in the South" theophany tradition (4 occurrences); the Pentateuch (either within the priestly itinerary as the wilderness of Sinai [14 occurrences] or within the context of the priestly legislation as Mount Sinai [15 occurrences]); and in post-exilic literature outside of the Pentateuch (3 occurrences). An examination of Sinai in these three contexts will provide insight into its formative tradition-historical development within exilic/post-exilic priestly tradition.

Sinai is referred to four times in archaic poetry, and always in the context of theophany (Judg 5:5; Ps 68:9, 18; Deut 33:2).[88]

---

[88] On the antiquity of these poems see W. F. Albright, "The Earliest Form of Hebrew Verse," *JPOS* 2 (1922) 69-86; "The Song of Deborah in Light of Archaeology," *BASOR* 66 (1936) 30; "A Catalogue of Early Hebrew Lyric Poems," *HUCA* 23 (1950-51) 14-24; *Yahweh and the Gods of Canaan: A Historical Analysis of Two Contrasting Faiths*, The Jordan Lectures (London: University of London, 1968) 13, 17. The arguments of Albright are expanded upon by F. M. Cross and D. N. Freedman, *Studies in Ancient Yahwistic Poetry*, SBLDS 21 (Missoula: Scholars Press, 1975) 13-27, 97-122. Hab 3:3-4 has also been included in this tradition because of its reference to Mount Paran, which is associated with Sinai in Deut 33:2 (see W. F. Albright, "The Psalm of Habbakuk," *Studies in O.T. Prophecy*, ed. H. H. Rowley [Edinburgh: University Press, 1950] 16). Hab 3:3-4 is not included in this study because Sinai is not specifically mentioned.

Judg 5:5 and Ps 68:9 describe Yahweh as "the one of Sinai" (*zeh sînay*); while Ps 68:18b states that "Yahweh came from Sinai. . . ." Several comments are necessary concerning these particular texts. First, see the form-critical analysis by Jeremias

These texts are characterized as the "March in the South" theophany tradition, because in each of them Sinai is a southern region from which God would appear to aid or to rescue Israel at a time of crisis.[89] The region of Sinai in these texts is not as precisely located as the presentation of Mount Sinai in the canonical Pentateuch would suggest. Rather, in the "March in the South" theophany tradition the region of Sinai is actually equated at different times with Seir, Edom, and Mount Paran.[90] The role of Sinai in the "March in the South" theophany tradition lays the groundwork for several initial conclusions concerning the tradition-historical roots of Sinai. First, it is clear from these texts that Sinai is anchored in a theophany tradition, which is deeply rooted in Israel's past. However, we must immediately add that at this stage of tradition Sinai is not a mountain, but a region. And finally, we can also conclude that the imagery of Yahweh in the "March in the South" theophany tradition is of a mobile God, who is able to leave his regional home in order to lead or to rescue Israel.

The mobile presentation of God in the "March in the South" theophany tradition would provide an excellent starting point for critically evaluating the static view of divine presence that is central to Zion. And this appears to be how it was used within

(*Theophanie*, 10-12), who describes these texts as representing the earliest *Gattung* of theophany (the report of Yahweh's coming and the reaction of nature in order to focus on the present). Second, for interpretation of the Hebrew *zeh* as representing the archaic pronoun *d* see W. F. Albright, "The Names Shaddai and Abram," *JBL* 54 (1935) 204; J. M. Allegro, "Uses of the Semitic Demonstrative Element Z in Hebrew," *VT* 5 (1955) 309-12; and F. M. Cross, "Yahweh and the God of the Patriarchs," *HTR* 55 (1962) 239 n.61, 255. But compare H. Birkeland, "Hebrew *Zae* and Arabic *Du*," *ST* 2 (1948) 201-2. Finally, the Hebrew of Ps 68:18b presents problems for interpretation. The MT reads, *'ǎdōnāy bām sînay baqqōdeš* ("Lord to them Sinai in the holy place/with the holy ones"). My translation assumes the following change in the *MT*: *'adōnāy bā' missînay*, which is similar to Deut 33:2— *yhwh missînay bā'*. For a similar solution to the Hebrew *bām* see S. Mowinckel, *Der Achtundsechzigste Psalm*, Avhandlinger utgitt an det Norske Videnskaps-Akademi 1 (Oslo: Jacob Debwad, 1953) 41; Clements, *God and Temple*, 24; and Cross, *Canaanite Myth and Hebrew Epic*, 102. In addition, there is debate whether *bqdš* translates "in the holy place" (Mowinckel, Clements), or "with the holy ones" (Cross).

[89] See Cross, *Canaanite Myth and Hebrew Epic*, 99-105.

[90] See Judge 5:4 where Yahweh is described as coming from Seir and as marching from Edom in the same context with Sinai, while Deut 33:2 describes the appearance of Yahweh from Sinai as also being from Seir and Mount Paran. Clifford (*Cosmic Mountain*, 115 n.16) writes concerning the reference to Mount Paran: "As is well known, *har* can mean a specific mountain or a mountainous terrain." He goes on to conclude that "in the March in the South passages. . .the writer had no specific mountain in mind, but a mountainous territory."

the priestly tradition, since the second context within the Hebrew Bible in which references to Sinai are clustered (and by far
the most prominent with 29 of the 36 references) is the priestly
legislation in the Pentateuch. This material underscores the
link between the "March in the South" theophany tradition and
priestly tradition, and provides insight into a transformation in
the use of Sinai, since it is referred to as both a region (the wilderness of Sinai) and a specific mountain (Mount Sinai). Priestly
tradents describe Sinai as a region fourteen times: the wilderness of Sinai is referred to twice in the itinerary list of Numbers
33 (Num 33:15, 16);[91] it occurs twelve additional times in
priestly texts either in the context of the itinerary (Exod 16;1;
19:1, 2; Num 10:12), or to designate that the wilderness of Sinai
is the place where cultic worship must be observed (the first
public worship, Lev 7:38; passover, Lev 9:1, 5; the place of cen-
sus, Num 1:1, 19; 3:4, 14; 26:64). The frequency of the wilderness of Sinai in texts that are clearly priestly indicates that it has
become an important cultic location within this tradition.[92]

The reason for the central role of Sinai within priestly tradition becomes clearer from an examination of the additional fif-
teen occurrences, where Sinai is transformed from a region to a
specific mountain. This transformation is evident in the priestly
legislation, when Mount Sinai is repeatedly designated as the
cosmic mountain of revelation, where Moses first received the
divine instructions for the cult (Lev 7:38; 25:1; 26:46; Num 28:6).
The transformation of Sinai from a region to a specific mountain
is also evident in the narrative context of the priestly legislation:
Sinai becomes the mountain of theophany in Exodus 19 (Exod
19:11, 18, 20, 23); it is the location of the Kabod Yahweh, which
provides setting for the initial revelation of the priestly legislation in Exodus 25-31 (Exod 24:16; 31:18); and it is the mountain

---

[91] There is debate whether the itinerary list in Numbers 33 is part of priestly tradition or an independent document. See, for example, Cross (*Canaanite Myth and
Hebrew Epic*, 308-9), who favors interpreting Numbers 33 as an independent document, and compare him to Noth (*History of Pentateuchal Traditions*, 220-21, and
Numbers, OTL [Philadelphia: Westminster, 1968] 242), who argues that Numbers
33 is a priestly compilation. This debate is of secondary importance to our discussion of Sinai within priestly tradition. The only difference it makes is whether the
tradition-historical development of Sinai is a three or four stage process: (1) the
"March in the South" theophany tradition where Sinai is a region; (2) [Numbers
33]; (3) priestly tradition in the Pentateuch where Sinai is a region and a mountain;
(4) post-exilic literature where Sinai is only a mountain. In either case the significance of Sinai for priestly tradition does not change.

[92] For further analysis of the *midbar* Sinai in priestly tradition see, among others,
Beyerlin, *Oldest Sinaitic Traditions*, 2; Hyatt, *Exodus*, 200, Clifford, *Cosmic Mountain*, 107-8.

of Covenant Renewal, which provides setting for the subsequent priestly legislation in Exodus 35-Numbers 10 (Exod 34:2, 4, 29, 32).[93]

The final context in which Sinai occurs in the Hebrew Bible illustrates how successful priestly tradents were in transforming Sinai from a region to a specific mountain. Sinai is referred to three times in post-exilic literature exclusively as a mountain (Neh 9:13-14; Sir 48:7; 2 Esdras 3:17-19).[94] These occurrences indicate that in the post-exilic period Mount Sinai had become part of Israel's *Heilsgeschichte* as the place of theophany, where Yahweh led Jacob from Egypt (2 Esdras 3:17-19)[95] and where Yahweh delivered Torah (Neh 9:13-14). Finally, the growing influence of Mount Sinai as the place of theophany is reflected in Sir 48:7, when it is even equated with Mount Horeb as the location of Yahweh's appearance to Elijah.

---

[93] The influence of priestly redactors in emphasizing Mount Sinai as the location of revelation is evident in three contexts within Exodus 19-34: in the initial revelation in Exodus 19, in the revelation of the Kabod in Exodus 24, and in the revelation of Covenant Renewal in Exodus 34. Each of these contexts employs similar imagery. For example, in the first context of Exodus 19 Mount Sinai is associated with the imagery of divine descent (*yrd*, Exod 19:18) to the "top of the mountain" (*'el-rō'š hāhār*, Exod 19:20), and the mediatorial role of Moses is subsequently called to the "top of the mountain" (*'el-rō'š hāhār*, Exod 19:20). In the second context of Exod 24:15b-18a Mount Sinai is also associated with the imagery of divine descent (*škn*, Exod 24:16a), to the "top of the mountain" (*běrō'š hāhār*, Exod 24:17) and the mediatorial role of Moses is stressed when he enters the cloud on the mountain (Exod 24:18a). In addition, the setting of the priestly legislation is emphasized in this context by the framing of Exodus 25-31 with reference to Mount Sinai (Exod 24:16; 31:18). In the third context of Exodus 34, Yahweh reappears on Mount Sinai for Covenant Renewal. Here again theophany incorporates the imagery of descent (*yrd*, Exod 34:5) and the mediatorial role of Moses is stressed when he is called to the "top of the mountain" (*'el-rō'š hāhār*, Exod 34:2). Furthermore, reference to Mount Sinai frames the legislation of Covenant Renewal in Exod 34:10-26 in much the same manner as the initial revelation of the priestly legislation in Exodus 25-31, only this time Mount Sinai is referred to twice, both before and after the legislation (Exod 34:2, 4, 29, 32). Finally, the descent of Moses from Mount Sinai (Exod 34:29) and his instruction of "all that Yahweh had spoken with him on Mount Sinai" (Exod 34:32) provides the context for the remainder of the priestly legislation in Exodus 35-Numbers 10.

[94] Mount Sinai is referred to in Ezra's prayer during Covenant Renewal in Neh 9:6-37, where he recounts Israel's *Heilsgeschichte*. In Neh 9:13-14, Mount Sinai is the location of and the place where Moses promulgated divine law to Israel. In the eulogy to Elijah in Sirach 48, Sinai is not only a mountain and the location of , but has even become equated with Mount Horeb. Consequently, Elijah is described in Sir 48:7 as the one "who heard rebuke at Sinai and judgment of vengeance at Horeb." Finally, Sinai is a mountain in 2 Esdras 3:17-19, where it is described as the place to which Yahweh led Jacob's descendants from Egypt in order to appear to them there.

[95] See Jeremias *Theophanie*, 107.

According to the preceding tradition-historical proposal, the transformation of Sinai as a specific mountain of revelation is best interpreted as an innovation by exilic/post-exilic priestly tradents, and as the final redaction in Exodus 19-24. Furthermore, it would appear that Mount Sinai has acquired at least two functions within priestly tradition. First, to provide a setting for the revelation of the priestly legislation, in much the same way as the first deuteronomistic redaction provided a setting for the deuteronomic legislation. Thus, we can conclude that these two redactions are both "pentateuchal" in nature, in that they both aim to anchor their distinct law-codes in the one revelation at the mountain in Exodus 19-24. Second, Mount Sinai functions to qualify the pre-exilic temple theology of Mount Zion. These two functions of Mount Sinai imply a theology of divine cultic presence which now requires interpretation.

B. *Divine Presence on Mount Sinai*

I hope to demonstrate in this section that Mount Sinai symbolizes a quality of divine cultic presence that is meant to provide a critique of Mount Zion within the Mountain of God tradition. As was the case with Mount Horeb, we will see here that Mount Sinai substitutes a metonymic relationship of contiguity between God and the mountain for the metaphorical relationship of resemblance between God and the mountain that was evident in the Mountain of God tradition. The result of this shift from metaphor to metonymy is that Mount Sinai does not symbolize the permanent dwelling place of a static God, but the impermanent dwelling place of a God who descends in fire from a heavenly temple to an earthly temple in order to be present with the worshipping community.

The distinction between Zion and Sinai that I have outlined above is implicit in the entire priestly redaction of Exodus 19-24, yet it reaches it clearest articulation in the account of theophany in Exod 24:15b-18a. Scholars have described this account of theophany as reflecting the Priestly Kabod theology, because of the introduction of the devouring fire of the Kabod Yahweh as the symbol of divine presence on the mountain.[96] The Kabod Yahweh will be our central focus of study and its interpretation will divide into two parts. First, the imagery of theophany in Exod 24:15b-18a will be examined. Second, the important role of theophany in Exod 24:15b-18a within the overall structure of the priestly redaction will be described.

---

[96] See most recently Mettinger, *The Dethronement of Sabaoth*, 80-115.

1. *The Kabod Yahweh and the Imagery of Theophany on Mount Sinai in Exod 24:15b-18a*

Two images are introduced in conjunction with the Kabod Yahweh in Exod 24:15b-18a. The reader is told that the fiery presence of the Kabod Yahweh is surrounded by a "cloud (*ānān*) and that its presence is best characterized as "tabernacling" (*škn*) on Mount Sinai. An examination of these images in relation to the Kabod Yahweh will illustrate the mobile character of God in priestly tradition, and how the permanent presence of God is separated from the mountain. Since these images are part of a "planned theological editing," they cannot be interpreted in isolation but must be seen as a development from the initial priestly reinterpretation of theophany in Exod 19:18. In view of this, our interpretation of the imagery of theophany in Exod 24:15b-18a will take its point of departure from Exod 19:18.

Within the overall structure of the priestly redaction, the theophany in Exodus 19:18 prepares the reader for the Kabod Yahweh in Exod 24:15b-18a by initiating a critique of Zion. Three points of contrast between the Mountain of God tradition in Exod 19:16ab-17 and the priestly redaction in Exod 19:18 provide important background for interpreting the theophany of the Kabod Yahweh in Exod 24:15b-18a.

First, the exclusive focus on the visual experience of theophany as fire at the summit of Mount Sinai provides an initial contrast to the thunder and the lightning in Exod 19:16ab-17, and it alerts the reader to the sacramental concerns of the priestly tradents, which will be developed further in the appearance of the Kabod Yahweh in Exod 24:15b-18a.

Second, the imagery of divine descent (*yrd*) contrasts with the static imagery of God as dwelling on the mountain in Exod 19:16ab-17. This imagery has tradition-historical roots in the Tent of Meeting tradition, where the motif of divine descent (*yrd*) to the door of the Tent of Meeting also played a central role.[97] The central place of the Tent of Meeting tradition for the priestly critique of Zion is underscored by the repeated use of the verb *yrd* throughout the priestly redaction of Exodus 19. That Yahweh is not a God who dwells on the mountain, but must descend in order to be present on Mount Sinai is under-

---

[97] Compare Mettinger, (*The Dethronement of Sabaoth*, 86) who discusses in detail the connection between priestly tradition and the Tent of Meeting tradition, but then concludes that the verb *yārad* is never used in connection with God within priestly tradition.

scored no less than four times within the priestly reinterpretation of the Mount Sinai tradition (Exod 19:11b, 15b, 18, 20). The
choice of this technical verb within the priestly redaction of Exodus 19-24 corresponds with the central role that the Tent of
Meeting tradition plays within the priestly legislation itself,
where the cult is described at different times as both the Tabernacle (*mškn*) and the Tent of Meeting (*'ōhel mô'ēd*).[98] The imagery of descent in the Tent of Meeting tradition is only the
starting point for the priestly critique of Zion, since this imagery
itself is qualified when it is replaced with the verb "to tabernacle" (*škn*) in the subsequent theophany of Exod 24:15b-18a.

And third, the personification of Mount Sinai as trembling
(*ḥrd*) at the divine descent suggests a metonymic relationship of
contiguity between God and the mountain as opposed to a metaphoric relationship of resemblance in which God is presented
as permanently dwelling on the mountain. This shift to metonymy foreshadows the impermanent presence of the Kabod
Yahweh that will be developed in the subsequent priestly description of theophany in Exod 24:15b-18a.

The introduction of the Kabod Yahweh, the cloud, and the
verb "to tabernacle" in Exod 24:15b-18a complete the critique
of Zion that was only inaugurated in Exod 19:18. The substitution of the Kabod in Exod 24:15b-18a to replace the direct equation of Yahweh with the fire in Exod 19:18 is an initial
qualification of divine presence on Mount Sinai.[99] The qualification of divine presence goes even further when the fiery Kabod
is engulfed in a cloud, which covers (*ksh*) it, and thus provides
yet an additional boundary between the sacred and the profane
at Mount Sinai.[100] Finally, the verb "to tabernacle" (*škn*) also
plays a central role in describing the divine presence on Mount
Sinai in Exod 24:15b-18a.[101]

[98] Exod 40:34-36 provides an excellent example of how these terms are used inter-
changeably by priestly tradents.

[99] R. Rendtorff ("The Concept of Revelation in Ancient Israel," *Revelation as History*, ed. W. Pannenberg [New York: Macmillan, 1968] 37) writes, "The seemingly
reasonable and often expressed opinion that the *kbwd* in the priestly texts ex-
presses a self-manifestation of Jahweh within the cult simply does not stand up on
examination."

[100] Compare Mann (*Divine Presence*, 257) who would interpret the function of the
cloud as being "closely related to that of consecration and communication." On
the tradition-historical roots of the cloud in ancient Near Eastern religion and in
Israel see Mendenhall, *The Tenth Generation*, 54-56, 209-14.

[101] On the translation of *škn* as "to tabernacle" see Cross, *Canaanite Myth and
Hebrew Epic*, 299.

The meaning of *škn*, however, is debated.[102] Although scholars agree that the verb is an important description of divine
presence within priestly tradition, there is debate whether it describes the permanent or impermanent cultic presence of God
for priestly writers. The issue is whether priestly tradition represents a point of continuity with the pre-exilic temple theology,
where God was envisioned as being permanently present in the
temple,[103] or a break with the past temple theology by describing the cultic presence of God as being impermanent.[104] This
debate becomes all the more important in view of the frequent
description of God's house in the priestly legislation as being the
tabernacle (*mškn*).[105] An interpretation of *škn* that is limited to
Exod 24:15b-18a does not provide clear criteria to address the
issues in this debate. However, when the use of *škn* in Exod
24:15b-18a is interpreted in conjunction with the account of
theophany in Exod 40:34-35, where the verb is also used, it becomes clear that the verb represents a break with pre-exilic
temple theology by emphasizing the temporary character of the
divine cultic presence.[106] Three details in particular concerning

---

[102] Although the verb "to dwell" (*yšb*) was the primary word for describing the
presence of God in the pre-exilic Zion-Sabaoth theology (i.e., Ps 132:13-14), the
verb "to tabernacle" (*škn*) could also be used, especially as a participle (i.e., Isa
8:18). The priestly writers, therefore, are reinterpreting older theological language, which provides the basis for debate. For further discussion of *škn* outside of
the priestly legislation see among others Cross, *Canaanite Myth and Hebrew Epic*,
299 *et passim*; and Mettinger, (*The Dethronement of Sabaoth*, 28, 83-87, 90-97)
who also includes a review of scholarship.

[103] So Mettinger, *The Dethronement of Sabaoth*, 88-97. Yet Mettinger does concede some contrast between the priestly use of *škn* and the pre-exilic term *yšb* in
that *škn* no longer designates the enthronement of God in the temple as *yšb* had.

[104] So F. M. Cross, "The Priestly Tabernacle," *BAR* 1 (1961) 224-27, and *Canaanite
Myth and Hebrew Epic*, 245, 299, 313; M. Görg, *Das Zelt der Begegnung: Untersuchung zur Gestalt der Sakralen Zelttradition Altisraels*, BBB 27 (Bonn: Hanstein, 1967) 97-124.

[105] Reference to the tabernacle occurs over 60 times in Exodus 25-31, 35-40.

[106] The accounts of theophany in Exod 24:15b-18a and in Exod 40:34-35 include
the same central images of the Kabod Yahweh, the cloud, and the verb "to
tabernacle."
   Exod 24:15b-16a reads:
   The cloud (*'ānān*) covered (*ksh*) the mountain
   and the Kabod Yahweh tabernacled (*škn*) on Mount Sinai
   Exod 40:34-35 reads:
   The cloud (*'ānān*) covered the Tent of Meeting
   and the Kabod Yahweh filled the Tabernacle
   Moses was not able to enter the Tent of Meeting
   because the cloud (*'ānān*) tabernacled (*škn*) on it
   and the Kabod Yahweh filled the tabernacle.
Such a precise repetition invites comparison, especially since these two theopha-

the way in which the verb *škn* is used in Exod 24:15b-18a and in Exod 40:34-35 support an interpretation of it as a qualification of pre-exilic Zion-Sabaoth theology.

The first noticeable feature about *škn* in these two texts is that the verb "to tabernacle" is not restricted in use to the Kabod Yahweh, but is also used to describe the presence of the cloud. Note, Exod 40:35 where the presence of the cloud on the Tent of Meeting is described with *škn*.

Second, the description of the cloud in Exod 40:36 as "ascending" (*'lh*) after it had "tabernacled" (*škn*) on the Tent of Meeting in Exod 40:35 suggests that *škn* does not describe a permanent presence within the priestly legislation, but an impermanent presence. The use of the same verb to describe the cultic presence of the Kabod Yahweh in Exod 24:15b-18a suggests that the Kabod, too, shares this semantic feature and thus represents an impermanent divine presence on Mount Sinai.

Third, the contrast in each text between *škn* and *'lh* (to ascend) suggests that the description of the Kabod Yahweh as tabernacling incorporates the imagery of descent.[107]

The three conclusions suggest that *škn* ("to tabernacle") within priestly tradition represents a break with past temple theology, since the imagery of descent does not allow for a static view of divine presence, while the temporary quality of the Kabod Yahweh forbids a permanent identification of God with the mountain. The verb *škn* provides yet a further qualification of the imagery of theophany in Exod 19:18, for now the presence of the Kabod Yahweh is more cautiously characterized as "descending and only temporarily dwelling" (*škn*) on Mount Sinai.

---

nies link the divine presence on Mount Sinai (Exod 24:15b-18a) with the priestly cult (Exod 40:34-35).

[107] The contrast between *'lh* and *škn* can be illustrated in each text as follows. The "tabernacling" of the Kabod Yahweh on Mount Sinai in Exod 24:15b-18a is contrasted twice to the ascent of Moses on the mountain:

    And Moses ascended (*'lh*) the mountain (Exod 24:15a)
    And the Kabod Yahweh tabernacled (*škn*) on Mount Sinai (Exod 24:16a)
    And Moses ascended (*'lh*) the mountain (Exod 24:18a)

The "tabernacling" of the cloud on the Tent of Meeting in Exod 34:35 also contrasts to its subsequent ascent in Exod 34:36:

    Moses was not able to enter the Tent of Meeting
    because the cloud tabernacled (*škn*) on it
    and the Kabod Yahweh filled the tabernacle (Exod 34:35)
    And when the cloud was taken up (*'lh*) from the tabernacle
    the people of Israel went on in their journey. (Exod 34:36)

See also Num 9:17, 19 which restates Exod 40:34-38. Finally, compare Mettinger, (*The Dethronement of Sabaoth*, 95) on the ingressive *Aktionsart* of *škn*.

Several conclusions concerning the quality of divine presence on Mount Sinai are possible from our study of the imagery of theophany in Exod 24:15b-18a. First, Mount Sinai and the Priestly Kabod theology contrast to the Mount Horeb and the Deuteronomic Name theology. Although both traditions redefine the presence of God with the verb "to tabernacle" (škn), in contrast to the Deuteronomic Name theology the Priestly Kabod theology focuses on the sacramental cult, rather than the name of God as the channel for divine presence.[108] Second, the central role of the cult in providing a safe channel for the presence of God on Sinai suggests closer tradition-historical links to Zion than Horeb, since the cult is also central in pre-exilic Zion-Sabaoth theology.[109] These tradition-historical links must not cover up a third conclusion: that Mount Sinai also provides a critique of Zion. When the reader is told that the Kabod Yahweh represents an impermanent presence of God (Exod 24:15b-18a), and furthermore that the tabernacle is a "copy" or "pattern" (tabnît) of God's permanent temple in heaven (Exod 25:9, 40), it becomes clear that no room is left for a confession of Yahweh Sabaoth as dwelling (yšb) permanently in the Jerusalem temple on Mount Zion.[110] The result of this is that Mount Sinai like Mount Horeb in deuteronomistic tradition, represents a shift from metaphor to metonymy in describing the relationship between God and the mountain.

2. The Kabod Yahweh as the Link between Narrative and Law in the Priestly Redaction of Exodus 19-24

Interpretation of the imagery surrounding the Kabod Yahweh provides only partial insight into the character of divine cultic presence being symbolized by priestly tradents. An examination of Exod 24:15b-18a within the overall structure of the priestly redaction will demonstrate how this unit is a hinge linking the preceding narrative in Exodus 19-24 with the subsequent priestly legislation in Exodus 25-31, 35-40, Leviticus, Numbers 1-10.

When interpreted in the context of the preceding narrative

---

[108] On the use of škn in Deuteronomy see Deut 12:11; 14:23; 16:2, 6, 11; 26:2. For discussion of the cult as a channel for revelation in priestly tradition see Rendtorff ("The Concept of Revelation in Ancient Israel," 37) who writes, ". . .from the priestly point of view, the appearance of Jahweh in his kbwd constitutes the establishment and the ordering of the cult, which alone makes possible the existence of sinful people before God."

[109] See Mettinger, The Dethronement of Sabaoth, 19-37.

[110] See Mettinger, The Dethronement of Sabaoth, 26-27.

in Exodus 19-24, the primary role of the Kabod Yahweh is to
provide a boundary between Yahweh and the people. Although
priestly redactors have presented a reinterpretation of theophany in Exod 19:18, this account does not function as the central
appearance of God. Rather, as was noted earlier, it ends ab-
ruptly in Exod 19:20-25 when Moses is commanded to ascend
Mount Sinai just at the moment when the reader expects the
divine promulgation of the Decalogue. Exod 24:15b-18a is an
important sequel, since it continues the emphasis on the visual
presence of God as fire, but qualifies that fiery presence as being
the Kabod Yahweh. With this qualification of divine presence,
the account of theophany in Exod 24:15b-18a does not end ab-
ruptly, but runs its full course, culminating in the revelation of
priestly legislation.

Thus, it would appear that the role of the Kabod Yahweh to
create distance between Yahweh and the people (and thus qualify the presence of God) is the point of focus when Exod 24:15b-
18a is read in the context of Exod 19:18, 20-25. As noted, however, this is a pivotal text within the priestly redaction; this suggests that Exod 24:15b-18 must also be read in the context of
priestly law.

The Kabod Yahweh plays a central role throughout the
priestly legislation (Exod 29:43; 40:34-35, Lev 9:6, 23), and in
this context its functions shifts from providing a boundary between Yahweh and the people to representing the presence of
God in the midst of the people. This function can be illustrated
by examining the four occurrences of the Kabod Yahweh within
the priestly legislation: in the initial theophany (Exod 24:15b-
18a), in the divine commands concerning the cult (Exodus 29),
after the construction of the tabernacle (Exodus 40), and in the
first public worship service (Leviticus 9).

The thematic development of the Kabod Yahweh within the
priestly legislation can be outlined as follows. The initial appearance of the Kabod Yahweh introduces the priestly legislation in Exod 24:15b-18a. In this opening account the
sacramental character of the Kabod Yahweh as being a "devouring fire" is underscored. Then the Kabod Yahweh is mentioned
a second time in Exod 29:43, where the function of the fiery
presence of the Kabod is explained. In Exod 29:43-46 the
reader is told that the fire of the Kabod Yahweh is for the purpose of sanctifying the cult, which will provide the means for
God to be present among the people.[111] After the initial con-

---

[111] The reference to Yahweh's Kabod as sanctifying the cult occurs in the larger

struction of the cult, the Kabod Yahweh is mentioned a third time, when its presence is transferred from Mount Sinai to the Tabernacle in Exod 40:34-35. The sanctification of the cult prepares the way for the final occurrence of the Kabod Yahweh, when it appears in the midst of the people during the first public worship in Leviticus 9:23b-24.

When these four occurrences of the Kabod Yahweh are interrelated, it becomes clear that the priestly legislation is not exploring how the Kabod Yahweh maintains distance between Yahweh and the people, but just the reverse. These four texts are probing how God can be present with Israel in the cult by means of the Kabod. Thus, the appearance of the Kabod Yahweh throughout the priestly legislation is a gradual process of descent from the summit of Mount Sinai through the Tabernacle into the midst of the people of Israel. Furthermore, when the function of the Kabod Yahweh as a sanctifying divine force (Exodus 29) is combined with the imagery of its descent into the midst of the people, an even larger design within the priestly redaction becomes apparent: The cultic theophany to all the people in Leviticus 9 actually completes the opening promise to Israel in Exod 19:5bb-6a that they would be a "kingdom of priests" and a "holy nation."

3. *Summary*

Four conclusions are possible at this point with regard to the symbolic function of Mount Sinai in representing the cultic presence of God.

First, we have seen that the introduction of the Kabod Yahweh on Mount Sinai is an innovation by priestly tradents meant to qualify Zion-Sabaoth theology. The imagery of divine mobility in the verbs "to descend" (*yrd*) and "to tabernacle" (*škn*) and the separation of God's permanent dwelling from the mountain have illustrated this point. The result of this imagery

context of Exod 29:38-46, where the daily burnt offering on the altar at the door of the Tent of Meeting is being described. This text separates into five parts: first, Yahweh outlines to Moses the type of offering that must be performed (Exod 29:38-41); second, Yahweh identifies the sanctuary as the location where he will meet with the mediator and the people because it is the place of sacrifice (Exod 29:42-43a); third, the function of the Kabod as sanctifying the cult and the priesthood is spelled out (Exod 29:43b-44); fourth, Moses is told that the sanctification of the cult by the Kabod Yahweh will allow for the divine presence "to tabernacle" (*škn*) among the people of Israel (Exod 29:45); and last, Yahweh promises that the divine presence in the sanctuary will lead Israel to knowledge (Exod 29:46). The logic of this text is actually worked out in the priestly legislation when the Kabod Yahweh does sanctify the cult and appear to the people in Leviticus 9.

is that Mount Sinai functions metonymically in representing a relationship of contiguity between God and the mountain.

Second, we have also seen that there are deep tradition-historical roots within the priestly critique of Zion. The Priestly Kabod theology includes two ancient traditions of theophany, namely the Tent of Meeting tradition and the "March in the South" theophany tradition. The use of these two traditions is not arbitrary, since each emphasizes the mobility of God in a different way. The Tent of Meeting tradition characterized the movement of God as a descent (*yrd*) to the door of the Tent of Meeting; the "March in the South" theophany tradition emphasized how the movement of God was a "going forth" to lead or to rescue Israel.

The two ancient traditions of theophany appear to have had a mutual effect upon each other in the formation of the Priestly Kabod theology. For example, on the one hand, the imagery of divine descent in the Tent of Meeting provided a means for priestly redactors to reinterpret Sinai within the "March in the South" theophany tradition from a region to a cosmic mountain in Exodus 19-24, because it actually reverses the mobile imagery of God from leaving a southern region to a descent upon a specific mountain. On the other hand, the "March in the South" theophany tradition provided a means for priestly redactors to expand the mobile character of Yahweh's presence beyond the imagery of a descent within the Tent of Meeting tradition, so that Yahweh both descends from heaven to meet Israel, and is also able to lead the people in the march from the wilderness of Sinai once the priestly legislation is established (Numbers 10).[112]

The combination of the Tent of Meeting tradition and the "March in the South" theophany tradition certainly provided an excellent starting point for a critique of the static imagery of divine presence in Zion-Sabaoth theology. The interrelationship of these traditions also lays the foundation for a more universal theology of divine presence, since God is able to descend from heaven in order to be present on Mount Sinai (Tent of Meeting tradition), and the Kabod Yahweh is also able to leave the cosmic mountain in order to be present with Israel in other locations ("March in the South" theophany tradition). The ability of the Kabod Yahweh to be present with Israel at other locations than the temple on the cosmic mountain corresponds with the universal focus of the priestly promise in the Proposal of

---

[112] Note here especially the function of the "pillar of cloud" to lead Israel in their wilderness journey (e.g., Exod 13:21; 14:19, 20, 24; Num 12:5). See Mann, *Divine Presence*, 256-57.

Covenant, where all the world was proclaimed to be the domain of Yahweh's rule.

Third, the character of divine cultic presence within priestly tradition can be summarized in the following manner: the Kabod Yahweh descends and dwells temporarily in the tabernacle (*škn*, Exod 24:16a), which is a copy (*tabnît*, Exod 25:9, 40) of the permanent home of God in heaven; its presence is described as fire (*'š*, Exod 24:17), which is covered and concealed by the cloud (Exod 24:15b, 16a; 40:34); the function of the Kabod Yahweh is two-sided—it provides distance between Yahweh and the people (Exod 24:15b-18a) and it sanctifies the cult (Exod 29:43) and ultimately the people (Lev 9:23b-24). The priestly account of theophany on Mount Sinai in Exod 24:15b-18a results in the following elaborate hierarchy among God-Moses-Israel:

MOUNT SINAI

HEAVEN

(Permanent Temple of God)

↓

The Kadob Yahweh "descends and temporarily dwells" (*škn*)
in a cloud on the summit of Mount Sinai
with a "copy" (*tabnît*) of the heavenly temple

SUMMIT OF MOUNT SINAI

(Moses the mediator)

"ascends" (*'lh*) to   "descends" (*yrd*) with
represent the people   a "copy" (*tabnît*) of
before God   the priestly legislation

BASE OF MOUNT SINAI

(The people of Israel)

Yahweh's "kingdom of priests" (*mamleket kŏhānîm*)
and "holy nation" (*gôy qādôš*)

Fourth, the cultic *Sitz im Leben* of the imagery of divine presence on Mount Sinai would appear to be the festival of the Day of Atonement in Leviticus 16. Lev 16:1-3 provides an introduction to the festival by underscoring how Yahweh can only be approached at certain times and only then by the mediator. When Aaron does enter the holy place, the reader is told that he

must take fire (*'š*, Lev 16:12) from the altar before Yahweh, and
that he must be sure to put incense on the fire, so that the
"cloud of incense" (*'nn hqṭrt*) covers (*ksh*) the mercy seat (Lev
16:13). These directions to Aaron create a series of parallels to
the theophany of the Kabod Yahweh on Mount Sinai which include the imagery of fire to describe the presence of God, the
cloud (of incense) to provide a boundary between the priestly
mediator and God, the limited access and danger of divine presence, and the similar purpose of the appearance of God to sanctify the people.

C. *Moses as Cultic Leader on Mount Sinai*

Moses is idealized as a mediator in the priestly redaction of
Exodus 19-24. Twice he is singled out as the one who must approach the presence of God alone on Mount Sinai: first in Exod
19:20-25, when Yahweh excludes all but Moses and Aaron to ascend the mountain, and in Exod 24:1-2, where Moses is once
again commanded to approach God alone. The idealization of
Moses as a priest, who maintains distance and clear boundaries
between Yahweh and Israel, is a central component within the
symbol of Mount Sinai. The reason for the central role of Moses
is very similar to what we have seen in deuteronomistic tradition. The breakdown of any metaphorical identification between God and the mountain in favor of a metonymic
relationship of contiguity accentuates the need for a mediator to
bridge the distance between God and Israel. Three aspects in
the idealization of Moses provide insight into his important role
as priestly mediator on Mount Sinai: the first is the central role
of Moses during the theophany of the Kabod Yahweh in Exod
24:15b-18a, the second is the movement of Moses on Mount Sinai, and the third is the shining face of Moses in Exod 34:29-35.

1. *Moses as Priestly Representative of Israel in Exod 24:15b-18a*

The mediatorial role of Moses as the representative of the
people reaches a climax in Exod 24:15b-18a. Comparison of this
text with Exod 19:18 will provide illustration, and Westermann's
analysis of Exod 24:15b-18a will provide a starting point for
comparison.[113] He would structure Exod 24:15b-18a; 25:1 in the
following manner:

(A) *The Approach of Yahweh* (Exod 24:15b-16aα)

[113] Westermann, "Die Herrlichkeit Gottes," 227-49.

The cloud (*'nn*) covered (*ksh*) the mountain
And the Kabod Yahweh tabernacled (*škn*) on
Mount Sinai

(B) *The Dwelling on the Mountain* (Exod 24:16ab)
The cloud (*'nn*) covered it six days

(C) *The Word from Yahweh* (Exod 24:16b)
And he (Yahweh) called to Moses on the seventh
day out of the midst of the cloud (*'nn*)

Exod 24:17   But the appearance of the Kabod Yahweh
was like a devouring fire (*'š*) on the top of
the mountain in the sight of the people of
Israel.

(A)') *The Approach of Moses* (Exod 24:18a)
Then Moses went (*bw'*) in the midst of the cloud
and he ascended (*'lh*) the mountain

(B') *The Dwelling on the Mountain* (Exod 24:18b)
And Moses was on the mountain forty days and
forty nights.

(C') *The Word of Yahweh* (Exod 25:1)
And Yahweh said to Moses. . .

Westermann has argued that Exod 24:15b-18a; 25:1 contains two symmetrical units (Exod 24:15b-16a and Exod 24:18a-25:1), each of which separates into a three-part sequence. The first part is the approach to the mountain ([A] Yahweh in Exod 24:15b-16aα and [A'] Moses in Exod 24:18a); the second part is the description of dwelling on the mountain ([B] Yahweh or the cloud in Exod 24:16ab and [B'] Moses in Exod 24:18a); and the third is the word of Yahweh from the mountain ([C] Exod 24:16b and [C'] Exod 25:1). In addition, Westermann noted that the two sequences are divided by the people's new perception of theophany as the Kabod Yahweh in Exod 24:17.[114]

The most striking feature of Westermann's analysis is that he has demonstrated how Exod 24:15b-18a is structured around the movement of Moses and Yahweh toward the mountain (A and A'). Westermann describes this movement as follows:

> The two movements go in opposite directions: the movement from above descends on the mountain; the movement from under (where the people are located) ascends the mountain. The movements come together as a *mô'ēd*, which makes possible the promulgation of the [divine] words to the mediator (translation by the author).[115]

114 Westermann, "Die Herrilichkeit Gottes," 231.
115 Westermann, "Die Herrilichkeit Gottes," 232.

Westermann's description of Exod 24:15b-18a as two move-
ments going in opposite directions could also have been applied
to the priestly redaction (Exod 19:18) of the Mountain of God
tradition (Exod 19:16ab-17). The combination of Exod 19:17
(the second verse of the Mountain of God tradition) and Exod
19:18 also described Yahweh and the people approaching the
mountain from opposite directions:

> Exod 19:17   Moses brought out ($y\d{s}$') the people from
> the camp to meet God.
> and they were stationed at the base of
> the mountain.
> Exod 19:18a   But Mount Sinai was wrapped in smoke be-
> cause Yahweh descended (yrd) on it in fire.

The similarities in form between Exod 19:17-18a and Exod
24:15b-25:1 accentuate differences between the two accounts.
In particular, the movement of Israel toward the cosmic mountain in Exod 19:17 and of Yahweh descending on Mount Sinai in
Exod 19:18a accentuated the problem of boundaries that had
already been stressed by Yahweh in Exod 19:12ab-13b during
the preparation for theophany. Consequently this attempt at a
môʿēd was aborted and instead Moses was required to ascend
the mountain alone in Exod 19:20 in order to receive even more
detailed instructions about boundaries, about the need for sanctification, and about the need for a priestly mediator. The
choice of Moses (and Aaron) as mediator in Exod 19:24 is played
out in the priestly description of theophany in Exod 24:15b-18a.
Here Moses no longer leads Israel out ot meet God as in Exod
19:17. Instead, he represents them before Yahweh as the mediator, by ascending the mountain alone. Thus the mediatorial
role of Moses becomes an important layer within the hierarchy
that priestly tradents have established between Yahweh and the
people at Mount Sinai. His role as the representative of the people is one important factor that allows the theophany in Exod
24:15b-18a to move ahead to the revelation of the priestly legislation in Exodus 25-31. However, the lengthy preparation required of Moses to enter the summit of Mount Sinai in Exod
24:15b-18a, and his initial inability to enter the Tabernacle in
Exod 40:34-35 when it was filled with the Kabod Yahweh underscore how even the mediator can approach God only at certain
times and even then only after proper purification.

2.   *Moses as Priestly Representative of Yahweh*

The function of Moses as mediator is not limited to his role as representative of the people before Yahweh, for he also acts in just the opposite role, namely as the representative of the divine presence to the people. This aspect of Moses' mediatorial role is conveyed in two ways in the priestly redaction: through the development of the verb "to descend" (*yrd*) as a description of the movement of Moses on Mount Sinai, and through the imagery of his shining face in Exod 34:29-35. Both of these motifs illustrate how Moses functions metaphorically in representing the divine fire at Mount Sinai.

First, a metaphorical relationship of resemblance is established between God and Moses with regard to their movement on Mount Sinai. Each is described with the verb "to descend" (*yrd*). The imagery of Moses as a priestly mediator who descends from the presence of God to the people is actually rooted in the Mountain of God tradition. In this account the reader is told that Moses ascended (*ʿlh*, Exod 19:3a) the mountain to God and that he descended (*yrd*, Exod 19:14) the mountain to the people in order to sanctify them in preparation for theophany. The priestly redaction in Exodus 19 builds on the imagery of descent in two ways in order to idealize the mediatorial role of Moses. First, priestly tradents develop the imagery of descent beyond the Mountain of God tradition by using *yrd* to describe Yahweh's approach to Mount Sinai in Exod 19:11b, 18, 20. With this new imagery of divine descent, the movement of Moses in Exod 19:14 becomes more than a spatial device to relocate the mediator with the people below, for now his descent also mirrors the movement of God.

Second, the descent of Moses into the midst of the people below actually completes the divine descent to the summit of Mount Sinai. This transfer of divine descent to Moses comes into focus when the verb *yrd* is examined throughout the priestly redaction of Exodus 19: the first occurrence of *yrd* predicts the theophany of Yahweh to all the people (Exod 19:11b), the second describes the event in the sight of all the people (Exod 19:18), the third stops the experience of theophany (Exod 19:20). In this third and final descent Yahweh twice tells Moses that the presence of God is too dangerous for the people and that Moses must complete the divine descent (*rēd*, Exod 19:21, 24). The result of this repeated divine command is that the descent of Yahweh to the people is transferred to Moses, the priestly mediator, who then fulfills the command by descending Mount Sinai in Exod 19:25 with the Decalogue.

An additional word is necessary at this point, for the correspondence between the movement of Moses and Yahweh in priestly tradition parallels deuteronomistic tradition, where the verb "to approach" (*bw* ') was used to describe the movement of both Yahweh (Exod 19:9a; 20:20) and Moses (Exod 19:7; 24:3). However, it also contrasts to deuteronomistic paranesis both by the choice of verb, and by the manner in which Moses receives his authority. In deuteronomistic tradition, it was not enough for Moses to be chosen by Yahweh; his authority had also to be authenticated by the people, who were required to hear the word of God in his message after he approached them (Exod 19:9a; 20:19). Thus, as the teacher of deuteronomic law, the authority of Moses was charismatically based. In contrast to this, charisma does not play a central role in the priestly idealization of Moses. As a priestly mediator, his authority rests with God alone (Exod 19:24), for it arises from the divine command that he descend the mountain to the people.[116]

Second, a metaphorical relationship of resemblance is also established between God and Moses with regard to the shining face of Moses in Exod 34:29-35. Although Exod 34:29-35 is outside the scope of our study, it warrants our attention because of its important location within the broader context of the priestly redaction of the Sinai Complex. Exod 34:29-314 is the priestly account of Moses' descent (*yrd*, Exod 34:29) from Mount Sinai with the priestly legislation (*šny lḥt h 'dt* "the two tablets of testimony," Exod 34:29) after Covenant Renewal. This final descent by Moses provides the context for the promulgation of the entire priestly legislation (Exodus 35-40, Leviticus, Numbers 1-10).[117] The authority of Moses, as a priestly mediator at Mount Sinai, is symbolized in this account through the imagery of his shining face (*qrn*).[118] The shining face of Moses is a metaphor of divine presence, for it represents a point of identification between himself and the fiery presence of God on Mount Sinai. The concluding verse of this account (Exod 34:35) informs the reader that whenever Moses promulgated law which he received from Mount Sinai he would uncover his face (which would then shine).[119]

In summary, as a cosmic mountain, Sinai not only signifies

---

[116] See also Terrien, *The Elusive Presence*, 133-34.

[117] For discussion and bibliography see Moberly, *At the Mountain of God*, 106-9.

[118] There is debate over the meaning of *qrn* which is used to describe the face of Moses. It may mean "horn" (see K. Jaroš, "Des Mose 'strahlende Haut': Eine Notiz zu Ex 34, 29, 30, 35," *ZAW* 88 [1976] 275-80) or "light" (see F. Dumermuth, "Moses strahlendes Gesicht," *TZ* 17 [1961] 244-47). The context suggests the latter reading, especially in view of the primary role of the Kabod Yahweh that Moses experienced on Mount Sinai.

[119] Thus the mask (*masweh*) of Moses does not represent the deity as, for example,

that the cult provides a point of contact (a metonymic relationship of contiguity) between the heavenly and earthly temples of God; it also signifies that Moses, as cultic leader, provides a point of identity (a metaphorical relationship of resemblance) for the divine cultic presence. He not only mirrors the movement of God, he even carries the fire of the Kabod Yahweh in his face.

D. *The Vision of Israel at Mount Sinai*

Mount Sinai also contains a vision of the people of God. One of the most prominent characteristics of Israel at Sinai is that they are a people, who have clearly seen God on the mountain. The visual emphasis of theophany was underscored by priestly redactors in the account of Israel's preparation, when Yahweh predicted in Exod 19:11b that the people would see the divine presence on Mount Sinai. The elaborate process of purification throughout the priestly redaction of Exodus 19 and in the restructuring of the deuteronomistic Covenant-Closing Ceremony into a Sanctification Ceremony of the people in Exodus 24 further reinforced the central importance of Israel as being a sanctified people. This emphasis continues throughout the priestly legislation where proper observance of the cult is underscored precisely because it aids in sanctifying the people (e.g., Lev 7:38). However, the clearest vision of Israel at Mount Sinai is stated by priestly redactors in the "Promise of Reward" within the Proposal of Covenant.

In the priestly "Promise of Reward" Yahweh's rule is proclaimed to be universal, while the vision of Israel as a purified people comes immediately to the foreground, when they are described as a "kingdom of priests" and a "holy nation." The vision of Israel at Mount Sinai in the priestly "Promise of Reward" comes into clearer focus when we compare it to the deuteronomistic promise in Exod 19:5ba. The deuteronomistic "Promise of Reward" in Exod 19:5ba can be illustrated in the following manner:

$$\begin{array}{c} \text{Yahweh} \\ \updownarrow \\ \text{(Israel)} \quad \leftrightarrow \quad \text{Nations} \end{array}$$

This diagram underscores how Israel's vertical relationship with Yahweh and their horizontal relationship to the nations is exclusive in focus, since their relationship with Yahweh as a

Gressmann (*Mose und seine Zeit*, 250) would argue. Rather it veils the divine light. See also Moberly, *At the Mountain of God*, 108.

"personal possession" (*sĕgullâ*) required that they be separate from the nations (*mikkól-hā'ammîm*).

The proclamation of Yahweh's universal rule in Exod 19:5bb is a challenge to the exclusive focus of the deuteronomistic promise, because the unique status of Israel as a "personal possession" of Yahweh, isolated from the other nations, conflicts with this larger vision of Yahweh's rule. The result is that Israel's unique status is redefined hierarchically, so that their promised exclusive relationship with Yahweh as his "personal possession" becomes the qualitatively different relationship that the people will have with God in contrast to the other nations— as a priest would have in the role of mediation. Furthermore, once Israel's unique relationship with Yahweh is redefined qualitatively, their previous separation from the other nations is also articulated hierarchically. The priestly vision of Israel as a "kingdom of priests" and a "holy nation" within the larger context of Yahweh's universal rule can be illustrated in the following manner:

Several concluding comments are in order at this point concerning the priestly vision of Israel at Mount Sinai. First, Israel's separation from the other nations according to the priestly "Promise of Reward" will no longer be geographical, but qualitative. They will be distinct from the nations in their priestly role of mediation within the larger realm of Yahweh's universal rule. Second, the hierarchical emphasis in the priestly vision of Israel at Mount Sinai corresponds well with the priestly concern with hierarchy that has been evident throughout their redaction of Exodus 19-24. Third, Israel's position in relation to the nations underscores a central point about hierarchy throughout priestly theology: it is never an end in itself, but always a necessary means to channel the presence of God wither to Israel (by means of Moses) or to the nations (by means of Israel). This insight leads to a fourth conclusion. The vision of Israel in the priestly "Promise of Reward" carries with it a mission, which is universal in scope. The necessary prerequisite for Israel to fulfill its priestly mission to the nations is the revelation of the priestly legislation on Mount Sinai. The priestly promise with its call to holiness, its universal vision of

Yahweh's rule, and its mission to the nations is a poignant theology for dispersed exiles.

E. *Conclusion*

We have seen in this section that Mount Sinai is a priestly symbol of divine cultic presence, which functions within the larger framework of the Priestly Kabod theology, and that it is meant to provide a qualification of Mount Zion within Zion-Sabaoth theology. It represents a qualification of the imagery of God as dwelling on the cosmic mountain in favor of a more transcendent view of God as descending (*yrd, škn*) from his heavenly temple to the summit of Mount Sinai. This qualification can be characterized as a shift in imagery from metaphor to metonymy. And as such, Mount Sinai symbolizes a rejection of the concept of unity that is inherent in Zion. In place of this concept of unity, the cultic presence of God on Mount Sinai is characterized as being the fiery Kabod Yahweh, which descends and only temporarily dwells on the mountain, but which is also able to leave Sinai in order to lead Israel in their wilderness travels. We have also seen that Moses is idealized as a priestly mediator at Mount Sinai, who, on the one hand, maintains distance and clear boundaries between the sacred and the profane, and, on the other hand, functions metaphorically in representing the presence of the Kabod Yahweh within the cult. Finally, Sinai also presents an ideal vision of the people of God as a holy people who mediate God's salvation in the larger context of the nations.

Chapter 5

DIVINE PRESENCE ON THE MOUNTAIN
IN THE CANONICAL SINAI COMPLEX

I
THE PROBLEM OF REPETITION IN THE
CANONICAL SINAI COMPLEX

In the preceding chapters I have sought to illustrate how the
Sinai Complex includes a history of redaction, which shows an
ongoing reflection about divine cultic presence. The tradition-
historical study has certainly confirmed the insight by Levenson
discussed in the opening chapter that the mountain setting is
central to this material, because it allows for both continuity and
change in Israel's theological discourse. The redaction history of
Exodus 19-24 from Zion through Horeb to Sinai has indeed illustrated how the mountain setting is a "mold into which new ex-
periences could be fit. . .without rupturing the sense of tradition
and continuity of historic identity."[1]

The rich diversity that we may wish to celebrate from a tradition-historical perspective raises a different set of problems
from a canonical point of view.[2] The central problem is that we
have created multiple texts in Exodus 19-24, which advocate
very distinct theologies of divine presence, while the movement
of the canonical Pentateuch would appear to be in the other
direction, namely that the Sinai Complex presents the one revelation of Torah on the mountain. Thus, the theological chal-

[1] Levenson, *Sinai and Zion*, 18.

[2] The problems of canon that I am addressing in this chapter arise from the stimu-
lating research in canonical criticism that has been undertaken in recent years
from somewhat different directions by B. S. Childs and J. A. Sanders. For representative work on canonical criticism by Sanders see *Torah and Canon* (Philadelphia:
Fortress Press, 1972) esp. ix-xx; and *From Sacred Story to Sacred Text* (Philadelphia:
Fortress Press, 1987). For Childs see "The Exegetical Significance of Canon for the
Study of the Old Testament," *Congress Volume: Göttingen 1977*, VTSup 29 (1977)
66-80; *Introduction to the Old Testament as Scripture* (Philadelphia: Fortress
Press, 1979) esp. 27-106; *The New Testament as Canon: An Introduction* (Philadelphia: Fortress Press, 1985) esp. 48-53 and for a round table discussion of his work
see *JSOT* 16 (1980).

lenge of the Sinai Complex from a canonical perspective cannot
in the end be addressed simply by undertaking a redaction-critical study which underscores diversity. Rather we must take an
additional step and at least raise the question of how these distinct traditions can be interrelated in any meaningful way since
that is what the canonical Pentateuch encourages us to do.

My aim in this chapter is to explore the interrelationship between the univocal claim of Torah, on the one hand, and the
diverse theologies which make up the substructure of the canonical Pentateuch, on the other, as these issues are reflected in
the Sinai Complex. However, the tension between the multiple
voices of tradition and the singular voice of canon goes beyond
the Sinai Complex, and actually poses a central problem for constructing a biblical theology of Torah in general. The problem is
not only theological, but also methodological. On the surface
the contrast between tradition-history and canon would seem to
force the reader either to follow the univocal claim of Torah and
thus construct an artificial theological unity to the material, or to
describe the diverse traditions within the canonical Pentateuch,
in which case a theology of Torah becomes a smorgasbord from
which the reader then picks and chooses. Such is the present
impasse in biblical studies between literary critics who often assume too quickly a unity to pentateuchal narrative by ignoring
the tradition history of the text, and tradition historians who
stress only the disunity of pentateuchal narrative at the expense
of the canonical text. A study of repetition within the Sinai
Complex may provide an avenue for moving beyond the present impasse, and, in the process, aid us in reaching the goal of
this chapter: to explore the interrelationship between tradition-
history and canon in the Sinai Complex.

Repetition is a promising avenue of study, because it is a
problem of interpretation that confronts the reader both tradition-historically and canonically. Consider first the problem of
repetition that arises from a tradition-historical study. Multiple
or repetitive texts of the same event that are stratified in canon
constitute a form of repetition, which would appear to subvert
the claims of Torah as being anchored in the one revelation of
God at the mountain. Our redaction-critical study of Exodus 19-
24 has demonstrated this by proposing three accounts of Israel's
encounter with God at the mountain. Yet, repetition is not simply a problem that comes into focus within Torah through tradition-historical interpretation. Rather, the canonical Pentateuch
itself introduces the problem of repetition by clearly separating
the priestly and deuteronomic legislations in Torah (and thus Si-

nai and Horeb) without harmonizing them. For example, in the canonical Pentateuch the revelation of the priestly legislation on Mount Sinai is one stage in Israel's wilderness travels (Exodus 35-Numbers 10), while the revelation of the deuteronomic legislation on Mount Horeb is a speech by Moses at the close of Israel's wilderness travels (Deuteronomy). Even this brief overview of Torah begins to illustrate that there is design in bringing together Sinai and Horeb by placing them within the chronology of a "story." Yet the story of Torah, itself, confronts the reader with a problem of repetition between Sinai and Horeb, since they are presented as the one divine revelation from the mountain in Exodus 19-24.

A definition of repetition in the next section of this chapter will provide a starting point for interpreting the central role of this trope within the canonical Sinai Complex.

II
A DEFINITION OF REPETITION

Repetition can be defined simply as "a re-use of the same word or group of words."[3] The moment that we pursue a more extended definition problems arise, because repetition is two-sided in its function: it simultaneously unifies and creates difference in literature. This dual function of repetition requires examination.

Repetition is a basic unifying device within literature. In fact it not only unifies literature in general, it also is meant to build emphasis.[4] And this is also true for biblical literature. The central role of repetition for creating emphasis is stated by J. Hillis Miller in his book, *Fiction and Repetition*, where he explores the function of recurrence within the English novel. He writes: "What is said two or more times may not be true, but the reader is fairly safe in assuming that it is significant."[5] By underscoring points of emphasis, repetition aids in unifying literature. The importance of repetition for unifying biblical literature was explored by James Muilenburg in his article, "Hebrew Rhetoric: Repetition and Style,"[6] and taken up anew more recently by Robert Alter, in his discussion of "The Techniques of Repeti-

---

[3] Ducrot and Todorov, *Encyclopedic Dictionary*, 278.

[4] See S. F. Fogle, "Repetition," *Princeton Encyclopedia of Poetry and Poetics*, ed., A. Preminger (Princeton: Princeton University Press, 1974) 699-701.

[5] J. Hillis Miller, *Fiction and Repetition: Seven English Novels* (Cambridge: Harvard University Press, 1982) 2.

[6] J. Muilenburg, "Hebrew Rhetoric: Repetition and Style," *Congress Volume: Copenhagen 1953*, VTSup 1 (1953) 97-111.

tion." Alter writes: "What we find. . .in biblical narrative is an
elaborately integrated system of repetitions, some dependent
on the actual recurrence of individual phonemes, words, or
short phrases, others linked instead to the actions, images, and
ideas that are part of the world of the narrative we 'reconstruct'
as readers but that are not necessarily woven into the verbal
texture of the narrative."[7] According to Alter, these repetitions
are used "by the Hebrew writers to reinforce each other and to
produce a concerted whole."[8] Thus, repetition in biblical literature, as in literature in general, is a basic unifying device.

On the other hand, repetition also creates difference within
literature. Bruce Kawin succinctly states this problem in his
book, *Telling it Again and Again*: "The growth of a work, even
from one identical line to another, makes exact repetition impossible. . . ."[9] What this means for a study of repetition is that
even though it is meant to unify literature and to create emphasis, contrast—or perhaps more appropriately, difference—is inherent to the trope. At best we can only discuss near-repetition
in literature.[10] The problem of difference in repetition has actually received more attention in the study of biblical narrative.
The reason for this particular focus is that repetition has been an
important avenue for recovering the tradition-historical development that is obliquely reflected in the present text. Even
though repetition is often used by biblical writers (and editors)
to unify the literature, for modern biblical scholars the difference between repetitions has been one avenue into the distinct
traditions that make up the canonical text. Thus, for example,
repetition was a primary concern to Wellhausen, since the difference between the repetitions created contradiction, which
for him was the starting point for isolating sources.[11]

---

[7] R. Alter, *The Art of Biblical Narrative* (New York: Basic Books, 1981) 95.

[8] Alter, *The Art of Biblical Narrative*, 95.

[9] B. F. Kawin, *Telling It Again and Again: Repetition in Literature and Film* (Ithaca: Cornell University Press, 1972) 7.

[10] Kawin, *Telling It Again and Again*, 7. See also Lotman, *The Structure of the
Artistic Text*, 104-36, esp. 135.

[11] For illustrations of Wellhausen's use of repetition in isolating literary sources see
his discussion of the Sinai Complex (*Composition*, 82-83, 94-96, 332) where he argues that any suggestion of Moses ascending the mountain twice in one source was
offensive (*anstössig*), and only possible if two parallel reports were combined.
Thus, he concluded that there were three sources in the Sinai Complex, because
Moses ascended the mountain that many times (Exod 20:21; 24:12; 34). Influencing
Wellhausen's assessment of repetition in the Sinai Complex is an assumption that
"primitive narrative" would not contain repetitions. For an evaluation of the notion of primitive narrative see T. Todorov, "Primitive Narrative," *The Poetics of
Prose* (Ithaca: Cornell University Press, 1977) 53-65, esp. 55.

The character of near-repetition, as a literary device that unifies and creates difference, requires still further distinctions in our definition, for it gives rise to what Miller describes as "two alternative theories of repetition": *mimesis* in which repetition is rooted in similarity, and *ungrounded doubling* in which repetition arises from difference.[12]

As mimesis, repetition is understood as being grounded in an archetypal model, so that difference is viewed in light of a preestablished identity—a third thing, if you will, which precedes the repetition. Identity is the point of departure (the archetype) and it gives rise to difference (the copies), and this, of course, is the basis for the concept of imitation. Because repetition is grounded in an archetype, the difference that comes into focus with each repetition is the result of willed, rational, and intentional action. Miller writes that within mimetic repetition, "memory works logically, by way of similarities which are seen as identities, one thing repeating another and grounded in a concept on the basis of which their likeness may be understood."[13] This statement leads to an important conclusion: a meaningful interpretation of a mimetic repetition will always lead the interpreter back to the archetype. Thus, in the end it is the archetype that is the point of emphasis.

Imitation plays no role in repetition as ungrounded doubling, because there is no archetypal model.[14] Instead, difference is the point of departure and it gives rise to similarity. In fact, by being ungrounded the repetition is only an "opaque similarity,"[15] which is neither willed nor intentional, but an involuntary action. Miller writes that in instances of repetition as ungrounded doubling memory works by forgetting, so that "one thing is experienced as repeating something which is quite different from it and which it strangely resembles."[16] This statement allows for the following conclusion: With the absence of an archetypal model, the interpreter of repetition as ungrounded doubling must search for meaning through the echoing of two dissimilar things. In other words, the meaning in the repetition "is neither in the first nor in the second nor in some ground which precedes both, but in between, in the empty

---

[12] Miller, *Fiction and Repetition*, 5. The following discussion draws heavily on Miller's work. For more extensive discussion see his opening chapter, "Two Forms of Repetition" and the secondary literature cited there.

[13] Miller, *Fiction and Repetition*, 8.

[14] Miller, *Fiction and Repetition*, 6.

[15] Miller, *Fiction and Repetition*, 9.

[16] Miller, *Fiction and Repetition*, 8.

space which the opaque similarity crosses."[17]

Both theories of repetition operate within the canonical Sinai Complex. In the following section the impact of the redaction-critical development in Exodus 19-24 from the Mountain of God tradition to the deuteronomistic and priestly redactions will provide the framework for a study of repetition as mimesis in the canonical form of the Sinai Complex. I hope to demonstrate how Zion is the point of identity in the Sinai Complex, even though it is subordinated in the canonical text and rejected as a constructive theology of divine presence in Torah. I also hope to demonstrate in this section how Horeb and Sinai are grounded in the archetype of Zion; and, as such, how they are copies which necessarily presuppose it. In the next section an examination of the story of Torah will provide the framework for a study of the second theory of repetition. I hope to demonstrate in this section how the presentation of Sinai and Horeb within Torah, where they are not harmonized but simply placed within the chronology of a story, is an instance of ungrounded repetition. Zion plays no role here as a point of identity, nor, in fact, is there a point of identity. Instead, the repetition of Sinai and Horeb within Torah creates an interplay of opaquely similar things, which in reality are fundamentally different. We will conclude this chapter by exploring how both forms of repetition encourage the reader to look for the center of Torah as a single revelation on the mountain, even though this center is never explicitly stated.

III
REPETITION AS MIMESIS IN THE CANONICAL SINAI COMPLEX

The central question in this section is whether a study of mimetic repetition provides a framework for interrelating the distinct traditions within the Sinai Complex into some kind of unity, as the canonical Pentateuch encourages the reader to do. Our study will proceed in two parts: first, we must clarify how the history of redaction in the Sinai Complex evinces mimetic repetition within the canonical text; and, second, we must explore the importance of mimesis for a theology of divine presence in Torah.

A. *Redaction as Mimesis*

The redactional study has illustrated how the structure of the

---

[17] Miller, *Fiction and Repetition*, 9.

Mountain of God tradition is carried through the subsequent redactions, and how it provides the point of critique for each of
them. This process creates mimesis in the canonical Sinai Complex.[18] Consider, first, how the Mountain of God tradition is the
archetype that precedes and functions as the *point of identity*
for the deuteronomistic and priestly redactions. It is tradition-
historically prior to the two redactions, and as such, it must be
viewed as having given rise to them. Second, in its role as an
archetype, the Mountain of God tradition has also become
subordinated to the deuteronomistic and priestly redactions in
the canonical Sinai Complex, since the latter two accounts are
meant to be subsequent reinterpretations of the former. And
third, as reinterpretations, the deuteronomistic and priestly redactions must be interpreted as being *copies* of the Mountain of
God tradition. What this means for an interpretation of the canonical text is that even though the deuteronomistic and
priestly redactions predominate as constructive theologies of divine presence, the Mountain of God tradition is not eliminated
in the canonical Sinai Complex. Indeed, it could not be eliminated, for it gives rise to each of the redactional copies.

The equation of redaction with mimesis provides one important starting point for investigating how the distinct voices that
make up the canonical Sinai Complex can be interrelated. Earlier we noted that a meaningful interpretation of mimetic repetition will always lead the interpreter back to the archetype,
with the result that, in the end, it is the archetype that is the
point of emphasis. This conclusion suggests that from the perspective of mimesis the Mountain of God tradition is the point of
emphasis for interpreting the canonical Sinai Complex, since as
the archetype it gives rise to the canonical text, and is the point
to which the interpreter must return. This conclusion has immediate theological implications, for it implies that from the

---

[18] Mettinger's (*The Dethronement of Sabaoth*, 16-17) application of cognitive dissonance theory to deuteronomistic and priestly traditions, as distinct responses to the
breakdown of Zion, would certainly fit well into a discussion of mimesis. Mettinger
writes that with the breakdown of Zion during the exile "the possibility did exist of
'explaining,' that is, of reinterpreting and rationalizing the dogma of divine presence." He continues, "Thus R. P. Carrol's (sic) assertion that 'dissonance gives rise
to hermeneutic' is most apropos." For Carroll's research on the topic see *When
Prophecy Failed: Reactions and Responses to Failure in the Old Testament Prophetic Traditions* (New York: Seabury Press, 1979) and "Prophecy and Dissonance:
A Theoretical Approach to the Prophetic Tradition," *ZAW* 92 (1980) 108-19. For
more broadly based research on the subject see L. Festinger, *A Theory of Cognitive
Dissonance* (Stanford: Stanford University Press, 1965).

perspective of mimesis Zion is the theological center of the canonical Sinai Complex.

B. *Zion as the Theological Center of the Canonical Sinai Complex*

The important role of the archetype in mimesis leads to what appears on the surface to be a rather peculiar conclusion when it is applied to the canonical Sinai Complex. It suggests that even though Sinai and Horeb function as constructive theological solutions in Torah to the problem of divine presence, as redactions they presuppose Zion, and will lead the reader back to Zion. A review of the theology of divine presence that is represented in the symbol of Zion (as compared to the symbols of Sinai and Horeb) will provide background for interpreting how Zion actually functions as the theological center within the canonical Sinai Complex.

Chapter 2 illustrated how Mount Zion functions as a metaphor in symbolizing the character of divine presence within the Mountain of God tradition. In particular, the imagery of God as dwelling on the mountain encouraged an identification between God and the mountain, which emphasized a theology of divine immanence. Chapters 3 and 4 demonstrated that both Mount Horeb and Mount Sinai qualify this theology of divine immanence by rejecting metaphor in favor of metonymy to describe the relation of God to the mountain. The result of this is that instead of the mountain symbolizing the dwelling place of God, it becomes the point of contact between God in heaven and the worshipping community on earth. Thus, both Horeb and sinai emphasize divine transcendence (although in different ways), and in the process, each qualifies the theology of divine immanence that is central to Zion. And by qualifying Zion, they *subordinate* it in the canonical Sinai Complex.

The subordination of Zion (rather than its elimination) establishes a temporal complexity in relation to the reader as a past, present and even future reality that is important for constructing a theology of divine presence in Torah. As a past reality Zion has an important unifying role as a constructive theology of divine presence. The positive interpretation of Zion arises from its role as an archetype, since it makes possible the qualified theologies of Horeb and Sinai and is actually their preestablished point of identity. Furthermore the past ideal of Zion spills over into the future, since the archetype is also the point to which the interpreter must return. The result is that within the canonical

Sinai Complex, the reader is encouraged to embrace Zion as both a past and future ideal.

Zion is rejected however as a present reality, since its subordination to Horeb and Sinai does not allow the reader to claim its realized theology of divine immanence in the present time. Instead, when constructing a contemporary theology of divine presence, the reader must leave behind metaphor and probe instead the metonymic symbols of Horeb and Sinai, which predominate in the canonical Sinai Complex. Yet even when the focus of the reader shifts from the past to the present, Zion still continues to play a unifying role in the canonical Sinai Complex. Its unifying role, however, is no longer constructive; as when Zion is seen as a past/future ideal. Rather, it acquires a negative role, by symbolizing what a theology of divine presence cannot be for the reader of Torah. The denial of Zion as a present reality underscores how mimesis alone is insufficient in creating a unified theology of divine presence within Torah, since the life of faith is not meant to be lived simply in the past and future, but also in the present. Consequently the interrelationship of Horeb and Sinai must also be examined independent of their archetype.

IV
REPETITION AS "UNGROUNDED DOUBLING" IN THE CANONICAL SINAI COMPLEX

A study of repetition as ungrounded doubling requires that we leave tradition-history behind and focus instead on the story of Torah and how the Sinai Complex is interwoven within it. Since Sinai and Horeb are clearly separated within Torah and left unharmonized, the problem of repetition is built into the structure of the canonical Pentateuch. And this problem of repetition cannot be solved through a study of mimesis. Instead, we must proceed along a different path and explore the dynamics of ungrounded doubling. In order to accomplish this goal, we must first clarify how the repetition of Sinai and Horeb in the story of Torah is an instance of ungrounded doubling. And second, we will examine how ungrounded doubling is the result of a priestly "canon-conscious redaction."

A.   Sinai and Horeb as "Ungrounded Doubling" in the Canonical Sinai Complex

Rarely are the cosmic mountain symbols of Mount Sinai and Mount Horeb distinguished from each other in the canonical

Pentateuch. The reason for this is certainly rooted in the structure of the canonical Pentateuch itself, which has combined the
two symbols into one story. The influence of Torah on interpreters is already evident in Sir 48:7, where Sinai and Horeb are
presented as the one mountain of revelation. Furthermore, a
review of the history of interpretation illustrates how interpreters right up to the present have tended to make the same identification as the author of Sirach. Dillmann, for example, in the
late nineteenth century concluded that there was no difference
between Sinai and Horeb, and that they were simply different
names for the same object.[19] Even more recently, scholars who
are aware of the divergent tradition-historical streams behind
Sinai and Horeb have, nevertheless, continued to interpret "Si-
nai/Horeb" as a single symbol,[20] which is then characterized as
the mountain of covenant,[21] law,[22] or even as the beginning
point of Israel.[23]

The powerful influence of the canonical Pentateuch upon interpreters to identify Sinai/Horeb as a single symbol becomes all
the more noteworthy when we remind ourselves that these
symbols have almost *nothing* in common. Mount Sinai emphasizes the visual presence of the Kabod Yahweh, the role of
Moses as a mediator who maintains distance and clear boundaries between Yahweh and Israel, and a universal vision of Israel
as a "kingdom of priests" and a "holy nation"; as compared to
Mount Horeb, which emphasizes the auditory presence of God,
the role of Moses as a commissioned teacher of deuteronomic
law, and an exclusive vision of Israel as being Yahweh's "personal possession." The only point of similarity between these
two symbols is in their deep structure, where both represent the
relationship of God to the cosmic mountain as being metonymic, rather than the metaphoric relationship of Zion, and it is
this point of similarity that propels them into their predominant
role within the canonical Sinai Complex. The result of their
central role in Torah is that just as Zion functions authoritatively
as a past/future ideal for the reader, Sinai and Horeb are meant
to function authoritatively in the reader's present time. Yet,
when we shift our focus to the present in order to interpret Sinai and Horeb (and thus leave Zion behind), we do not leave

[19] Dillmann, *Exodus*, 31.
[20] See Terrien (*The Elusive Presence*, 106-60) for a significant departure from this
trend.
[21] Levenson, *Sinai and Zion*, 16-86.
[22] Donaldson, *Jesus on the Mountain*, 31-35.
[23] Cohn, *The Shape of Sacred Space*, 43-61.

behind the problem of repetition. Rather, the problem changes form: from mimesis to ungrounded doubling. Note how these very distinct symbols have been carefully separated from each other in the canonical Pentateuch, even while the story forces an opaque similarity by presenting them as the one revelation at the mountain.

A heightened demand for interpretation results from repetition as ungrounded doubling, in that the reader of Torah is really given no choice about whether Sinai and Horeb are indeed the one mountain of revelation. Instead, they must be brought together. This situation is quite different from the willed and intentional action of repetition as mimesis, where the reader of Torah appears to have more choice in whether to probe the tradition-history of Exodus 19-24. Cohn in his book, *The Shape of Sacred Space*, illustrates both the contrast between mimesis and ungrounded doubling and the involuntary quality of the latter with regard to Sinai and Horeb. In the chapter entitled, "The Sinai Symbol" he informs the reader that he is aware of the distinct tradition-historical backgrounds of Sinai and Horeb, but that his quest for a canonical reading of Sinai and Horeb does not require a probe into their differences. Thus Cohn sees repetition as mimesis in the canonical text, but chooses not to pursue it. The reason given for this choice is that biblical compilers regard these symbols as being equivalents, and therefore Cohn's study of the final form of the text demands that he, too, treat the symbols as being identical.[24] But they are not identical, and the reason for Cohn's seemingly self-conscious choice not to pursue tradition history actually arises from the involuntary quality of repetition as ungrounded doubling in the canonical text.

The powerful influence of ungrounded doubling also aids in unifying Torah. That unity, however, is neither a willed choice between the two symbols of Sinai and Horeb, nor a harmonization of them into an archetype. Rather, it is an involuntary interplay of opaquely similar things, which, although fundamentally different, must be interrelated. The heightened demand for interpretation that is implicit in ungrounded doubling requires a more detailed probe at the level of literary devices in order to describe in more detail just how the distinct symbols of Sinai and Horeb have been interrelated in the canonical Sinai Complex.

---

[24] Cohn, *The Shape of Sacred Space*, 44.

B. *The Priestly Redaction as a "Canon-Conscious Redaction"*

I hope to demonstrate in this section that the literary devices which have given rise to ungrounded doubling in the Sinai Complex are the result of priestly tradents and that these devices are "canon-conscious." Our study will proceed in two part: first, the term canon-conscious requires definition; then, the canon-conscious character of the priestly redaction must be illustrated in the Sinai Complex.

1. *A Definition of "Canon-Conscious Redaction"*

The term canon-consciousness was introduced by Seeligmann in an investigation into the "Voraussetzungen der Midraschexegese" within the very formation of the Hebrew Bible. He argued that the oldest midrashic exegesis actually developed organically out of the biblical literature, and, in order to illustrate this thesis, he suggested that late developments in the Hebrew Bible must be studied both from the perspective of the history of literature and from a more psychological point of view. He proposed that certain literary devices (such as flexibility of narratives, wordplays based on ambiguity, and the adaptation of motifs), which were part of the late formation of the Hebrew Bible, were actually constitutive of the oldest midrash. Seeligmann also proposed that these devices provided insight into a certain psychological attitude of the late editor/exegetes, which he defined as a canon-consciousness (*Kanonbewusstseins*). A characteristic of this canon-consciousness is that the term Torah becomes laden with content, which categorically demands an interpretation. This impinging character of Torah on late editors was, according to Seeligmann, because of the stabilizing and fixing of biblical tradition and its status as a Holy Word. Thus, for Seeligmann, canon consciousness is a hermeneutic concerning the intention of late biblical writers, editors, or exegetes.[25]

Childs acknowledged Seeligmann's notion of canon-consciousness in his *Introduction to the Old Testament as Scripture*. In so doing he also redefined the term to reflect a more intrinsic hermeneutic of intentionality. Consequently, what is constitutive of canon-consciousness for Childs is not a perceived attitude on the part of late biblical editors toward an emerging authoritative text, but the present shape of the literature itself. More precisely, canon-consciousness designates devices in the text

[25] I. L. Seeligmann, "Voraussetzungen der Midraschexegese," *Congress Volume: Copenhagen 1953*, VTSup 1 (1953) 150-81, esp. 150-52.

which have ordered older tradition in such a way that the material is loosened from its historical moorings in order to function authoritatively in the reader's present time. This temporal shift from past tradition to continually present tradition is a new function for the literature, according to Childs, and the effects of this new function are built in the structure of the canonical text. Canon-consciousness, therefore, actually becomes a poetics of canon for Childs, and a qualified form of redaction becomes an important area of study within this new poetics.[26]

Childs argued that redactional techniques within the Hebrew Bible can be distinguished on a spectrum between two poles which must be carefully distinguished.[27] At one end of the spectrum there are signs of redaction in the biblical text, which indicate that tradition was reinterpreted by an editor to fit a particular historical context. The social, political and economic forces that influenced the editor are often open to the interpreter in this type of redaction.[28] At the other end of the spectrum there are signs of redaction in which no historically specific references or political forces are evident to the reader of the biblical text.[29] In this case, the interpreter is confronted with a layered text, which shows both signs of reinterpretation and perhaps indications of an attempt to unify the material. According to Childs these redactional techniques are important

---

[26] Childs, *Introduction to the Old Testament*, 59-60.

[27] Childs ("The Exegetical Significance of Canon for the Study of the Old Testament," 68) brings out this contrast by comparing redaction to canon. He writes, "The method of redactional criticism seeks to discern from the peculiar shape of the biblical literature signs of intentional reinterpretation. . .which can be related to an editor's particular historically conditioned perspective. A canonical method also makes use of the peculiar shape of the literature, often in direct dependence upon redactional analysis." But, ". . .canonical analysis focuses its attention on the effect which the different layers have had on the final form of the text. . . ."

[28] Childs (*Exodus* 404-09) provides an example of this type of redaction in his discussion of the second commandment in the Decalogue (Exod 20:4-6). Childs attributed two problems of syntax in Exod 20:4-6 to redaction—the relation of the prohibition against images to what follows in v. 4 and the plural suffix ("them") in v. 5. These redactional techniques provided Childs with "a good example of how the recognition of a historical dimension leading up to the. . .final form can bring. . .interpretation. . .into sharper focus." He concluded that the editor of Exod 20:4-6 was responding to a fresh challenge of Canaanite religion in the style of Deuteronomy.

[29] Childs (*Exodus*, 501-03) provides examples of this type of redaction in his discussion of Exodus 24. The juxtaposition of Moses in Exod 24:1a to the seventy elders in Exod 24:1b-2, the harmonization of Exod 24:1-2, 9-11 with Exod 24:3-8 through framing, and the addition of Exod 24:12 show signs of redaction, but no social, political, or economic forces are evident in the editor's work.

devices in describing a poetics of canon.[30]

Seeligmann and Childs lay important groundwork for our study of the priestly redactions as being canon conscious. Seeligmann has correctly raised the question of whether different forces might not be influencing the transformation of biblical tradition in its later stages of development, and whether these forces might not be evident in certain types of literary devices that are now embedded in the canonical text. Childs has gone a step further by turning Seeligmann's insights even more rigorously to the canonical text in his quest for what I have described as a poetics of canon: that is, devices built into the structure of canon which loosen the text from its mooring in the historical past and thus encourage its reading in the continual present of the reader. The insights of Childs with regard to redaction are particularly interesting for this study, since we too, wish to make a distinction between types of redaction in contrasting the deuteronomistic and priestly redactions of Exodus 19-24. His emphasis on anonymity (of historical, political, and economic factors) as the decisive quality in separating canonical versus non-canonical redaction is not helpful for this study, since in attempting to anchor their distinct law codes in the revelation at the mountain in Exodus 19-24, both the deuteronomistic and priestly redactions evince this quality. For example, neither redaction is overtly signed and furthermore the past character concerning the revelation at the mountain is maintained. Yet both redactions do reinterpret older tradition for a new generation, which theoretically could extend to the reader's present time. Thus, other criteria are necessary if we are to distinguish between the deuteronomistic and priestly redactions with regard to canon-consciousness.

Sheppard, in an article entitled, "Canonization: Hearing the Voice of the Same God through Historically Dissimilar Traditions," may provide criteria by which we can distinguish between the two redactions in Exodus 19-24. Sheppard defined canon-conscious redactions as "attempts by editors to relate one canonical book or part of a book to some other canonical book or collection of books" for the purpose of hearing them together.[31] He writes:

These redactions reflect occasional efforts to over-

[30] Childs, *Exodus*, 503.
[31] G. T. Sheppard, "Canonization: Hearing the Voice of the Same God through Historically Dissimilar Traditions," *Int* 36 (1982) 21-33 esp. 23. See also *Wisdom as a Hermeneutical Construct*, BZAW 151 (Berlin: de Gruyter, 1980) 109-10.

come. . .the apparent independence of biblical traditions
by introducing an overt literary link between them, one
which exceeds the actual historical connections original
to the different literatures.[32]

These canon-conscious literary links are not aimed at harmonizing distinct traditions. Rather, Sheppard concludes that they
"enhance the presumption of biblical unity by creating explicit
interpretative contexts between books and groups of books."[33]
Thus, the end result of a canon-conscious redaction is "not to
solve but to heighten the demand for interpretation."[34]

2. *Priestly "Canon-Conscious Redactions" in the Canonical Sinai Complex*

I hope to demonstrate in this section that the heightened demand in Torah to interpret Sinai and Horeb as the one mountain of revelation, even though they are fundamentally
different, is the result of a canon-conscious priestly redaction, in
which priestly tradents have displaced Horeb with Sinai, while
they have also created literary links between them; and that the
simultaneous action of displacement and linkage is what has
given rise to the central role of ungrounded doubling between
Sinai and Horeb in the canonical Pentateuch. A review of spatial form devices within the priestly redaction will provide a
point of departure for a more detailed study of the canon-conscious literary links between the deuteronomic and priestly
legislations.

Earlier it was noted how the priestly redaction is spatial in
form, that is, how it repeatedly disrupts the flow of the narrative
in order to provide more specific information either about the
setting of Mount Sinai or about the function of characters within
the setting. With the predominance of spatial form devices, the
vertical structure of the mountain became the organizing axis in
the narrative over plot and chronology, which provided a narrative context for the revelation of the priestly legislation on the
summit of Mount Sinai. If we expand our perspective to the
larger context of Torah, it becomes clear that spatial form devices serve an additional literary purpose, which is to displace
Horeb with Sinai, while also creating links between the two.
The displacement of Horeb with Sinai is made clearly evident
by the predominance of Sinai in the surface structure of Exodus

---

[32] Sheppard, "Canonization," 23.
[33] Sheppard, "Canonization," 25.
[34] Sheppard, "Canonization," 25.

19-24. It is, after all, the Sinai Complex and not the Horeb Complex that is the object of study in the canonical Pentateuch. The literary links between Sinai and Horeb that result from spatial form devices are less obvious, and this function is our central task in describing the canon-conscious quality of the priestly redaction.

This much is clear at the outset concerning the character of the literary links between Sinai and Horeb: displacement and linkage by means of spatial form devices should not be interpreted as subordination. On the contrary, in describing the structure of narratives in which spatial form devices are central, Mickelsen concluded that they were best likened to an orange, since the scenes of such narratives are frequently segments of equal value in which the internal movement is circular around a central core subject.[35] If we apply this insight to the canonical Sinai Complex, it would appear that by giving spatial form techniques a central role as linking devices in the canonical Sinai Complex, priestly tradents have certainly created a story, but it is a story that is more concerned with setting and characters than it is with presenting a unified flow of events. Consequently, the revelation of distinct legislations on Sinai and on Horeb are placed only loosely within a chronological framework, with the result that they appear to revolve around the core subject of the narrative, which is the one revelation at the mountain, and in this way they maintain equal value. Such a structure has strong effects upon the reader, for it gives rise to ungrounded doubling. The prominence of this form of repetition forces the reader "to project not so much forward ('what happens next') as backward or sideways" in order to uncover the progression of the Sinai complex,[36] and this heightened demand for interpretation actually "enhance(s) the presumption of biblical unity" between Sinai and Horeb.[37] Although they are fundamentally different and left unharmonized in the canonical Pentateuch, Sinai and Horeb are experienced as being opaquely similar.[38]

Spatial form devices, as a means of linking the deuteronomic and priestly legislations, give rise to a whole series of ungrounded doublings in the canonical Sinai Complex, which must

[35] D. Mickelsen, "Types of Spatial Structure in Narrative," *Spatial Form in Narrative*, ed. by J. R. Smitten and A. Daghistany (Ithaca: Cornell University, 1981) 64-67.
[36] Mickelsen, "Types of Spatial Structure in Narrative," 37.
[37] Sheppard, "Canonization," 25.
[38] Miller, *Fiction and Repetition*, 9.

be explored in more detail in the following sections. Two things
will become clear from this study. First, we will see that the
combination of the deuteronomic and priestly legislations in the
canonical Sinai Complex occurs in two stages, which consist of
an initial promulgation of law to establish covenant in Exodus
19-24 and a subsequent (and more detailed) promulgation of law
within the setting of Covenant Renewal in Exodus 32-34. Second, we will see that ungrounded doubling plays a central role
throughout the canonical Sinai Complex in enhancing the presumption of biblical unity. There are two promises within the
Proposal of Covenant, two interpretations of the Decalogue,
two initial accounts concerning the revelation of law, two versions of the tablets, and finally, two legislations of Covenant
Renewal.

a. *Revelation of Law at the Mountain of God
    in Exodus 19-24*

The redaction-critical study of Exodus 19-24 has underscored
how the structure of this material is rooted in the three-part sequence of the Mountain of God tradition, which consisted of Introduction, Preparation, Purification and Theophany, and
Sacrificial Ritual. The redaction-critical study has also illustrated
how the structure of the Mountain of God tradition has become
a framework for introducing legislation into the account of theophany at the mountain, and that because of this transformation, the three-part sequence of the Mountain of God tradition
becomes a progression in the revelation of law: from a Proposal
of Covenant, through a theophany which includes the revelation of the Decalogue, to a still more detailed revelation of law.
This reinterpretation was initiated by deuteronomistic tradents,
but also followed by priestly redactors, which suggests that we
should look for the effects of a priestly canon-conscious redaction precisely at each of these three points, since it is at these
crucial junctures that we would expect both displacement and
linkage between the distinct law codes.

1) *The "Promise of Reward" in the Proposal of Covenant.*
The first signs of the canon-conscious character of the priestly
redaction are evident in the Proposal of Covenant. The interaction between the deuteronomistic and priestly redactions comes
into focus obliquely within the structure of this introductory episode, when what appears to be a firmly fixed vertical hierarchy
between characters in Exod 19:1-3a (with Yahweh and Israel
clearly separated by the mountain, while Moses moves vertically

between them) actually gives way by the end of the episode to a much more vague presentation of Moses in Exod 19:7 as simply conveying speech between Yahweh and Israel.

The ambiguity in structure provides the backdrop for a much clearer point of contact between the two redactions in the "Promise of Reward." Earlier we noted how both deuteronomistic and priestly tradents have anchored a divine promise in the Proposal of Covenant to function as an introduction to their respective legislations, with the deuteronomistic promise in Exod 19:5ba and the priestly promise in Exod 19:5bb-6a. Although these distinct promises are still clearly evident in the canonical text, priestly tradents have created links between the two, and even forced a new reading of the deuteronomistic promise.

The links between the two promises come into focus through a brief review of each. The deuteronomistic "Promise of Reward" in Exod 19:5ba portrays a relationship between Israel and Yahweh which excludes the nations. And this is a problem, for the logic of this ideal leaves no room for the priestly promise in repetition 19:5bb-6a with its proclamation of Yahweh's universal rule and its accompanying vision of Israel as priests within this world. Consequently, the addition of the priestly promise creates conflict, which actually forces a new reading of the exclusivity within the deuteronomistic promise. In particular, when the deuteronomistic promise is read in conjunction with the priestly promise, the implications of social exclusivity in the former must be reinterpreted as a qualitative exclusivity, as a priest might have in the role of mediation. Such a vision, however, is hardly exclusive, for it actually implies a mission to the nations.

The addition of the priestly promise is perhaps the strongest instance of displacement by priestly tradents, and as such it raises questions whether it qualifies as being canon-conscious. My reason for this hesitation is that the priestly redaction in Exod 19:5bb-6a not only disrupts the flow of the narrative in order to add new material and to create literary links between the two promises, but actually goes a step further and forces a new reading of the deuteronomistic promises. In taking this extra step, it raises the question of whether there is subordination in the relationship of the two promises. We will leave the question unanswered, and simply add that one reason for this movement toward subordination might be the prominent role that the deuteronomistic redaction is playing in providing a context for the priestly promise.

2) *Theophany and the Revelation of the Decalogue.* The canon-conscious links between the deuteronomistic and priestly redactions in the second episode are clear at a number of points. We will see that in contrast to the "Promise of Reward," priestly redactors create a parity between the two interpretations of theophany, with the result that the revelation of the Decalogue becomes shared Torah.

Links between the deuteronomistic and priestly interpretations of theophany are created immediately in the account of preparation. The two redactions are combined in the canonical text as distinct speeches by Yahweh (Exod 19:9aa, 10:aa, "And Yahweh said to Moses"), with separate introductions (Exod 19:8b, 9b, "And Moses returned/reported the words of the people to Yahweh"). In this way the two speeches are isolated from each other syntactically, which provides clear boundaries between their distinct interpretations of theophany. Exod 19:8b-9a stresses the need for Israel to hear the speech of Yahweh and acquire faith in Moses, while the appearance of Yahweh is described as an approach (*bw'*) on a thick cloud. Exod 19:9b-15 stresses the need for the people to be sanctified and for the mountain to be sealed off, while the future appearance of Yahweh is described as a descent (*yrd*) on Mount Sinai "before the eyes of all the people." The two accounts of preparation appear to have equal status in the canonical text; perhaps the reason for this is that the Mountain of God tradition is providing the context for the distinct redactions in contrast to the "Promise of Reward" in the Proposal of Covenant, where the priestly promise built more directly upon the deuteronomistic redaction.

The separate interpretations of the preparation for theophany are carried through into the description of the event itself. Earlier we saw how the deuteronomistic (Exod 19:19) and priestly (Exod 19:18) redactors emphasized different aspects of the account of theophany within the Mountain of God tradition (Exod 19:16ab-17), and how the combination of these redactions result in a chiastic framework that can be summarized as follows.

(A) Description of theophany as thunder (*qlt*), lightning (v. 16a)
(B) Fear (*ḥrd*) of the people (v. 16b)
  (C) Moses leading Israel to the mountain (v. 17)
  (C') Priestly reinterpretation of theophany as

> a divine descent in fire on Mount Sinai (v.
> 18a)
> (B') Priestly personification of the mountain as
>   trembling (*ḥrd*) (v. 18b)
> (A') Deuteronomic reinterpretation of theophany as
>   speech (*ql*) between Moses and God (v. 19)

The priestly redaction disrupts the deuteronomistic reinterpretation of theophany, while also providing links to it. The diagram illustrates how each redaction emphasizes different aspects of the Mountain of God tradition with the result that their distinct interpretations of theophany are placed side by side in a chiasmus and thus not really interacting with each other. This arrangement is reminiscent of the relationship between the deuteronomistic (Exod 19:8b-9a) and priestly (Exod 19:9b-15) accounts of the preparation for theophany that we have just discussed, where a similar juxtaposition occurs in the form of distinct divine speeches.

The parity between the two accounts of theophany continues through the promulgation of the Decalogue, thus creating conflicting interpretations without providing a clear indication of which reading is primary. The conflicting interpretations of the Decalogue come into clearest focus when one compares the contrasting portrayals of Moses which presently frame the Decalogue. The priestly interpretation of Moses as a mediator precedes the Decalogue in Exod 19:20-25, where he is described as descending Mount Sinai and promulgating the legislation to the people. Here the Decalogue must be interpreted as having been revealed to Moses alone, and this corresponds with his role as mediator throughout the priestly legislation. In contrast to this, the authentication of Moses as a teacher of law occurs after the Decalogue in Exod 20:18-20. In the deuteronomistic account Moses receives the Decalogue through conversation with God in the midst of all the people, who hear the law as direct speech of God, and then authenticate him as an authoritative teacher. This latter portrayal of Moses corresponds with his role throughout deuteronomistic tradition.

The conflicting interpretations of the Decalogue in the canonical Sinai Complex are the result of priestly tradents, for they are the ones who have disrupted the flow of the narrative within the deuteronomistic redaction to include their own interpretation concerning the revelation of the Decalogue in Exod 19:20-25. Yet, their displacement of the deuteronomistic interpretation is accompanied by linkage in the form of the conflicting narrative contexts for the Decalogue. Thus, for example, if the priestly redaction is emphasized, the reaction of the people to the direct words of God after the promulgation of the Decalogue seems out of place, since Moses is really the one presenting the Decalogue to them. But, conversely, if the deuteronomistic redaction is emphasized, the ascent of Moses on Mount Sinai in the middle of theophany appears to be a "dismal anti-climax,"[39] since it would then appear to be followed by the direct speech of God to Israel.

The result of the conflicting narrative contexts of the Decalogue is that "undecidability" is inherent to the canonical text so that in the end the reader must choose which of the two interpretations will be emphasized. It must be immediately added that once a decision is made, whatever interpretation of the Decalogue is rejected automatically forces a qualification of the chosen reading. And this situation leads to two conclusions. First, the conflicting narrative contexts of the Decalogue are an instance of ungrounded doubling, and the effect of this form of repetition is to heighten the demand for interpretation. Second, the quality of undecidability within the canonical text suggests that the Decalogue has become shared Torah of the deuteronomic and priestly legislations. This conclusion is supported by noting the synoptic tradition of the Decalogue in Exod 20:2-17 and Deut 5:6-21, and even further reinforced by noting that the account of the giving of the Decalogue in Deut 5:6-21 reflects the same mutual claim of deuteronomistic and priestly tradents, since in Deut 5:4-5a the reader encounters the same contextual ambiguity in being told that the Decalogue was both direct speech of God to Israel and mediated divine speech through Moses.[40]

3) *The Initial Revelation of Law as a Covenant Closing and Sanctification Ceremony.* The canon-conscious links between the deuteronomic Book of the Covenant and the priestly Tabernacle Cult are somewhat different from the Proposal of Covenant and the narrative context of the Decalogue. Priestly redactors have not forced a reinterpretation of the deutero-

---

[39] See Childs, *Exodus*, 368.

[40] Deut 4:4-51 reads, "Yahweh spoke with you face to face at the mountain, out of the midst of the fire, while I stood between Yahweh and you at that time, to declare to you the word of Yahweh." The contrast in imagery here is striking. See Childs (*Exodus*, 351) who notes that the contrast is all the more striking because the deuteronomistic pattern of Yahweh speaking the Decalogue directly to Israel is consistent elsewhere. For further discussion see, among others, von Rad, *Deuteronomy*, 55; Perlitt, *Bundestheologie*, 81 n.1; Hossfeld, *Dekalog*, 255; Mittmann, *Deuteronomium*, 132, n.1.

nomistic redaction as they did in the Proposal of Covenant, nor
have they laid claim to the Book of the Covenant as they did
with the Decalogue. Instead, priestly tradents provide pointers
beyond the Book of the Covenant that prepare the reader for
the subsequent priestly legislation in Exodus 25-31. These
pointers are evident at a number of junctures in Exodus 24.

One way in which priestly tradents link their legislation to
the Book of the Covenant, while also pointing the reader ahead,
is by framing the Covenant Closing Ceremony in Exod 24:3-7
with new material in Exod 24:1-2, 9-11. The insertion of Exod
24:1-2 disrupts the movement of the deuteronomistic redaction
by inserting a new divine speech to Moses after the revelation of
the Book of the Covenant.

The insertion of Exod 24:1-2 results in the following structure to the third episode in Exodus 19-24. The episode begins
with an initial speech by Yahweh addressed to Moses, who is
being commissioned to convey the legislation of the Book of the
Covenant (Exod 20:22-23:33) to Israel. This speech is inaugurated with the following form:

> *wayyō 'mer yhwh 'el-mōšeh*
> *kōh tō 'mar 'el-běnê yiśrā'ēl*
> And Yahweh said to Moses,
> "Thus you will say to the children of Israel"

The priestly redaction expands the episode by adding a second
speech by Yahweh addressed to Moses alone (Exod 24:1-2), in
which he is called to be separate from the people. This speech
begins with the following form:

> *wě 'el-mōšeh 'āmar*
> and to Moses he said,

The syntax of this phrase has caused problems for interpreters.
Childs summarizes the problem when he writes: "One would
expect a different Hebrew construction for the beginning of a
new section, such as *wayyō 'mer 'el mōšeh*."[41] Noth even concluded that an entire section fell out of the text because of the
uneven syntax.[42] I would suggest however that the redactional
addition of Exod 24:1-2 is canon-conscious, and that the syntax
serves a function for priestly redactors by clearly separating this
second speech of Yahweh to Moses, the mediator, from the first
speech of Yahweh to Moses, the commissioned teacher of

[41] Childs, *Exodus* 498.
[42] Noth, *Exodus*, 196.

deuteronomic law. Not only is the second speech of Yahweh in Exod 24:1-2 clearly separated from the deuteronomic legislation by syntax, it also forces the reader to move beyond the Covenant-Closing Ceremony to the vision of the heavenly temple in Exod 24:9-11, since this event is the fulfillment of the divine command in Exod 24:1-2.

Another way in which priestly tradents link their legislation to the revelation of the Book of the Covenant, while also moving the story ahead, is by adding a new conclusion to the Covenant-Closing Ceremony. In particular, the final proclamation and acceptance of the deuteronomic legislation in Exod 24:7 is used as a transitional device by the priestly redactors to incorporate the blood ritual in Exod 24:6, 8. The incorporation of this ritual takes the reader beyond a Covenant-Closing Ceremony and in the process also adds a new dimension of sanctification to the ceremony on analogy to the Sanctification Ceremony of priests in Lev 8:22-30. The new motif of sanctification then takes over to become the point of focus for the remainder of Exodus 24, as preparation for the revelation of the priestly legislation in Exodus 25-31.

The sequence of events in Exodus 24 illustrates an overall design of priestly tradents to move the reader beyond the revelation of deuteronomic law, with its promulgation in a Covenant-Closing Ceremony, in order to incorporate the priestly legislation into the events of Exodus 19-24. The disruptions of the deuteronomistic redaction, with the additional speech to Moses in Exod 24:1-2 and with the blood ritual in Exod 24:6, 8, converge in Exod 24:9-11, since this text both fulfills the new command to Moses in Exod 24:1-2, and continues the sequence of the Sanctification Ceremony of the priests in Lev 8:22-30, where blood purification also progresses to a meal before God.

In conclusion, with the addition of the priestly material in Exodus 24, what is a Covenant-Closing Ceremony when read in light of the Book of the Covenant is simultaneously a Sanctification Ceremony for the subsequent revelation of the priestly legislation. Wellhausen describes well the effect of the priestly canon-conscious redaction in Exodus 24, when he writes of Exod 24:3-8 that what appears to have been "a formal closing of the promulgation of the law. . . presently is a brief intermezzo."[43] Both perceptions hold firm in the canonical text because both law codes are meant to be anchored in the events of Exodus 19-24.

[43] Wellhausen, *Composition*, 83.

b. *The Legislation of Covenant Renewal in Exodus 32-34*

Although this study has been limited to Exodus 19-24, an interpretation of priestly canon-conscious redactions within the
formation of the canonical Sinai Complex requires that we expand our scope and include the account of Covenant Renewal
in Exodus 32-34. Exodus 19-24 itself provides good reason for
expanding our focus, because of the introduction of the motif of
the tablets in Exod 24:12. This motif links the initial revelation
of law in Exodus 19-24 with the legislation of Covenant Renewal
in Exodus 32-34, while it also functions as a unifying device
throughout Exod 24:12-34:35.[44] The motif of the tablets separates Exod 24:12-34:35 into a four-part sequence in which first,
the command to receive the tablets is given (Exod 24:12); second, the reception of the tablets is noted (Exod 31:18); third,
their destruction is narrated as a result of Israel's sin (Exod
32:15-19); and fourth, they are reissued to Moses during Covenant Renewal (Exod 34:1, 4, 28-29).

We should also note that in spite of the unifying function of
this motif, the tablets themselves are described with a variety of
terms throughout Exod 24:12-34:35 (*lḥt, ḥlḥt, šny lḥt*, etc.),[45]
and that two distinct traditions in particular are discernable in
the canonical text, namely the "(two) tablets of stone" (*[šny] lḥt
h'bn*, Exod 24:12; 31:18; 34:1, 4) as a signifier of deuteronomic
legislation,[46] and the "two tablets of testimony" (*šny lḥt h'dt*,
Exod 31:18; 32:15-16; 34:4, 29) as representing priestly legislation.[47] Thus, the motif of the tablets in the canonical text has
not been harmonized, and this insight provides a starting point
for the present study. Our interpretation of Covenant Renewal
will begin with an examination of the motif of the tablets of
stone in deuteronomistic tradition, and this will be followed by a
description of the two tablets of testimony in priestly tradition.
I hope to demonstrate that the distribution of the two tablets of
testimony in Exod 24:12-34:35 reflects a canon-conscious at-

[44] See Perlitt, *Bundestheologie*, 203-7.

[45] The variety of terminology has prompted past interpreters to seek the origin of
the motif of the tablets in Exod 24:12-34:35 on the basis of subtle distinctions
among the different terms. See, for example, S. Lehming, "Versuch zu Ex. xxxii,"
VT 10 (1960) 16-50. Most recently Hossfeld (*Dekalog*, 145-46) has interpreted four
levels of tradition on the basis of the distinct terminology.

[46] See Perlitt, *Bundestheologie*, 203-07. Deuteronomy also refers to the tablets as
"the two tablets" (*šny lḥwt*) in Deut 9:17; 10:3; as "the tablets" (*lḥt*) in Deut 10:2, 4,
5; and finally as "the tablets of the covenant" (*lḥt hbryt*) in Deut 9:9, 11.

[47] See Cross, *Canaanite Myth and Hebrew Epic*, 313.

tempt by priestly redactors to link the deuteronomic and priestly legislations as the one legislation of Covenant Renewal.

1) *The Motif of the "Tablets of Stone" in Deuteronomistic Tradition.* The influence of deuteronomistic redactors in Exod 24:12-34:35 is strong.[48] Not only is there a clear link between Covenant Renewal in Exodus 32-34 and in Deuteronomy through the use of the motif of the tablets of stone (Exod 24:12; 31:18; 34:1, 4, 28; Deut 4:13; 5:22; 9:9, 10, 11, 15; 10:1, 3), but in addition the two texts in Deuteronomy (Deut 9:9-19; 10:1-4), which recount the events of Covenant Renewal, follow the same four-part pattern.[49] Thus an interpretation of the "tablets of stone" requires that we examine both texts in determining what legislation deuteronomistic tradents are referring to through the use of this motif.

Two aspects of the story in Exodus suggest that the Decalogue is the content of the tablets of stone. First, we should note that Moses has already inscribed the Book of the Covenant during the Covenant-Closing Ceremony in Exod 24:4. Thus there is no need for an additional ascent in Exod 24:12 unless Yahweh intends to inscribe the Decalogue on the tablets of stone. This conclusion is supported at the close of Covenant Renewal in Exod 34:27-28, where the contents of the tablets of stone are designated explicitly as being the "ten words," which form the basis for covenant.[50]

The recounting of Covenant Renewal in Deuteronomy also suggests that the content of the tablets of stone are the Decalogue. In fact, Deuteronomy is unambiguous on this point, since the Decalogue is consistently referred to as the words on the

---

[48] See Perlitt, *Bundestheologie*, 203-32.

[49] The four-part pattern in Deut 9:9-19; 10:1-4 can be illustrated as follows: first, Moses is described as ascending the mountain to receive the tablets of stone (Deut 9:9); then, he is given the tablets of stone, on the mountain after forty days and nights (Deut 9:11/Exod 31:18); third, he descends the mountain and shatters the tablets (Deut 9:15-16/Exod 32:15-16); and finally, Moses receives new tablets of stone (Deut 10:1-4/Exod 34:1-4, 27-29). Deut 10:1-4 further reinforces a comparison to Exodus 34 through a series of verbal parallels: in each account Moses is commanded to cut "tablets of stone" like the first (Deut 10:1/Exod 34:1); Yahweh states that he will write again all the words which were on the previous tablets that Moses shattered (Deut 10:2/Exod 34:1); and Moses is presented as executing the commands of Yahweh (Deut 10:3/Exod 34:4).

[50] For an interpretation of Exod 34:27-28 within deuteronomistic tradition rather than as a kernel of older J tradition (as for example Noth, *Exodus*, 265-66; or more recently Halbe, *Das Privilegrecht Jahwes*, 270-315 have argued) see Perlitt, *Bundestheologie*, 207, 228-32. Compare, also Zenger, *Sinaitheophanie*, 97-98; and Hossfeld, *Dekalog*, 208-10.

tablets, which form the basis of covenant. The tablets of stone are first equated with the Decalogue in Deut 4:13 through the reference to the ten words. Then, after Moses recounts the words of the Decalogue in Deut 5:6-21, he concludes in Deut 5:22 that Yahweh wrote these words on "two tablets of stone" before giving them to himself. The tablets of stone are linked with the Decalogue in the context of the golden calf in Deuteronomy 9, where Moses once again recounts how Yahweh gave him the two tablets of stone after forty days and nights on the mountain, and that these tablets contain "all the words" that Yahweh had spoken on the mountain out of the midst of fire (Deut 9:11).[51] The tablets of stone are still associated with the Decalogue when Moses recounts the Covenant Renewal Ceremony of Exodus 34 in Deut 10:1-5. He states in Deut 10:4 that the words on the new tablets were the ten words, which Yahweh had spoken earlier to Israel from the midst of the fire. And finally, the framing of the entire account of the Horeb Theophany in Deuteronomy with the reference to the ten words (Deut 4:13; 10:4) underscores even further that the Decalogue is the content of the tablets of stone.

2) *The Motif of the "Two Tablets of Testimony" in Priestly Tradition.* This is clearly a priestly designation, since their cultic law is frequently described as the "testimony" (*hā'ēdut*, Exod 25:16, 21, 22; 26:33, 34; 27:21; 30:6, 36).[52] The motif of the two tablets of testimony occurs three times in Exod 24:12-34:35 (Exod 31:18; 32:15; 34:29), and an examination of the distribution of this motif will illustrate two things: first, how priestly redactors have followed the four-part sequence of the motif of the tablets of stone in deuteronomistic tradition; and second, how the incorporation of the priestly two tablets of testimony displaces the deuteronomistic interpretation and in the process introduces ambiguity, which allows for the incorporation of the priestly legislation as being part of the content of the tablets.

Priestly redactors first introduce ambiguity with regard to the content of the tablets of stone through the syntax of Exod 24:12, which reads:

And Yahweh said to Moses,

---

[51] The tablets of stone are not specifically mentioned in either Exod 32:15-19 or Deut 9:17. Yet this event must be included within the sequence of each account since it is presupposed in the command of Exod 34:1/Deut 10:1-4 for Moses to cut new tablets of stone like the first, which he shattered.
[52] Cross, *Canaanite Myth and Hebrew Epic*, 313.

"Ascend the mountain to me and wait there.
And I will give you the tablets of stone (*luḥōt hā'eben*)
and the Torah (*wĕhattôrâ*)
and the commandment (*wĕhammiṣwâ*)
which I wrote to instruct them."

This syntax presently allows for two readings. If the *waw* connecting "the Torah and the commandment" to the "tablets of stone" is an explicative,[53] then these terms are merely further descriptions of the Decalogue, which is the unambiguous designation of this term in Deuteronomy. However, if the *waw* is read as a conjunction,[54] then other legislation besides the Decalogue is being included on the tablets of stone. The problem of syntax at least suggests that the command for Moses to receive the tablets of stone has been expanded,[55] with the result the reader must now determine what Torah is in fact included on the tablets of stone.

The ambiguity introduced in the syntax of Exod 24:12 becomes even more pronounced when the motif of the two tablets of testimony first appears in Exod 31:18 in conjunction with the tablets of stone. The presence of both terms gives rise to two possible interpretations, depending on which term is stressed. According to a deuteronomistic interpretation of Exod 31:18, Moses is called up the mountain in Exod 24:12 after the Covenant-Closing Ceremony to receive the Decalogue as codified law (i.e., the tablets of stone), which Yahweh had previously spoken directly to the people during theophany. According to a priestly interpretation of Exod 31:18, Moses is receiving new cultic legislation (i.e., the tablets of testimony in Exodus 25-31) to confirm the presence of Yahweh, which now becomes possible only after the Sanctification Ceremony of the people. Neither interpretation can be easily rejected, so that the reader is once again left to determine the content of the tablets in the canonical text.

Ambiguity continues into the account of the golden calf in Exodus 32. The problem is that although Moses ascended the mountain in Exod 24:12 to receive the tablets of stone, when he descends the mountain in Exod 32:15, he has the two tablets of testimony in his hands. Once again the reader must decide between two possible interpretations. A deuteronomistic interpretation of the construction of the golden calf and the

---

[53] *GKC* 154a, n.1b.
[54] *GKC* 154a.
[55] See Noth, *Exodus*, 199-200; Zenger, *Sinaitheophanie*, 77; Childs, *Exodus* 499.

shattering of the tablets must be viewed in the context of the Decalogue. In this case Israel's construction of the golden calf breaks the covenant because it is a violation of the prohibition against images in the first commandment of the Decalogue.[56] The golden calf can also be interpreted as a rival cult to the priestly legislation, with the result that the calf becomes a challenge to the presence of Yahweh. In this case the shattering of the two tablets of testimony symbolizes the inability of God "to tabernacle" with Israel.[57]

Finally, the ambiguity over the content of the tablets is carried through the Covenant Renewal Ceremony in Exodus 34. On the one hand, it appears that Exod 34:27-28 is making explicit reference to the Decalogue in describing the ten words. Yet, when Moses actually descends the mountain in Exod 34:29, he once again is carrying the two tablets of testimony, and no mention is made of the Decalogue. Instead, the descent of Moses with the tablets of testimony provides the setting for the promulgation of priestly law in Exodus 35-Numbers 10, which was initially revealed to Moses in Exod 35-31, but lost in the incident of the golden calf.[58]

We have seen that the motif of the tablets of stone in the deuteronomistic redaction of Exod 24:12-34:35 has provided the context for a subsequent priestly redaction. Priestly tradents have inserted the motif of the two tablets of testimony to incorporate their legislation into the revelation of law in Exodus 19-24 (Exodus 25-31) and into the Covenant Renewal Ceremony of Exodus 34 (Exodus 35-Numbers 10). In addition, the priestly redaction is canon-conscious, since it attempts to relate the deuteronomic and priestly legislations as the content of the tablets by creating ambiguity in the canonical Sinai Complex. The result of the priestly canon-conscious redaction is that the content of the tablets in the canonical Sinai Complex is the one lit-

---

[56] For an example of this interpretation of the tablets see Perlitt, *Bundestheologie*, 203. The prohibition against images is also central to the account of the Decalogue in Deuteronomy 4-5 (see esp. Deut 4:15-19, 23, 28).

[57] For examples of this interpretation see O. Hvidberg-Hansen, "Die Vernichtung des Goldenen Kalbes und der Ugaritische Ernteritus," *AcOr* 33 (1971) 22-23; Mann, *Divine Presence*, 154-55; and Moberly, *At the Mountain of God*, 46-110.

[58] Note also the priestly portrayal of Moses that accompanies the account of his descent with the two tablets of testimony. The reader is told that Moses actually mirrors the Kabod Yahweh as he promulgates the priestly legislation of Covenant Renewal. For an interpretation of *qrn* in the description of Moses' face as light which symbolizes divinity see Hab 3:4; and compare also Dumermuth, "Moses strahlendes Gesicht," 244-47.

erary Torah, which contains both the deuteronomic and priestly law codes.

C. *"Sinai/Horeb" as the Theological Center To the Canonical Sinai Complex*

As authoritative theologies of divine cultic presence in the canonical Sinai Complex, Sinai and Horeb are presented as being the one mountain of revelation in the wilderness. Yet the story of the one revelation is not a unified narrative. At many points priestly redactors have gone out of their way not to harmonize the distinct symbols of Sinai and Horeb. This is evident in the overall structure of the canonical Sinai Complex, where Sinai and Horeb are carefully separated as distinct stages in Israel's wilderness travels, and it is evident within the carefully constructed narrative of Exodus 19-24. Frequently priestly tradents have created ambiguity which forces the reader to acknowledge conflicting interpretations in the canonical text. Through ambiguity, priestly tradents encourage the reader to interpret the Decalogue as shared Torah, and the content of the tablets as both deuteronomic and priestly legislation. They even encourage the reading of Exodus 24 as both a Covenant-Closing Ceremony and a Sanctification Ceremony.

The predominance of ambiguity within the canonical Sinai Complex suggests that a unified theology of divine presence, embedded within the text, is rejected. The central role of ungrounded doubling in creating this ambiguity suggests that the ideal of a unified interpretation is, nevertheless, forced upon the reader, since the priestly canon-conscious literary links between deuteronomic and priestly legislation actually enhance the presumption of biblical unity. In this way, repetition as ungrounded doubling actually aids in unifying Torah. That unity is neither a willed choice between the two symbols of Sinai and Horeb, nor a harmonization of them into an archetype. Rather, the heightened demand to interpret creates an involuntary interplay of opaquely similar things, which, although fundamentally different, must be interrelated.

V
CONCLUSION

My aim in this chapter has been to explore how repetition encourages the reader to look for the theological center of the Sinai Complex, even when this center is never explicitly stated. We have seen that in a certain respect biblical writers have chosen to "talk around" the subject of divine cultic presence by actually presenting several perspectives in the canonical Sinai Complex. The choice of biblical writers to "talk around" the subject of divine presence, rather than to advocate a single position, should in no way be viewed as a retreat from their task; it merely underscores the inability of language to have the final word on the subject. And I would venture that it is precisely because of this point that repetition acquires such a central role in the canonical Sinai Complex. Kawin, in his book *Telling It Again and Again*, states the point well in quoting Qoheleth: " 'Man cannot utter it,' but he can utter around it. He can, through repetition, 'make it manifest.' "[59] Our exploration of mimesis and ungrounded doubling has underscored a number of ways in which repetition within the canonical Sinai Complex makes manifest the presence of God.

Our study of mimesis has underscored the important role of tradition history in the canonical Sinai Complex by demonstrating how redaction creates mimesis, and how mimetic repetition plays a key role in interrelating the distinct traditions within this material. We saw in particular how the Mountain of God tradition acquires a unifying function as an archetype in the canonical Sinai Complex, through its subordination to the deuteronomistic and priestly redactions. The result of this subordination is an inner relationship between traditions, in which a theology of divine presence in Torah is presented to the reader as a movement from divine immanence in Zion (metaphor) to the qualified presence of Horeb and Sinai (metonymy). Canon, therefore, from the perspective of mimesis is "frozen motion," and this insight underscores how insufficient it would be simply to interpret the qualified theologies of divine presence in Horeb and Sinai without taking into account their tradition-historical relationship to Zion as it is reflected in the canonical Sinai Complex.

Thus, from the perspective of mimesis, Zion, with its theology of divine immanence, is the theological center in the canonical Sinai Complex, even though it is subordinated to the subsequent redactions. When it is anchored in the past, Zion unifies the canonical Sinai Complex as an ideal archetype that makes Horeb and Sinai possible; in the present Zion provides a critical point of unity between Horeb and Sinai, by representing what a theology of divine presence cannot be; and finally, as a future hope Zion once again becomes an ideal. And is this not

[59] Kawin, *Telling It Again and Again*, 7-8.

also the role of Zion in the larger canon, where the utopian ideal of divine immanence is anchored in the *Urzeit* of the garden and shot off into the distant future through apocalyptic visions of the *Endzeit*, even while the reader is denied it as a present reality?

The denial of Zion as a present reality underscores how mimesis alone is insufficient to create a unified theology of divine presence within Torah. However, when we shift our focus from the past to the present (and thus leave Zion behind) we do not leave behind the problem of repetition. It simply changes form from mimesis to ungrounded doubling between Sinai and Horeb. Unlike mimesis, ungrounded doubling allows neither for subordination between the elements that make up the repetition, nor for an archetype that might provide a basis for interpretation. Instead, we saw that ungrounded doubling arises from a priestly canon-conscious redaction, in which priestly tradents displace the deuteronomistic interpretation of divine presence on Horeb with their own vision of Sinai, while also creating links between the two. The result of this redaction is that the fundamentally different symbols of Sinai and Horeb are presented to the reader as being the one revelation of God on the mountain. This presumption of biblical unity in the story of Torah actually heightens the demand for interpretation, so that a quest for unity becomes almost involuntary on the part of the reader.

The inherent relationship between text and reader (between canon and community) that arises from ungrounded doubling serves an important function in probing the present reality of God within the worshipping community, for it implies that in the end the unity of Sinai/Horeb cannot be located in the text, but must be fashioned by the reader into an opaque similarity in light of the text. This conclusion was already implicit in our examination of the metonymic quality of the symbols of Sinai and Horeb, since if the text gave the final word concerning the character of divine presence, it would itself become another form of Zion. Biblical writers and editors have resisted this temptation, and instead of shifting the metaphorical and immanent presence of God from cult to text, they have chosen to "talk around" the subject of divine presence, and thus make it manifest through repetition.

Chapter 6

THE SOCIAL CONTEXT OF THE CANONICAL
SINAI COMPLEX

Our study of cosmic mountain symbolism in the Sinai Complex requires that we move beyond the literature itself and explore the social context that has given rise to it. The reason for
this extrinsic focus is because symbols are inherently institutional and sociological. This aspect of symbols was underscored
in the opening chapter when we noted that symbols only exist
for a well defined group of users.[1] And, indeed, this social aspect
of symbols has already entered our study at a number of points.
For instance, frequent reference has been made in the preceding chapters to deuteronomistic and priestly editors in Exodus
19-24. We noted that the compilation of the two Mosaic legislations is usually assigned to the later pre-exilic/exilic (Deuteronomistic) and exilic/post-exilic (Priestly) periods, even though
each contains material from earlier periods. We have seen how
these traditions contain very different visions of what Israel
should be, and how each tradition has claimed divine authority
for its version of the Mosaic legislation by anchoring its law code
in the account of theophany in Exodus 19-24. We also noted
that the two legislative traditions reflect contrasting theologies
of divine presence that are critical of pre-exilic Zion-Sabaoth
theology, and that each is anchored in its own particular cultic
Sitz im Leben. Finally, past research into the social context of
deuteronomistic and priestly traditions would add a geographical distinction between the two during the exilic period. It is
argued that deuteronomistic tradition is associated with a group
in Palestine in contrast to priestly tradition, which is associated
with a Babylonian group.[2] These differences result in the fol-

---

[1] Ducrot and Todorov, *Encyclopedic Dictionary*, 100.
[2] For arguments in favor of a Palestinian setting of the exilic compilation of the
deuteronomic legislation see M. Noth, *Überlieferungsgeschichtliche Studien I: Die
Sammelnden und bearbeitenden Geschichteswerke in Alten Testaments*, Schriften
der Königsberger Gelehrten Gesellschaft 18/2; 2nd ed. (Tübingen: Max Niemeyer,
1957) 96-107; E. Janssen, *Juda in der Exilzeit: Eine Beitrag zur Frage der Entstehung des Judentums*, FRLANT 69 (Göttingen: Vandenhoeck und Ruprecht,

lowing contrasting profiles of two groups:

	"Deuteronomistic Group"	"Priestly Group"
(1) Location	Palestine	Babylon
(2) Authorittive Law	Deuteronomic Legislation	Priestly Legislation
(3) Cultic *Sitz im Leben*	The law is supported by an interpretation of the presence of God as speech (Name Theology) revealed on Mount Horeb	The law is supported by an interpretation of the presence of God as fire (Kabod Theology) revealed on Mount Sinai
(4) Leadership	Leaders are idealized as charismatic teachers of law	Leaders are idealized as priestly mediators of law
(5) Social Vision of Israel	Exclusive in focus	Universal in scope

A thorough analysis of the developing social contexts of the "Deuteronomistic" and "Priestly" groups is well beyond the scope of this study, and such an analysis will not be part of this chapter. However, our study would be incomplete if we did not at least begin to probe the more limited social context of the canonical Sinai Complex, and for this Gottwald provides a point of departure. He writes in an article entitled, "Social Matrix and Canonical Shape," that "the very act of canonization. . .is. . .a thoroughly social act conditioned by a social locus in which this particular canon won out over other possible canons or over against resistance to canonization itself."[3] And because canonical literature is not socially disinterested, Gottwald argues that the interpreter must look for *two types* of social tensions within the text: one tension concerns conflicts over what is included and excluded within the canonical text; the other tension concerns the interrelationship of traditions that are in fact included within the canonical text.[4] Gottwald cautions that without seeing these social tensions within the text "canonical criticism may lapse into harmonization that simply accepts a communal decision to validate a collection and arrangement of

1956) 26-54; H. W. Wolff, "The Kerygma of the Deuteronomic Historical Work," *The Vitality of Old Testament Traditions*, W. Brueggemann and H. W. Wolff, 2nd ed. (Atlanta: John Knox Press, 1982) 84. However, compare Ackroyd (*Exile and Restoration*, 66-68) who is less certain about the location of the deuteronomistic tradents. For arguments in favor of a Babylonian setting for the exilic compilation of the priestly legislation see O. Eissfeldt, *The Old Testament: An Introduction*, 206-7; Ackroyd, *Exile and Restoration*, 85; and J. G. Vink, "The Date and Origin of the Priestly Code in the Old Testament," 50 *et passim*.
[3] N. K. Gottwald, "Social Matrix and Canonical Shape," *TToday* 42 (1985) 315.
[4] Gottwald, "Social Matrix and Canonical Shape," 315.

literature as somehow overcoming, flattening out, and resolving all the prior and continuing socio-religious struggle in the community."[5] And such a development, he concludes, may in the end actually obscure the nature and purpose of canonical authority.[6]

The tension of competing traditions *within* the canonical text that was noted by Gottwald is of particular interest for our study because of the argument in the previous chapter concerning the canon-conscious character of the priestly redaction, with its two aims: to provide a narrative context for priestly legislation, and to relate the deuteronomic and priestly legislations as one Torah. Thus, central to our definition of canon-consciousness is the acknowledgement that within the canonical Sinai Complex there is tension between competing traditions. In fact, the absence of literary unity (which appears to be a central component of the canon-conscious character of the priestly redaction) suggests that the canonical Sinai Complex might be aimed more at unifying distinct groups than at harmonizing the literature itself. And this tendency raises the more social based question concerning what type of relationship is being envisioned between the Deuteronomistic and Priestly groups in the canonical Sinai Complex.

Our exploration into the social context of the canonical Sinai Complex will separate into two sections; in each section the canon-conscious character of the priestly redaction will remain a central point of focus. In the first section, we will interpret the participants in the Vision of God on the mountain in Exod 24:9-11 as representing a compromise between the Deuteronomistic and Priestly groups, which gives canonical status to both of their legislations. We will see how the vision of social unity as a compromise between distinct and even competing groups in the exilic and post-exilic periods is the result of the canon-conscious priestly redaction. The second section will change the focus of study from profiling the distinct groups in Exod 24:9-11 to raising the question of the occasion for the priestly redaction. Here, we can do little more than note general circumstances which allow for an association of the priestly redaction (and thus the canonical Sinai Complex) with the mission of Ezra.

[5] Gottwald, "Social Matrix and Canonical Shape," 315.
[6] Gottwald, "Social Matrix and Canonical Shape," 316-17.

I

THE PARTICIPANTS IN THE VISION OF GOD
ON THE COSMIC MOUNTAIN IN
EXOD 24:9-11

Exod 24:9-11 recounts a Vision of God and a meal on the cosmic mountain in which Moses, Aaron, seventy elders, and Nadab and Abihu all participate. The large cast of characters presently included in this text has caused problems for past interpreters. Noth concluded that reference to so many characters was striking in such a short pericope, and what was even more problematic for him was that not all the characters appeared to have a clear function in the canonical text.[7] I would certainly agree with Noth that there are a striking number of characters in Exod 24:9-11, and that their numbers have most certainly grown in the tradition-historical development of this text. I would disagree, however, with his conclusion that some of the characters lack function in the canonical text.

My aim in this section is to demonstrate that all the participants in Exod 24:9-11 have clear function in the canonical text. The important role of Moses will be explored in the following section when we interpret his role in Exod 24:9-11 in light of the social function of Ezra. Thus, our interpretation of the "leaders of the people of Israel" (*ăṣîlê běnê yiśrā'ēl*) in Exod 24:9-11 within this section will separate into three parts: the seventy elders, Aaron, and Nadab and Abihu. I hope to demonstrate that the seventy elders and Aaron represent the Deuteronomistic and Priestly groups, and that Nadab and Abihu represent a canon-conscious priestly compromise which is meant to forge links between the two groups.

A. *The Seventy Elders*

Interpretation of the seventy elders as representing the Deuteronomistic group will proceed in two stages. First, a brief summary of the role of the elders (*zěqānîm*) in general as representatives of the people in the history of Israel will provide a starting point for interpreting the seventy elders in Exod 24:9-11. And second, an interpretation of the two additional instances in which the seventy elders are mentioned in the He

---

[7] Noth, *History of Pentateuchal Traditions*, 186. For further discussion see Perlitt, *Bundestheologie*, 183; Nicholson, "The Antiquity of the Tradition in Exodus xxiv 9-11," 75; Zenger *Sinaitheophanie*, 73; Vriezen "Exegesis of Exodus xxiv 9-11," 106; and H. Valentin, *Aaron*, 400.

brew Bible, namely Num 11:16 and Ezek 8:11, will provide more specific background for identifying them in Exod 24:9-11.

In his article, "Exodus 24,9-11 als Beispiel lebendiger Erzähltradition aus der Zeit des babylonischen Exil," Ruprecht provides a summary of the leadership role of elders in Israelite history, and he concludes that they most clearly represented the people at two particular points—in the premonarchical and exilic periods. Two stories in particular suggest that elders may have enjoyed a central role of leadership in the premonarchical period, during the transition to the monarchy. The elders play a central role as the representatives of Gilead in the story of Jephthah (Judg 11:4), and they assume a leadership role in making a request to Samuel for a monarch (1 Sam 8:4).[8] The elders appear to retain some local judicial power during the monarchy period, where they also represent the people in public worship.[9] But, according to Ruprecht, they reemerge in the exilic period with new importance both in public worship and in governing the people. The central role of the elders in Deuteronomy as the ones who not only receive the law from Moses (Deut 31:9), but also must adjudicate disputes in light of it (e.g., Deut 19:12; 21:2, 3, 4; 21:19, 20; 22:15, 16, 17; 25:7, 8, 9) points to their growing power in this period. And furthermore the appearance of the elders in later post-exilic texts would certainly add support to the presentation of them in Deuteronomy as being significant representatives of the people in matters of both law and worship. Note, for example, how Ezra specifically mentions the governing power of the elders (Ezra 2:68; 3:12) and how Yahweh is described as appearing from Mount Zion before the elders in Isa 24:23.[10]

The growing power of elders in governing the people and in public worship in the exilic period is also reflected in the two instances of the seventy elders in Num 11:16 and Ezek 8:11. Numbers 11 explores the judicial power of the seventy elders in a positive light, while Ezekiel 8 presupposes the influence of this group in matters of worship by providing an argument against their role in the cult.

---

[8] Ruprecht ("Exodus 24,9-11 als Beispiel lebendiger Erzähltradition," 142-43) includes the additional references—Judg 21:16; 1 Sam 8:4; 15:30; 30:26; 2 Sam 3:17; 5:3; 17:4, 15; 19:12.

[9] Ruprecht "Exodus 24,9-11 als Beispiel lebendiger Erzähltradition," 143.

[10] Ruprecht ("Exodus 24,9-11 als Beispiel lebendiger Erzähltradition," 143) notes other texts which include Jer 29:1 (where the prophet addresses the elders in the exile) and Ezek 8:1; 9:6; 14:1; 20:1-3 (where the elders of Judah come and sit before the prophet).

"Seventy from the elders of Israel" (šibʿîm ʾîš mizziqnê yiśrāʾēl) are "set aside" for special divine favor in Num 11:16. This text provides an immediate contact to Exod 24:9-11 by the mention of this special group of seventy, and the contact is made even more firm when the seventy elders are described with the verbal form of the noun ʾaṣîl that was used to describe the leaders on the mountain in Exod 24:11b.[11] More detailed information concerning this group is gained from Num 11:16b where the seventy elders are described as "elders of the people" (ziqnê hāʿām), and "scribes" (sōṭĕrāyw).[12] After their introduction, the reader is told in Num 11:17 that these seventy elders are special because they have received a portion of Moses' spirit for the purpose of assisting him in the government of the people. Thus they are teachers and judges and this authority of theirs is illustrated charismatically in their commission by Moses, for when the spirit of Moses is given to them, they all prophesy momentarily (Num 11:25).

"Seventy elders of Israel" (wĕšibʿîm ʾîš mizziqnê bêt yiśrāʾēl) are also mentioned in Ezek 8:11 in the context of public worship. Ezekiel describes them judgmentally as having censors in their hands as they offer sacrifices to idols (Ezek 8:10-11).[13] In fact, according to the prophet, they are one of the causes for divine judgment (Ezek 8:12).[14] Whether the seventy elders of Israel in Ezekiel 8 represent "an institution, sanctified by ancient tradition," as Zimmerli has argued, is difficult to confirm.[15] But the later addition to the text of a specific leader—Jaazaniah ben-Shaphan—does suggest that a particular group of "seventy elders" was active during the exilic period and that their leader could be named.[16] Ezekiel 8 offers two additional insights into the identity of the seventy elders of Israel. First, this group must be distinguished from the elders of Judah (wĕziqnê yĕhûdâ) in Ezek 8:1, who are sitting before the prophet. And second, the severe judgment of the seventy elders of Israel by Ezekiel suggests that this group may very well represent "a presumptuous intrusion into the cultic sphere" during the exilic period, which was opposed by a priestly group whom Ezekiel

---

[11] For discussion see Vriezen, "Exegesis of Exodus xxiv 9-11," 110.

[12] For discussion see Noth, Numbers, 87.

[13] For discussion of the images of reptiles and beasts in this passage see Zimmerli, Ezekiel I, 240-41.

[14] Zimmerli, Ezekiel I, 241.

[15] Zimmerli, Ezekiel I, 240.

[16] See Zimmerli, (Ezekiel I, 241) for a description of Jaazaniah ben-Shaphan as a redactional insertion.

represented.[17]

When we combine the bits and pieces of information that have risen to the surface in our brief overview of elders in general and the seventy elders in particular, a profile begins to emerge of the role of elders in the exilic period that provides important insight for interpreting the function of the seventy elders in Exod 24:9-11. The seventy elders are charismatic in possessing the spirit of Moses and thus they are able to judge the people, while they are also described as scribes. In addition, they are distinguished from the "elders of Judah," with their own particular leader. Furthermore, the seventy elders also participate in public worship, which is interpreted as a cause of divine judgment by Ezekiel.

This profile, I would suggest, corresponds to the Deuteronomistic group. Elders play an important role both in the deuteronomistic redaction of Exodus 19-24 and in the book of Deuteronomy, and in addition the deuteronomistic tradents emphasized the presence of God as speech and the role of Moses as a charismatic teacher in order to provide a narrative context for the deuteronomic legislation. The presence of the seventy elders on the mountain with Moses in Exod 24:9-11 would provide canonical status for their legislation, and would also firmly anchor their leadership role both in the cult and in governing the people.

B. *Aaron*

The prominent role of Aaron both as the high priest of Israel and as the brother of Moses is judged to be one of the latest tradition-historical developments in the Pentateuch, and it is considered to be the contribution of priestly theologians in the exile.[18] In view of this overall assessment of Aaron in the Pentateuch, his presence on the mountain in Exod 24:9-11 is considered to be a late addition to the text. A closer look at the role of Aaron and the priestly families who trace their lineage through him will illustrate how Aaron functions in Exod 24:9-11 as the representative of the Priestly group.

The function of Aaron in Exod 24:9-11 as the representative of a Priestly group can be described in more detail by examining the late priestly genealogy of Levi in Exod 6:14-24, which in-

[17] See Zimmerli, *Ezekiel I*, 241.
[18] Noth, *History of Pentateuchal Traditions*, 178-82; Valentin, *Aaron*, 409-10 *et passim*.

troduces the genealogy of Aaron.[19] In this genealogy Aaron has assumed a prominent role as the brother of Moses (Exod 6:20), and he is described as having four sons: Nadab, Abihu, Eleazar, and Ithamar (Exod 6:23). The listing of Aaron's four sons in this genealogy provides a starting point for interpreting more specifically the function of Aaron in Exod 24:9-11. In particular note that of Aaron's four sons, only Nadab and Abihu are specifically mentioned in Exod 24:9-11. Eleazar and Ithamar are absent. This particular configuration of priestly representatives in Exod 24:9-11 suggests that Nadab and Abihu acquire a unique function in the present text in distinction from Aaron, since they are specifically mentioned. Further, the absence of Eleazar and Ithamar suggests that Aaron should be interpreted as representing these latter two sons in the public worship service. In other words the absence of Eleazar and Ithamar in a context where two of Aaron's sons are specifically mentioned provides the basis to conclude that Aaron does not simply represent the priesthood in general in Exod 24:9-11, but that he specifically represents the priestly families of Eleazar and Ithamar, who, in turn, represent the Priestly group.

An additional word is necessary concerning Eleazar and Ithamar and their representation through Aaron in Exod 24:9-11. There is certain symmetry in the presentation of Eleazar and Ithamar in the genealogy of Aaron (Exod 6:24), which is reinforced in their equal representation through Aaron in Exod 24:9-11. This symmetry is noteworthy, because these characters represent the priestly families of Zadok and Abiathar, who were rivals in the pre-exilic cult of Jerusalem to the point where the priestly family of Abiathar was banished from Jerusalem.[20] The balance of these rival priestly families suggests that the Priestly group (which we have placed in the exilic/post-exilic periods;) might very well represent a compromise of the priestly family of Zadok (who held power in the pre-exilic cult) and the priestly family of Abiathar (who lost power to the Zadokites in the pre-exilic period, but who are specifically mentioned as being part of the group that accompanies Ezra on his return from Babylon).[21] Such a compromise between competing priestly families should

[19] Compare also Ezra 8:2; 1 Chronicles 5, 24. See Vink, "The Priestly Code," 34-35.
[20] For discussion see R. De Vaux, *Ancient Israel: Its Life and Institutions* (New York: McGraw-Hill, 1961) 372-86, esp. 372 74.
[21] Note how the priestly genealogies of Aaron, which balance the rival families of Zadok and Abiathar, are also tied to Ezra's mission in Ezra 8:2, where the two families are described as returning with Ezra from Babylon. See De Vaux, *Ancient Israel*, 396-97 and Vink, "The Priestly Code," 37.

caution us not to interpret even the distinct groups as being ho-
mogeneous, but to see social tension within their very
formation.[22]

C. *Nadab and Abihu*

At this point in our study we have accounted for the representation of both the Deuteronomistic and Priestly groups in the
seventy elders and in Aaron. Moses, of course, is functioning as
an ideal for both groups, and thus his presence in Exod 24:9-11
is also accounted for. However, the presence of Nadab and
Abihu has caused problems for past interpreters. They clearly
represent the priesthood along with Aaron, but their presence
in such an important event does not conform to an expected
Tendenz of a priestly redaction, because the only event for
which they are remembered outside of Exod 24:9-11 is their
apostasy during public worship in Lev 10:1-2, where they are
killed by Yahweh.[23] In view of this situation, Nadab and Abihu
have been judged to lack function in the canonical form of Exod
24:9-11.[24]

---

[22] de Vaux (*Ancient Israel*, 396) suggests, for example, that some form of compromise between the priestly families of Zadok and Abiathar was reached during the
exile.

[23] Beyerlin (*Oldest Sinaitic Traditions*, 16, n. 105) states both the problem and the
reigning solution, namely that these characters are in the text because they are so
deeply rooted in this tradition. He writes: "The hypothesis that Nadab and Abihu
were only inserted by the Priestly redactor. . .is hardly correct, since both are dis-
qualified in Lev x 1. Their names would have been omitted at such a central point
of the tradition as Exod xxiv 1a, if their position had not been securely attested
from an early date." See also Nicholson, "The Antiquity of the Tradition in Exodus
xxiv 9-11," 75, and "The Origin of the Tradition in Exodus xxiv 9-11," 152.

[24] Noth (*History of Pentateuchal Traditions*, 162, 186-87) concluded that Nadab
and Abihu were part of the independent tradition of Exod 24:1, 9-11 and not the
product of a priestly redaction. He reasoned that these characters were harmonized with Aaron by priestly redactors who incorporated them into the genealogies
of Aaron when the latter was added to Exod 24:1, 9-11, and that once this harmonization took place, Nadab and Abihu no longer had function in the text. R. Gradwohl ("Das 'Fremde Feuer' von Nadab und Abihu," *ZAW* 75 [1963] 289-95) has
taken a different approach for uncovering the tradition-historical background of
Nadab and Abihu by focusing on Leviticus 10, where their death is narrated. He
concluded that the two sons of Aaron are a veiled reference to the two sons of
Jeroboam I, Nadab and Abijah, and thus they represent a priestly polemic from the
exilic period against the cult set up by Jeroboam I. The problem with this interpretation is that Abihu and Abijah are not the same. In fact, if near parallels are the
criterion for comparison then there is yet another analogy, namely the sons of
Shammai, Nadab and Abishur in the genealogy of Judah found in 1 Chr 2:28-30.
For a similar interpretation to Gradwohl's see M. Aberbach and L. Smolar, "Aaron,
Jeroboam, and the Golden Calves," *JBL* 86 (1967) 134.

My aim in this section is to demonstrate that Nadab and Abihu do have a function in the present form of Exod 24:9-11 as characters who represent a limitation of priestly power in public worship, and that consequently they reflect a compromise between Aaron (the Priestly group) and the seventy elders (the Deuteronomistic group), which is embedded in the canonical text itself.

An overview of the occurrences of Nadab and Abihu in the Hebrew Bible will illustrate their peculiar role in the canonical Pentateuch. Nadab and Abihu are mentioned ten times in the Hebrew Bible (Exod 6:23-24; 24:1, 9; 28:1; Lev 10:1-2; Num 3:2, 4; 26:60; 1 Chr 5:29; 24:1). Only once do they have a clearly defined role, namely in Lev 10:1-2, where they offer "strange fire" (*'ēš zārâ*) before Yahweh during public worship, for which they are immediately destroyed by fire from God. In addition to the ten specific references to Nadab and Abihu, two further instances in the Pentateuch should be noted, since Leviticus 16 and Numbers 16 refer to the circumstances of the death of these characters without specifically mentioning their names. Thus we can broaden the scope of our study of Nadab and Abihu to twelve instances in the Hebrew Bible. These references can be divided between the Pentateuch (Exod 6:23-24; 24:1, 9; 28:1; Lev 10:1-2; 16; Num 3:2, 4; 16; 26:60) and Chronicles (1 Chr 5:29; 24:1). The distinction between the pentateuchal references and Chronicles will highlight a slightly different perspective on these characters, which will aid us in seeing their role as compromise characters in the canonical Pentateuch. The presentation of Nadab and Abihu in the Pentateuch will be examined before the occurrences in Chronicles.

As we have already noted, the starting point for interpreting the function of Nadab and Abihu in the Pentateuch must be Lev 10:1-2, where their apostasy and subsequent deaths are narrated. The account of the death of Nadab and Abihu takes place in the larger context of public worship, which begins in Leviticus 9. This worship service is inaugurated with sacrifices that are offered by Moses, Aaron and his sons, and the elders of Israel (*lĕziqnê yiśrā'ēl*) in Lev 9:1-21. Thus we should note that the public service of worship includes the same cast of characters as Exod 24:9-11.

The sacrifices in Lev 9:1-21 are followed by a cultic theophany in Lev 9:22-24, which takes place before the Tent of Meeting. Three features of this theophany are noteworthy and they provide the immediate context for the cultic actions of Nadab and Abihu in Lev 10:1-2. First, the authoritative role of Aaron is emphasized in his close association with Moses, in his ability to enter the Tent of Meeting, and in his leadership role during the sacrifices. Second, the priestly vision of the cultic presence of God as the Kabod Yahweh is underscored. And third, the primary focus of the appearance of the Kabod Yahweh is to "all the people" (*hā'ām*, vv. 22, 23; *kŏl-hā'ām*, v. 24), and not simply to Aaron and Moses, or even to the priesthood in general. It is in the midst of this public theophany that Nadab and Abihu are distinguished from Aaron, Moses, and the rest of the priesthood by undertaking their own cultic ritual. The activity is described in the following manner:

> Now Nadab and Abihu, the sons of Aaron
> each took his censer (*maḥtātô*)
> and put fire ('*ēš*) in it,
> and laid incense (*qĕtōret*)
> and offered strange fire ('*ēš zārâ*) before Yahweh
> which was not commanded them.
> And fire came forth from before Yahweh,
> and devoured them.
> And they died before Yahweh. (Lev 10:1-2)

It is difficult to interpret the apostasy of Nadab and Abihu from the description of their actions.[25] The most that we can conclude from this is that their transgression is associated with an incense offering, which they present before Yahweh on their own initiative.

The larger context in which their actions are narrated provides a few more clues for interpretation. In particular, the juxtaposition of their separate action in Lev 10:1-2 to the preceding focus on "all the people" (*kŏl-hā'ām*) in Lev 9:24 suggests that they are killed for offering private sacrifices during public worship, which shifted the focus away from "all the people." This interpretation is reinforced by the events which immediately follow their deaths. When Moses interprets the death of Nadab and Abihu to Aaron in the following verse, he turns the focus back on "all the people," when he states to Aaron:

biqrōbāy 'eqqādēš

---

[25] Gradwohl ("Das 'Fremde Feuer' von Nadab and Abihu," 288-92) suggests that their offense is that their fire did not come from the altar. But the text gives no indication of this. J. C. H. Laughlin ("The "Strange Fire" of Nadab and Abihu," *JBL* 95 [1976] 559-65) sees both a priestly polemic and a polemic against Zoroastrian religion in the emphasis on fire.

wĕ'al-pĕnê kŏl-hā'ām 'ekkābēd
Among those who draw near me I will show myself
holy
and before all the people I will be glorified. (Lev 10:3)[26]

The narrative context of Lev 10:1-2 suggests that Nadab and
Abihu are killed by Yahweh for overstepping their priestly role
in public worship by offering private sacrifices. Their death,
therefore, is not being praised by Moses "as having contrib-
uted. . . to the glorification of Yahweh."[27] Instead, it is a reproach against the priesthood for having shifted the focus of
public worship away from the people. Several additional features of Leviticus 10 support this conclusion. First, after the interpretation of the death of Nadab and Abihu by Moses in Lev
10:3, the reader is told that Aaron held his peace (*wăyyiddōm*)
at the words of Moses. Second, Moses commands that the bodies
of Nadab and Abihu be carried out of the camp. And finally,
Aaron, Eleazar, and Ithamar are not allowed to mourn the death
of Nadab and Abihu, lest they die and anger come upon all the
people. Instead, Moses declares that "all the people of Israel,"
who are "the brothers of the priests" (*wa'ăḥêkem*), will mourn
their death.
     Lev 10:1-2 provides the necessary background for interpret-
ing the function of Nadab and Abihu in Exod 24:9-11. Although
they are clearly priestly characters, they stand in contrast to
Aaron (as well as Eleazar and Ithamar) by representing a limitation of priestly power in public worship. This limitation of
priestly power is vividly symbolized in their divine execution
when they overstep the priestly office by offering private sacrifices of incense during public worship.
     However, the limitation of priestly power in public worship
is also carefully qualified in the canonical Pentateuch both in
Leviticus 16 and in Numbers 16, where the death of Nadab and
Abihu is referred to without the characters being specifically

---

[26] Cross (*Canaanite Myth and Hebrew Epic*, 204) describes this saying as being
"highly eliptical, even mysterious." M. Noth (*Leviticus*, OTL [Philadelphia: Westminster, 1965] 85) described the unit as a traditional and proverbial expression in
parallelistic form. In this case, the two prepositional phrases—*biqrōbay* and *wĕ'al
pĕnê kŏl-hā'ām*—should be interrelated in some way. The ambiguity arises in determining who is being referred to in the first prepositional phrase, "among those
who draw near to me." It could be a reference to the priest who are being admon-
ished not to exclude the people from the cult. In this case the reference would be
to the incense offerings of Nadab and Abihu. A second possibility is that the two
lines are parallel, in which case the reference is to all the people. The emphasis on
"all the people" in the present context favors the second reading.
[27] So Aberbach and Smolar, "Aaron, Jeroboam, and the Golden Calves," 134.

named. An examination of the account of the Day of Atonement in Leviticus 16 and the rebellion of Korah, Dathan, and Abiram in Numbers 16 will illustrate how each of these texts is meant to emphasize the important role of the priests in public worship, and thus qualify the message implied in the death of Nadab and Abihu.

Leviticus 16 consists of instructions to Aaron concerning his special cultic role on the Day of Atonement. This text is aimed at underscoring the unique and central role of the high priest over against the people, and thus presents a contrast to Lev 10:1-2. In view of this, it is strange that this text would begin by making reference to the death of Nadab and Abihu in the opening verse. This reference makes more sense when we note that the death of these characters is given a slightly different interpretation. The reader is not told that they were killed because they brought "strange fire" near to Yahweh, but simply that they died "in drawing near to God." Lev 16:1b plays down the specific cause of the death of Nadab and Abihu, and uses this qualified interpretation to accentuate the special role of the high priest. The reader is given the impression that since Nadab and Abihu died simply from "drawing near to God" the presence of God is dangerous, and that a special high priest like Aaron, who is specially sanctified (Lev 16:2-14), is required to represent the people before God on the Day of Atonement.

The emphasis on the role of Aaron as high priest in Leviticus 16 is applied to the priests in general through the account of the rebellion of Korah, Dathan, and Abiram in Numbers 16. Although this narrative has certainly undergone a complex tradition-historical development, in its canonical form it too appears to be aimed at qualifying the message implied in the death of Nadab and Abihu by underscoring the need for the priesthood in public worship.[28] A brief overview of Numbers 16 will illustrate this point.

The power of the priesthood is challenged at the outset of this story when an argument is presented to Moses that all the congregation of Israel is holy, and that therefore all the people should be equal in worship (Num 16:3). This argument is reminiscent of Moses' reproach to Aaron in Lev 10:3 immediately

---

[28] For discussion of the possible tradition-historical development of this narrative as reflecting disputes between priestly families see G. W. Coats, *The Murmuring Motif in the Wilderness Traditions of the Old Testament: Rebellion in the Wilderness* (Nashville: Abingdon Press, 1968) 257-60; Noth, *Numbers*, 120-31; Cross, *Canaanite Myth and Hebrew Epic*, 205-6.

after the death of Nadab and Abihu. However, in Numbers 16
Moses takes on a somewhat different role. Instead of supporting
this challenge to priestly power, as Lev 10:3 might suggest he
would, he defers an answer to God. Thus, Moses instructs those
who oppose priestly power, to "take censers, put fire in them
and put incense upon them before " (Num 16:6), which mirrors
the actions of Nadab and Abihu in Lev 10:1-2. When the rebel-
lious group follows the instructions of Moses they too are destroyed by Yahweh as were the sons of Aaron.

There are clear literary links between the death of Nadab
and Abihu in Lev 10:1-2 and the rebellion by Korah, Dathan,
and Abiram in Numbers 16.[29] Yet, in spite of these links, reference to Nadab and Abihu is avoided in Numbers 16 as was the
case in Leviticus 16. Numbers 16 also departs from Lev 10:1-2
by playing down the negative interpretation of their death as
was the case in Leviticus 16, only this time the qualified interpretation is used to accentuate the power of the priesthood in
general, rather than the special role of the high priest. The aim
of Numbers 16 to underscore the special status of the priesthood
becomes particularly evident in the conclusion to the story. After the earth has swallowed the group that has challenged
priestly power, the reader is told that their censers were ham-
mered out as a covering for the altar. The reason for this action
is stated in Num 16:40a: "so that no one who is not a priest, who
is not of the descendants of Aaron, should draw near to burn
incense before Yahweh."

In summary both Leviticus 16 and Numbers 16 have made
reference to Lev 10:1-2 in such a way as to qualify the message
implied in the death of Nadab and Abihu—that they represent a
limitation of priestly power in public worship. Leviticus 16 af-
firms the special role of Aaron as high priest, while Numbers 16
makes it clear that there is a sharp distinction between the
priesthood in general and the laity.

As we stated at the outset, reference to Nadab and Abihu is
not limited to the Pentateuch, but extends into Chronicles. The
reference to these characters in Chronicles is noteworthy because no mention is made of their cultic transgression in Lev
10:1-2. Twice in Chronicles they are referred to as being sons of
Aaron and in each of these contexts their names are placed
alongside those of Eleazar and Ithamar. In 1 Chr 5:29 they are
referred to without comment, while in 1 Chr 24:1 their lack of
progeny is simply explained as the result of their premature

---

[29] See Gradwohl, "Das 'Fremde Feuer' von Nadab und Abihu," 290.

deaths. These two references to Nadab and Abihu in Chronicles suggest that their function in representing a limitation of priestly power in public worship is limited to the Pentateuch.

D. *Conclusion*

We have reached a point where we can summarize the role of the participants in Exod 24:9-11, and in the process we can also make several conclusions concerning both the canon-conscious quality of the priestly redaction and the social context of the canonical Sinai Complex.

First, we must conclude that all the characters have function in the canonical form of Exod 24:9-11. The seventy elders represent the Deuteronomistic group, while Aaron represents the Priestly group, which consists of at least the priestly families of Zadok and Abiathar. In addition we have seen that Nadab and Abihu have a specific function in the canonical text in distinction from Aaron. In particular, although they are priestly representatives, they now stand between Aaron and the seventy elders by symbolizing a limitation of priestly power in public worship, which reflects a compromise with regard to the cult between the Deuteronomistic and Priestly groups, each of whom anchor their authority in Moses. This compromise is carefully qualified in Leviticus 16 and in Numbers 16, and it is limited to the Torah.

Second, the function of Nadab and Abihu provides additional insight into the canon-conscious quality of the priestly redaction. At this point in our study we can conclude that canon-consciousness is not simply a literary attempt to link "one canonical book. . .to some other canonical book," but is also an attempt to link competing groups, which are profiled in the literature. The unexpected function of Nadab and Abihu in Exod 24:9-11 provides an illustration of how the priestly redactors are attempting to create such a link between themselves and the Deuteronomistic group. Rather than undercutting the position of the seventy elders in Exod 24:9-11, they have taken into account the authority of the competing group by the manner in which they have shaped the canonical text. This of course is true not simply of the characters in Exod 24:9-11, but also of the relationship between the deuteronomistic and priestly redactions throughout the canonical Sinai Complex.

The third and final conclusion concerns the date and social context of the canon-conscious priestly redaction. Earlier we noted that although the priestly legislation may in fact contain pre-exilic tradition, its compilation and present redactional context should be placed in the exilic/post-exilic periods. Ezekiel 8 suggests that a date for a compromise between the Deuteronomistic and Priestly groups should be sometime later than the exilic period. The reason for this is that the severe judgment against the seventy elders of Israel by the prophet Ezekiel would imply that these groups are still competing for authority during the exilic period. In view of this situation, the most likely date for such a compromise would be the post-exilic period, and there are several reasons for associating the priestly redaction (and the canonical Sinai Complex) with the mission of Ezra.

II
THE "CANON-CONSCIOUS" PRIESTLY
REDACTION
AND THE MISSION OF EZRA

The association of priestly tradition with the mission of Ezra is hardly a novel thesis. One of the central features of Ezra's mission, as it is described in Ezra 7-10 and in Nehemiah 8-10, is that he is commissioned by Artaxerxes to return to Jerusalem and "to make inquires about Judah and Jerusalem according to the law of. . .God, which is in [his] hand" (Ezra 7:13). This particular reference to the law of God in the hands of Ezra has prompted scholars to conclude that Ezra actually possessed codified religious law, and that it might very well have been either the priestly source,[30] or the Pentateuch as a whole.[31] I too am suggesting that the law book of Ezra is the Pentateuch, but I would add that it is a Pentateuch which is self-consciously formed by priestly redactors to combine the authoritative religious legislation of the distinct Deuteronomistic and Priestly groups into one literary Torah. A number of literary, tradition-historical, and social factors support this conclusion.

A starting point for associating the mission of Ezra with the Pentateuch is the frequent reference to a written Torah. Note, for instance, how in the commissioning of Ezra by Artaxerxes reference is made to a particular "law of God" that Ezra "holds in his hands" (Ezra 7:12). This law, we are told, is the "Torah of Moses" (Ezra 7:6) and the "Torah of Yahweh" (Ezra 7:10). Furthermore, when we read on in v. 10, we learn that the mission of Ezra is to teach this Torah to Israel. Yet to conclude from this

[30] See, for example, G. Fohrer, *History of Israelite Religion* (New York: Nashville, 1972) 358.
[31] So Wellhausen, *Prolegomena*, 497.

reference that the "Torah" of Ezra is the Pentateuch is premature. In fact the present study has illustrated how this "Torah" could very well be the deuteronomistic legislation, since Moses plays a primary role in it,[32] or perhaps even the priestly legislation. Nevertheless, closer examination of the character of Ezra in Ezra 7-10 and the content of his message in Nehemiah 8-10 suggests that this "Torah of Moses" is a combination of these legislations, and thus that the mission of Ezra concerns the promulgation of the canonical Sinai Complex.

One reason for associating the mission of Ezra with the Pentateuch is his characterization in Ezra 7-10 and its correspondence to Moses in the canonical Pentateuch. In our interpretation of the deuteronomistic and priestly redactions we have seen how Moses is idealized in each tradition in distinctive roles as teacher of deuteronomic law and mediator for priestly law, and how these roles are combined in the canonical Pentateuch. Thus the character of Moses is one means for combining these legislative traditions, and this is also true in the characterization of Ezra. Like Moses, he is described as being both a priest (hakkōhēn) and a scribe (sōpēr) in Ezra 7:1-6. These similar characteristics raise the question of whether Ezra and his mission might not in fact represent the social compromise between the Deuteronomistic and Priestly groups that is envisioned in the "literary" Moses of the canonical Pentateuch, and also reflected in the participants in the Visio Dei of Exod 24:9-11.

The account of Ezra reading the "Torah of Moses" to Israel in Nehemiah 8-10 adds further support for associating his mission with the promulgation of the Pentateuch. First, the setting of Covenant Renewal in Nehemiah 8-10 for the reading of Torah is similar to the canonical Sinai Complex, where Covenant Renewal in Exodus 34 is also the spring board for the revelation of the priestly (Exodus 35-Numbers 10) and deuteronomic (Book of Deuteronomy) legislations. In the canonical Pentateuch, both of these legislations are the content of Covenant Renewal. This similarity raises the question of whether the reading of Torah by Ezra and the ceremony of Covenant Renewal in Nehemiah 8-10 might not be the Sitz im Leben for the promulgation of the Pentateuch. This hypothesis is supported by an examination of the content of Ezra's review of Heilsgeschichte in his penitential prayer of Nehemiah 9. Clearly this prayer reviews the primary

---

[32] This view was advocated by U. Kellermann, "Erwägungen zur Esragesetz," ZAW 80 (1968) 373-385.

sequence of the Pentateuch. However, what is particularly interesting from our study of the canonical Sinai Complex is that when Ezra recounts Exodus 19-24 in this prayer, his description of the revelation of Torah includes both deuteronomistic and priestly interpretations of the event. Thus, we read in Neh 9:13 that Yahweh not only descended (*yrd*) on Mount Sinai, but also spoke (*dbr*) from heaven. This imagery suggests that it is the one literary Torah of the deuteronomic and priestly legislations that is being promulgated in Nehemiah 8-10 as the "Law of Moses."

Finally the historical and social context of the mid- to late fifth century B.C.E. also provide the necessary milieu for the type of compromise that I have argued is reflected in the priestly redaction.[33] It is clear that there is a history of conflict in Judah between distinct groups in the exilic and post-exilic periods, which surfaced over the construction of the temple, and continued to linger throughout the fifth century B.C.E.[34] These

---

[33] A more exact date for the mission of Ezra would require further literary-critical and historical research. For example the arrangement of the texts in Nehemiah 8-10 and in Ezra 7-10 presents a series of literary-critical problems. Ezra and Nehemiah appear together in Nehemiah 8-10 because of the Covenant Renewal ceremony in Nehemiah 8, which is led by Ezra. But the present position of Nehemiah 8 has been judged to be the result of later redactors, who have moved it from its original position between Ezra 8 and 9 in order to associate the mission of Nehemiah with the mission of Ezra. The redactor(s) responsible for this has been judged to be the chronicler (D. J. Clines, *Ezra, Nehemiah, Esther*, NCB [Grand Rapids: Eerdmans, 1984] 9-12); or the compiler of First Esdras (J. M. Myers, *Ezra-Nehemiah*, AB 14 [Garden City, NY: Doubleday, 1965] xlii); or a Maccabean redactor, because Flavius Josephus is unaware of any connection between Ezra and Nehemiah (S. Mowinckel, *Studien zu Buche Ezra-Nehemiah I* [Oslo: Universitatesforlaget, 1964] 45, 50-59). The literary-critical complexities create further historical problems in determining the chronology of Nehemiah and Ezra. One chronology would place the mission of Ezra (458 B.C.E.) before Nehemiah during the reign of Artaxerxes I (so F. M. Cross, "A Reconstruction of the Judean Restoration," *JBL* 94 [1975] 4-18 and Sh. Talmon, "Ezra and Nehemiah," *IDBSup* [Nashville: Abingdon, 1976] 317-28). Another chronology would reverse the two missions and thus place the mission of Ezra (398 B.C.E.) after the mission of Nehemiah during the reign of Artaxerxes II (so J. H. Hayes and J. M. Miller, *Israelite and Judean History*, OTL [Philadelphia: Westminster, 1977] 503-9 and K. Galling, *Studien zur Geschichte Israels im Persischen Zeitalter* [Tübingen: J.C.B. Mohr (Paul Siebeck), 1964] 149-84).

[34] Interpretation of the conflicts in the exilic and post-exilic periods would certainly have to extend beyond the groups that have been profiled in this study. For example, the problem of the "people of the land" has not been addressed (see Ezra 4:4), or the contrast in the Elephantine Papyri between the *gērîm* and the *'ezrāḥîm*. For discussion of these conflicts see, among others, E. W. Nicholson, "The Meaning of the Expression *'am hā'āreṣ* in the Old Testament," *JSS* 10 (1965) 59-66; R. J. Coggins, "The Interpretation of Ezra 4:4," *JTS* 16 (1965) 124-27; Cazelles, "La mission

unresolved conflicts would provide one important motivation for a canon-conscious priestly redaction that is aimed at combining distinct legislations into one literary Torah during the mission of Ezra.[35] In addition, there is an outside factor in the motivation of a canon-conscious priestly redaction during this time period, namely Persian law. The commissioning of Ezra by Artaxerxes to promulgate a codified religious law in Jerusalem has precedent within Persian policy, if the Demotic Papyrus #215 cols c:6-16 is historically reliable.[36] This papyrus contains a decree from Darius to the Egyptian officers, priests and scribes to codify the past Egyptian law of the Pharaohs, of the temple, and of the people (as a basis for provincial law?). The commissioning of Ezra and his subsequent mission to promulgate a Torah might very well be similar to the circumstances reflected in the Demotic Papyrus #215, in which case the "Torah of Moses" would most certainly be a compromise containing all of Israel's religious law, both deuteronomic and priestly.[37]

In conclusion, by advocating that the mission of Ezra is a promulgation not only of the canonical Sinai Complex, but of the canonical Pentateuch as a whole, I am actually associating this mission with priestly tradition, since I have argued that the priestly redaction is canon-conscious. My association of the mission of Ezra with a canon-conscious priestly redaction certainly requires much more detailed tradition-historical study of the Pentateuch as a whole, as well as further study of the historical

d'Esdras," 131; and Grelot, "La dernière étape de la rédaction sacerdotale," 177-79. Ackroyd (*Exile and Restoration*, 149-52) is probably correct when he argues that the conflicts throughout this period should not be too closely identified within one particular group, but that there are probably a number of competing groups in the exile. The present study would support this conclusion, since we have already identified three groups—the priestly families of Zadok and Abiathar, as well as a Deuteronomistic group, which itself probably also breaks down into smaller factions.

[35] For discussion of the aim of Ezra's mission as unifying distinct and rival groups see Cazelles, "La mission d'Esdras," 113-40; Ackroyd, *Exile and Restoration*, 87; and Vink, "The Priestly Code," 51-56.

[36] W. Spiegelberg, *Die Sogenannte Demotische Chronik: Des Pap, 215 der Bibliothèque nationale zu Paris* (Leipzig: J. C. Hinrichs'sche Buchhandlung, 1914) 30-31. See also Hayes and Miller, *Israelite and Judean History*, 515.

[37] The independence of Egypt from the Persians provides further motivation for such a commission to Ezra, since it places the religious disputes in Judah within a larger political context, in which the Persian empire required a stable province on the western border. See Galling, *Studien zur Geschichte Israels im Persischen Zeitalter*, 156. For further discussion of the influence of Persian policy as a possible factor in the mission of Ezra see N. K. Gottwald, *The Hebrew Bible: A Socio-Literary Introduction* (Philadelphia: Fortress, 1985) 434-38.

circumstances concerning the role of Ezra in the post-exilic period. However, the similarities that I have noted between Ezra
and Moses and between the setting of Covenant Renewal for
the promulgation of law in the canonical Sinai Complex and in
the mission of Ezra, encourage further investigation into the
mission of Ezra as the social context for the formation of Torah.
As Gottwald has already reminded us at the outset of this chapter, further study of this period may prove important for understanding the very nature and purpose of canonical authority
itself.

Chapter 7

REDACTION AND THEOLOGY IN THE CANONICAL SINAI COMPLEX

I
REDACTION IN THE SINAI COMPLEX

I stated in the opening chapter that one of my aims in this study was to reassess the tradition history of the Sinai Complex, by advocating that its development was a process of redaction rather than the interweaving of distinct sources. In addition, I suggested that a reassessment of the role of redactors would provide the methodological basis for interpreting not only tradition history, but also the canonical form of the Sinai Complex. In order to achieve these goals I have sought to demonstrate two things: first, that pentateuchal redactors were not "passive tradents," whose primary aim was to preserve tradition, but that they were creative theologians, who have critically transformed tradition; and second, that the canonical Sinai Complex is not "incomprehensible," but, to use Rendtorff's terminology, the result of "planned theological editing." My tradition-historical interpretation of Exodus 19-24 can be summarized in the following manner.

I have argued that the elaborate account of theophany in the canonical form of Exodus 19-24 is rooted in a pre-exilic Mountain of God tradition. This account of theophany included an account of Israel's arrival at an unnamed cosmic mountain (Exod 19:2b-3a); their two-day preparation for theophany (Exod 19:10-11a, 12aa, 13b-15a), along with a description of theophany itself as a thunderstorm (Exod 19:16-17); and, finally, a sacrificial ritual by the "young men of Israel" at the base of the unnamed mountain (Exod 24:4ab-5). Thus, Exodus 19-24 was originally an account of theophany and sacrifice, and not the occasion for the promulgation of divine law.[1] My conclusion that this Mountain of God tradition is a pre-exilic account of theophany arises primarily from the imagery of divine presence that is assumed in the description of theophany. In particular, the static and per-

---

[1] See, for example Levin, "Der Dekalog am Sinai," 189.

manent presence of God, as a thunderstorm on the cosmic
mountain, corresponds most closely with the Zion-Sabaoth theology of the pre-exilic Jerusalem cult. Whether the Mountain of
God tradition is one episode in a larger pre-exilic epic (a JE
Epic?) is a question that must remain open in the absence of a
more broad based study of the tradition-historical development
of the Pentateuch.

What has become clear from this study is that the theology of
divine presence represented in Mountain of God tradition is
critically evaluated by deuteronomistic and priestly tradents,
who also seek to anchor their distinctive legislations in the theophany of Exodus 19-24 as the content of the mountaintop revelation to Moses. Although our study did not explore the
tradition-historical development of the deuteronomic (Book of
the Covenant, Book of Deuteronomy) and priestly (Exod 25-31,
35-Numbers 10) legislations, nevertheless, by focusing on the
tradition history of Exodus 19-24, I have argued that each law-
code emerges into Torah by means of a "pentateuchal" redaction; and that the formative period in the compilation of these
law codes within the story of Torah is the late pre-exilic/exilic
(deuteronomistic) and exilic/post-exilic (priestly) periods. These
redactions of the Mountain of God tradition can be summarized
in the following manner.

Deuteronomistic redactors significantly expand the pre-exilic Mountain of God tradition by anchoring the deuteronomic
legislation in this event, so that theophany in Exodus 19-24 becomes an occasion for covenant and the promulgation of law.
Consequently, the arrival of Israel at the cosmic mountain becomes the setting for a divine Proposal of Covenant, in which
Israel is envisioned as being an exclusive people (Exod 19:3b-
5ba, 6b-8a); theophany becomes an occasion for the promulgation of law (Exod 19:8b-9a, 19; 20:1-20); and the sacrificial ritual
is transformed into a Covenant-Closing Ceremony (Exod 20:21-
23:33; 24:3-4aa, 7). Furthermore, we have seen that the deuteronomistic redactors do not simply transform a pre-exilic narrative about theophany and sacrifice into an account of theophany
and law; in so doing they have also qualified Zion-Sabaoth theology with a vision of the impermanent auditory presence of God,
which corresponds to Mount Horeb.

Priestly redactors provide yet further additions to the
deuteronomistic account of theophany and law, in order also to
anchor their legislation in this event. Under the influence of
priestly redactors, the revelation at the mountain is given a new
setting in the "wilderness of Sinai" and the initial Proposal of

Covenant acquires yet another promise, which is universal in scope (Exod 19:12a, 5bb-6a). In it we are told that Israel will be a holy nation, and that this kingdom of priests will not be separate from, but will actually be in service to the other nations. In addition theophany becomes an experience of the impermanent presence of God as fire on Mount Sinai (Exod 19:11b, 12ab-13, 15b, 16aa, 18, 20-25), while the deuteronomistic Covenant-Closing Ceremony is reframed into a Sanctification Ceremony of the people (Exod 24:1-2, 6, 8, 9-11, 15b-18a), which culminates in the revelation of the priestly legislation (Exodus 25-31).

My conclusion that the theophany of Yahweh on Mount Sinai is a priestly innovation, which is meant to qualify Zion-Sabaoth theology, is perhaps the most startling tradition-historical conclusion to arise from this study. However, it is not without precedent. The peculiar distribution of the references to Mount Sinai in the Hebrew Bible and the absence of Mount Sinai in the pre-exilic prophetic literature were already problems for Wellhausen.[2] And, furthermore, the persistence of these problems for any tradition-historical study of the roots of Mount Sinai is evident when we note that they still provided the starting point for von Rad's penetrating essay on "The Form-Critical Problem of the Hexateuch,"[3] and have recently been brought to light again by Booij,[4] whose conclusions overlap at several points with the present study.

The additional description in Chapters 5-6 of the priestly redaction as being canon-conscious provided a means for interpreting the canonical Sinai Complex in light of its tradition-historical development. I have used the term canon-conscious to account for redactional devices by priestly tradents, which indicate that they are not simply attempting to create a narrative context for their legislation, but are also attempting to relate the deuteronomic and priestly legislations as one literary Torah. At times priestly redactors have forced new readings to create a link between the distinct legislations and the groups profiled within them, as, for example, in the two promises within the Proposal of Covenant, where priestly redactors forced the reader to qualify the exclusive focus of the deuteronomic promise. At other times, priestly redactors have created ambiguity, which forces the reader to acknowledge conflicting interpretations in the canonical text. Through ambiguity, priestly tradents encourage the reader to interpret the Decalogue as shared To-

---

2 Wellhausen, *Prolegomena*, 343-45.
3 Von Rad, "Problem of the Hexateuch," 1-25.
4 Booij, "Mountain and Theophany," 1-3.

rah, and the content of the tablets as both deuteronomic and priestly legislation. They even encourage a reading of Exodus 24 as being both a Covenant-Closing and a Sanctification Ceremony. Finally, our study of canon-conscious redaction has underscored how priestly tradent were willing to use the priestly figures of Nadab and Abihu in an unexpected way—as compromise characters, whose presence in Torah now creates a link between competing groups.

We have seen in this study that the aim of canon-conscious priestly tradents has certainly been to fashion a story—a narrative of law if you will, which we are encouraged to read as a single whole. Yet the story of the one revelation in Exodus 19-24 is not a unified narrative, since at many points priestly redactors have gone out of their way not to harmonize the dissimilar traditions. Instead, the canonical Sinai Complex confronts the reader with distinct versions of what might best be described as the "Mosaic Legislation," through a two-stage process. The revelation of law begins in Exodus 19-24 with the shared Torah of the Decalogue, the deuteronomic Book of the Covenant and the priestly Cultic Legislation. This initial revelation is followed by the legislation of Covenant Renewal in Exodus 34, which provides an overarching structure to the remainder of the Pentateuch. The revelation of the priestly legislation on Mount Sinai is one stage in Israel's wilderness travels, while the revelation of the deuteronomic legislation on Mount Horeb is a speech by Moses at the end of Israel's wilderness travels. Thus, there is design in bringing together these potentially competing traditions by placing them within the chronology of a story, but the distinct law-codes themselves are not harmonized.

Such design suggests that neither tradition-history nor literary criticism can be ignored in any interpretation of the canonical Sinai Complex. I would hope that this study aids in calling into question the dichotomy that is developing in contemporary biblical study between tradition-historians, who stress only the disunity of pentateuchal narrative and thus ignore the canonical text, and literary critics, who often assume too quickly a unity to pentateuchal narrative by ignoring the tradition history of the text.[5]

---

[5] For a more detailed examination of this problem in contemporary biblical studies see Damrosch, *The Narrative Covenant.*

II
Theology in the Sinai Complex

My second aim in this study has been to interpret the theologies of divine presence in the Sinai Complex through an investigation of cosmic mountain symbolism in Exodus 19-24. Our study of the mountain setting has underscored both how the mountain functions as a signifier of divine presence, and how the symbolic character of the mountain changes at the hands of different tradents. These insights have provided the basis for identifying three theologies of divine cultic presence in the tradition-historical development of the Sinai Complex, which are associated with distinct cosmic mountains. I have argued first, that the static and permanent presence of God in the Mountain of God tradition, as dwelling on the cosmic mountain, symbolizes a metaphoric relationship of resemblance between God and the mountain, which is reminiscent of Mount Zion in pre-exilic Israel; second, that the mobile imagery of God in the deuteronomistic redaction, as "approaching" (bw ') the mountain in order to speak with Moses and Israel, symbolizes a metonymic relationship of contiguity between God and the mountain, which is similar to the impermanent auditory presence of the "Name" on Mount Horeb; and third, that the mobile imagery of God in the priestly redaction, as "descending" ($yrd/škn$) on the mountain in fire, symbolizes a metonymic relationship of contiguity, which is similar to the impermanent visual presence of the Kabod on Mount Sinai.

If the results of this tradition-historical analysis hold, then they must have an effect on biblical theology in a number of ways, and I would like to conclude by pointing out three theological implications, which strike me as being fruitful avenues for further research.

First, on a critical note, this study calls into question the opposition that is frequently advocated in biblical theology between Sinai and Zion, Moses and David, law and temple. Our redaction-critical study of Exodus 19-24 would suggest that Sinai and Horeb must be interpreted as theological qualifications of Zion, and, furthermore, that Sinai has actually come to represent a tempered priestly theology.

Second, the tradition history of the Sinai Complex from Zion to Sinai/Horeb, without the elimination of the former, suggests that a theology of divine presence should also incorporate this developmental component of the canonical text. What this would imply is that a biblical theology of divine presence which finds its starting point in an affirmation of divine transcendence is a misreading of pentateuchal theology, even though theologies of divine transcendence predominate in the canonical Sinai Complex in the form of Sinai and Horeb. Rather, the starting point for a theology of divine presence must be the divine immanence of Zion, for it makes possible the qualifications of Sinai/Horeb. Thus, this study suggests that a biblical theology of divine presence must be seen as being a movement from Zion to Sinai/Horeb, from metaphor to metonymy, from immanence to transcendence, with an ideal of a return to divine immanence.

Finally, the canonization of the distinct symbols of Sinai and Horeb as constructive theologies of divine presence which must be interrelated by the reader raises a variety of questions about the relationship of word and sacrament in contemporary worship. Our study of repetition as ungrounded doubling, has underscored how the canonical Sinai Complex is unequivocal in its two-fold demand that these distinct forms of divine presence not be harmonized, nor that either exist at the cost of the other. The present study has certainly not exhausted this avenue of research, nor its potential effects for constructing a theology of word and sacrament for contemporary worship.

BIBLIOGRAPHY

Aberbach, M. and Smolar, L. "Aaron, Jeroboam, and the Golden Calves." *JBL* 86 (1967): 129-40.

Ackroyd, P. R. *Exile and Restoration: A Study of Hebrew Thought of the Sixth Century B.C.* OTL. Philadelphia: Westminster, 1968.

Albright, W. F. "A Catalogue of Early Hebrew Lyric Poems." *HUCA* 23(1950-51): 14-24.

———— "The Earliest Form of Hebrew Verse." *JPOS* 2 (1922): 69-86.

———— "The Names Shaddai and Abram." *JBL* 54 (1935): 173-204.

———— "The Psalm of Habbakuk." In *Studies in Old Testament Prophecy*, edited by H. H. Rowley, pp. 1-18. Edinburgh: University Press, 1950.

———— "The Song of Deborah in Light of Archaeology." *BASOR* 66 (1936): 30.

———— *Yahweh and the Gods of Canaan: A Historical Analysis of Two Contrasting Faiths.* The Jordan Lectures. London: University of London, 1968.

Allegro, J. M. "Uses of the Semitic Demonstrative Element Z in Hebrew." *VT* 5 (1955): 309-12.

Alter, R. *The Art of Biblical Narrative.* New York: Basic Books, 1981.

Althann, R. "A Note on Exodus 19,12ab-13." *Bib* 57 (1976): 242-46.

Arndt, W. F. and Gingrich, F. W. *A Greek-English Lexicon of the New Testament and Other Early Christian Literature.* Chicago: University of Chicago Press, 1957.

Auerbach, E. *Moses.* Amsterdam: G.J.A. Ruys, 1953.

Bächli, O. *Israel und die Völker. Eine Studie zum Deutero-nomium.* ATANT 41. Zürich: Zwingli Verlag, 1962.

Baentsch, B. *Das Bundesbuch: Ex. xx 22-xxiii 33: Seine ur-sprüngliche Gestalt, seine Verhältnis zu den es umgebenden Quellschriften und seine Stellung in der alt-testamentlichen Gesetzgebung.* Halle: Max Niemeyer, 1892.

———— *Exodus-Leviticus-Numeri.* HKAT. Göttingen: Vanden-hoeck und Ruprecht, 1903.

Baltzer, K. *The Covenant Formulary in Old Testament, Jewish, and Early Christian Writings.* Translated by D. E. Green. Philadelphia: Fortress Press, 1971.

Bandstra, B. *The Syntax of the Particle Ky in Biblical Hebrew and Ugaritic.* Ph.D. dissertation, Yale University, 1982.

Barr, J. "Theophany and Anthropomorphism in the Old Testament." *VT* 7 (1959): 31-38.

Barth, C. "Theophanie, Bundschliessung und neuer Anfang am dritten Tage." *EvT* 28 (1968): 521-33.

Bauer, J. B. "Könige und Priester, ein heiliges Volk (Ex 19,6)." *BZ* 2 (1958): 283-86.

Beer, G. *Exodus.* HAT 3: Tübingen: J.C.B. Mohr (Paul Siebeck) 1939.

Begg, C. T. "The Destruction of the Calf [Exod 32,20/Deut 9,21]." In *Das Deuteronomium: Entstehung, Gestalt und Botschaft*, edited by N. Lohfink, pp. 208-51. BETL 68. Leuven: Leuven University Press, 1985.

———— "The Literary Criticism of Deut 4, 1-40: Contributions to a Continuing Discussion." *ETL* 56 (1980): 10-55.

Begrich, J. "*Berit*: Ein Beitrag zur Erfassung einer alttestamen-tlichen Denkform." *Gesammelte Studien zum Alten Testament.* TBü 21. München: Chr. Kaiser Verlag, 1964. pp. 55-66.

Beyerlin, W. *Origins and History of the Oldest Sinaitic Tradi-tions.* Translated by S. Rudman. Oxford: Basil Blackwell, 1965.

———— "Die Paranese im Bundesbuch und ihre Herkunft." In *Gottes Wort und Gottes Land: Festschrift für Hertsberg,* edited by H. G. Reventlow, pp. 9-29. Göttingen: Vanden-hoeck und Ruprecht, 1965.

Birkeland, H. "Hebrew *Zae* and Arabic *Du.*" *ST* 2 (1948): 201-2.

Blenkinsopp, J. "The Structure of P." *CBQ* 38 (1976): 275-92.

Blum, E. *Die Komposition der Vätergeschichte.* WMANT 57. Neukirchen-Vluyn: Neukirchener Verlag, 1984.

Booij, Th. "Mountain and Theophany in Sinai Narrative." *Bib* 65 (1984): 1-26.

Braulik, G. "Literarkritik und archäologische Stratigraphie: Zu S. Mittmanns Analyse von Deuteronomium 4,1-40." *Bib* 59 (1978): 351-83.

—— *Die Mittel deuteronomischer Rhetorik-erhoben aus Deuteronomium 4,1-40.* AnBib 68. Rome: Pontifical Biblical Institute, 1978.

Bright, J. *A History of Israel.* 3d ed. Philadelphia: Westminster Press.

Brockelmann, C. *Hebräische Syntax.* Neukirchen Kreis Moers: Verlag der Buchhandlung des Erziehungsvereins, 1956.

Brown, S. J. *The World of Imagery: Metaphor and Kindred Imagery.* New York: Russel & Russel, 1966.

Buber, M. *Moses.* Oxford: University Press, 1946.

Carroll, R. P. *When Prophecy Failed: Reactions and Responses to Failure in the Old Testament Prophetic Traditions.* New York: Seabury Press, 1979.

—— "Prophecy and Dissonance: A Theoretical Approach to the Prophetic Tradition." *ZAW* 92 (1980): 108-19.

Caspari, W. "Das priesterliche Königreich." *TBl* 8 (1929): 105-10.

Cassuto, U. *A Commentary on the Book of Exodus.* Jerusalem: Magnes Press, 1967.

Cazelles, H. "Alliance du Sinai, alliance de l'Horeb et renouvellement de l'alliance." In *Beiträge zur alttestamentlichen Theologie: Festschrift für W. Zimmerli,* edited by H. Donner, R. Hanhart, and R. Smend, pp. 69-79. Göttingen: Vandenhoeck und Ruprecht, 1977.

—— *Etudes sur le code d'alliance*. Paris: Letouzey et Anè, 1946.

—— "La mission d'Esdras." *VT* 4 (1954): 113-40.

—— "Moïse devant l'histoire." *Moïse: l'homme de l'alliance*, pp. 11-27. Paris: Desclee, 1955.

—— " 'Royaume des prêtres et nation consacrée.' Exode (19,6)." In *Humanisme et foi chretienne*, pp. 541-45. Melanges scientifiques du Centenaire de l'Institut Catholique de Paris. Paris: Ch. Kennenigiessar et Y. Marchasson, 1975.

Childs, B. S. *The Book of Exodus*. OTL. Philadelphia: Westminster Press, 1974.

—— "The Exegetical Significance of Canon for the Old Testament." *Congress Volume: Göttingen 1977*. VTSup 29 (1977): 66-80.

—— *Introduction to the Old Testament as Scripture*. Philadelphia: Fortress Press, 1979.

—— *The New Testament as Canon: An Introduction*. Philadelphia: Fortress Press, 1985.

—— "Response to Reviewers of Introduction to the Old Testament as Scripture." *JSOT* 16 (1980): 52-60.

Clements, R. E. "Deuteronomy and the Jerusalem Cult Tradition." *VT* 15 (1965): 300-12.

—— *God and Temple*. Philadelphia: Fortress Press, 1965

Clifford, R. J. *The Cosmic Mountain in Canaan and the Old Testament*. HSM 4. Cambridge: Harvard University Press, 1972.

Clines, D. J. *Ezra, Nehemiah, Esther*. NCB. Grand Rapids: Eerdmans, 1984.

Coats, G. W. "Moses versus Amalek: Aetiology and Legend in Exod. XVII 8-16." *Congress Volume: Edinburgh, 1974*. VTSup 28 (1975): 29-41.

—— *The Murmuring Motif in the Wilderness Traditions of the Old Testament: Rebellion in the Wilderness*. Nashville: Abingdon, 1968.

—— "The Wilderness Itinerary." *CBQ* 34 (1972): 135-52.

—— *Moses: Heroic Man, Man of God*. JSOTSup 57. Sheffield: JSOT Press, 1988.

Coggins, R. J. "The Interpretation of Ezra 4:4." *JTS* 16 (1965): 124-27.

Cohn, R. *The Shape of Sacred Space. Four Biblical Studies*. AAR Studies in Religion 23. Missoula: Scholars Press, 1981.

Coppens, J. "Exode, XIX,6: un royaume ou une royauté de prêtres?" *ETL* 53 (1977): 185-86.

Cross, F. M. *Canaanite Myth and Hebrew Epic: Essays in the History of the Religion of Israel*. Cambridge: Harvard University Press, 1973.

—— "The Priestly Tabernacle." *BAR* 1 (1961): 224-27.

—— "A Reconstruction of the Judean Restoration." *JBL* 94 (1975): 4-18.

—— "Yahweh and the God of the Patriarchs." *HTR* 55 (1962): 225-59.

—— and Freedman, D.N. *Studies in Ancient Yahwistic Poetry*. SBLDS 21. Missoula: Scholars Press, 1975.

Dahood, M. "Hebrew-Ugaritic Lexicography III." *Bib* 46 (1965): 313.

—— "Hebrew-Ugaritic Lexicography VII." *Bib* 50 (1969): 341.

—— "The Phoenician Background of Qoheleth." *Bib* 47 (1966): 267.

Damrosch, D. *The Narrative Covenant: Transformations of Genre in the Growth of Biblical Literature*. New York: Harper and Row, 1987.

Davies, G. I. "The Wilderness Itineraries and the Composition of the Pentateuch." *VT* 33 (1983): 1-13.

—— *The Way of the Wilderness: A Geographical Study of the Wilderness Itineraries in the Old Testament*. SOTSMS 5. London: Cambridge, 1979.

De Vries, S. J. *1 Kings*. Word Biblical Commentary 12. Waco: Word Books, 1985.

—— "The Time Word *maḥar* as a Key to Tradition Development." *ZAW* 87 (1975): 65-79.

———— *Yesterday, Today and Tomorrow: Time and History in the Old Testament.* Grand Rapids: Eerdmans, 1975.

———— "A Review of Recent Research in the Tradition History of the Pentateuch." SBLASP 26 (1987): 459-502.

Diessler, A. "Die Perikope von Bundeschluss (Ex 24,1-11), eine Einweisung in den Gottesdienst des Gottesvolk." *Erbe und Auftrag* 53 (1977): 361-66.

Dillmann, A. *Die Bücher Exodus und Leviticus.* HAT. Leipzig: S. Hirzel, 1880.

Donaldson, T. L. *Jesus on the Mountain.* JSNTSup 8. Sheffield: JSOT Press, 1985.

Douglas, M. *Purity and Danger. An Analysis of the Concepts of Pollution and Taboo.* London: Routledge and Kegan Paul, 1978.

Driver, S. R. *The Book of Exodus.* The Cambridge Bible. Cambridge: University Press, 1929.

Ducrot, O. and Todorov, T. *Encyclopedic Dictionary of the Sciences of Language.* Translated by C. Porter. Baltimore: The Johns Hopkins University Press, 1979.

Dumermuth, F. "Biblische Offenbarungsphänomene." *TZ* 21 (1965): 1-21.

———— "Moses strahlendes Gesicht." *TZ* 17 (1961): 244-47.

Ehrlich, A. B. *Randglossen zur Hebräischen Bibel: Erster Band Genesis und Exodus.* Leipzig: J.C. Hinrichs, 1908.

Eissfeldt, O. *Die Komposition der Sinai-Erzrählung Exodus 19-34.* Sitzungsberichte der Sächsischen Akademie der Wissenschaften zu Leipzig 113/1. Berlin: Akademic-Verlag, 1966.

———— *The Old Testament: An Introduction.* Translated by P. R. Ackroyd. New York: Harper and Row, 1965.

Eliade, M. *The Sacred and the Profane: The Nature of Religion.* New York: Harcourt, Brace and Co., 1959.

Engnell, I. *Gamla Testamentet I: En Traditionshistorik Inleding.* Stockholm: Svenska kyrkans diadonistyrelses bokforlag, 1945.

Fensham, F. C. *Exodus:* De Prediking van het Oude Testament. Nijkerk: Uitgeverij G.F. Callenbach, 1970.

Festinger, L. *A Theory of Cognitive Dissonance.* Stanford: Stanford University Press, 1965.

Fishbane, M. *Biblical Interpretation in Ancient Israel.* Oxford: Clarendon, 1985.

Fogle, S. F. "Repetition." In *Princeton Encyclopedia of Poetry and Poetics*, edited by A. Preminger, pp. 699-701. Princeton: Princeton University Press, 1974.

Fohrer, G. " 'Priesterliches Königtum', Ex 19,6." *TZ* 19 (1963): 359-62.

——— *History of Israelite Religion.* Nashville: Abingdon, 1972.

Friedman, N. "Symbol." In *Princeton Encyclopedia of Poetry and Poetics*, edited by A. Preminger, pp. 833-36. Princeton: Princeton University Press, 1974.

Friedman, R. E. *The Exile and Biblical Narrative.* HSM 22. Chico: Scholars Press, 1981.

——— "Sacred History and Theology: The Redaction of Torah." In *The Creation of Sacred Literature*, edited by R. E. Friedman, pp. 25-34. University of California Publications: Near Eastern Studies 22. Berkeley: University of California Press, 1981.

——— *Who Wrote the Bible?* New York: Summit Books, 1987.

Galling, K. *Studien zur Geschichte Israels im Persischen Zeitalter.* Tübingen: J.C.B. Mohr (Paul Siebeck), 1964.

Genette, G. *Figures of Literary Discourses.* European Perspectives. Translated by A. Sheridan. New York: Columbia University Press, 1982.

Gese, H. "Bemerkungen zur Sinaitradition." *ZAW* 79 (1967): 137-54.

Glueck, N. "The Theophany of the God of Sinai." *JAOS* 56 (1936): 462-71.

Gordon, C. H. *Ugaritic Textbook.* AnOr 38. Rome: Pontificium Institutum Biblicum, 1965.

Görg, M. "Die Gattung des sogenannten Tempelweihspruches (1 Kg 8, 12f.)." *UF* 6 (1974): 55-63.

────── *Das Zelt der Begegnung: Untersuchung zur Gestalt der Sakralen Zelttradition Altisraels.* BBB 27. Bonn: Hanstein, 1967.

Gottwald, N. K. *The Tribes of Yahweh: A Sociology of the Religion of Liberated Israel, 1250-1050 BCE.* Maryknoll, NY: Orbis Books, 1979.

────── "Social Matrix and Canonical Shape." *Ttoday* 42 (1985): 307-21.

────── *The Hebrew Bible: A Socio-Literary Introduction.* Philadelphia: Fortress Press, 1985.

Gradwohl, R. "Das 'Fremde Feuer' von Nadab und Abihu." *ZAW* 75 (1963): 288-96.

Greenberg, M. "Hebrew sĕgullā Akkadian sikiltu." *JAOS* 71 (1951): 172-74.

Grelot, P. "La dernière étape de la rédaction sacerdotale." *VT* 6 (1956): 174-89.

────── "Le papyrus pascal d'Eléphantine et le problème du Pentateuque." *Vt* 5 (1955): 250-65.

Gressman, H. *Die Anfänge Israels.* Die Schriften des Alten Testaments 1/2. Göttingen: Vandenhoeck und Ruprecht, 1914.

────── *Mose und Seine Zeit.* FRLANT 1. Göttingen: Vanderhoeck & Ruprecht, 1913.

────── "Die Aufgaben der alttestamentlichen Forschung." *ZAW* 1 (1924): 1-33.

Grewel, H. *Mosegeschichten.* Handbücherie für den Religions Unterricht 9. Gütersloh: Gerd Mohn, 1971.

Haag, H. "Das 'Buch des Bundes' (Ex 24,7)." In *Das Buch des Bundes: Aufsätze zur Bibel und zu ihrer Welt*, edited by B. Lang, pp. 226-33. Düsseldorf: Patmos, 1980 = *Wort Gotes in der Zeit. Festschrift für Karl Herrmann Schelke*, herausgegbenen von H. Feld, pp. 22-30. Düsseldorf: Patmos, 1973.

Haelvoet, M. "La theophanie du Sinai." *ETL* 29 (1953): 375-81.

Halbe, J. *Das Privilegrecht Jahwes Ex 34,10-26: Gestalt und Wesen, Herkunft und Wirken in vordeuteronomischer Zeit.* FRLANT 114. Göttingen: Vandenhoeck und Ruprecht, 1975.

Haran, M. "The Nature of the '*Ohel Mô'edh*' in the Pentateuchal Sources." *JSS* 5 (1960): 50-65.

—— *Temples and Temple-Service in Ancient Israel: An Inquiry into the Character of Cult Phenomena and the Historical Setting of the Priestly School.* Oxford: Clarendon Press, 1978.

Hayes J. H. and Miller, J. M. *Israelite and Judaean History.* OTL. Philadelphia: Westminster, 1977.

Heinisch, P. *Das Buch Exodus.* Das Heilige Schrift des Alten Testaments 1. Bonn: Peter Hanstein Verlagsbuchhandlung, 1934.

Held, M. "A Faithful Lover in an Old Babylonian Dialogue." *JCS* 15 (1961): 11-26.

Hensel, H. *Die Sinaitheophanie und die Rechtstraditionen in Israel.* Ph.D. dissertation, Heidelberg, 1971.

Hermission, H.- J. *Sprache und Ritus im Altisraelitischen Kult: Zur 'Spiriritualisierung' der Kultbegriffe im Alten Testament.* WMANT 19. Neukirchen-Vluyn: Neukirchener, 1965.

Hossfeld, F.- L. *Der Dekalog: Seine späten Fassungen, die originale Komposition und seine Vorstufen.* OBO 45. Göttingen: Vandenhoeck und Ruprecht, 1982.

Huffmon, H. B. and Parker, S. B. "A Further Note on the Treaty Background of Hebrew *yāda'.*" *BASOR* 184 (1966): 36-38.

Hurvitz, A. "The Evidence of Language in Dating the Priestly Code." *RB* 81 (1974): 24-56.

—— *A Linguistic Study of the Relationship Between the Priestly Source and the Book of Ezekiel.* Cahiers de la Revue Biblique 20. Paris: J. Gabalda, 1982.

Hvidberg-Hansen, O. "Die Vernichtung des Goldenen Kalbes und der Ugaritische Ernteritus." *AcOr* 33 (1971): 5-46.

Hyatt, J. P. *Exodus.* NCB. London: Oliphants, 1971.

Jakobson, R. "Two Aspects of Language and Two Types of

Aphasic Disturbances." Pp. 55-82 in R. Jakobson and M. Halle, *Fundamentals of Language*. Janua Linguarum 1. The Hague: Mouton, 1956.

Janssen, E. *Juda in der Exilzeit: Ein Beitrag zur Frage der Entstehung des Judentums*. FRLANT 69. Göttingen: Vandenhoeck und Ruprecht, 1956.

Jaroš, K. "Des Mose 'strahlende Haut': Eine Notiz zu Ex 34:29, 30, 35." *ZAW* 88 (1976): 275-80.

Jensen, P. *Die Kosmologie die Babylonier*. Strasbourg: Trübner, 1890.

Jepsen, A. *Untersuchungen zum Bundesbuch*. BWANT III/5. Stuttgart: W. Kohlhammer, 1927.

Jeremias, J. *Der Gottesberg: Ein Beitrag zum Verstandnis der biblischen Symbolsprache*. Gütersloh: C. Bertelsmann, 1919.

Jeremias, J. *Theophanie: Die Geschichte einer alttestamentlichen Gattung*. WMANT 10. Neukirchen-Vluyn: Neukirchener Verlag, 1965.

Johnston, W. "Reactivating the Chronicles Analogy in Pentateuchal Studies, with Special Reference to the Sinai Pericope in Exodus." *ZAW* 99 (1987): 16-37.

Junker, H. "Das allgemeine Priesterum." *TTZ* 56 (1947): 10-15.

Kasher, M. M. *Encyclopedia of Biblical Interpretation IX: A Millennial Anthology. Exodus*. New York: American Biblical Encyclopedia Society, 1970.

Kaufmann, J. "Probleme der israelitische-jüdischen Religionsgeschichte." *ZAW* 48 (1930): 23-43.

Kautzsch, E., ed. *Gesenius' Hebrew Grammer*. 2d Eng. ed. Translated by A. E. Cowley. Oxford: Clarendon Press, 1978.

Kawin, B. F. *Telling It Again and Again: Repetition in Literature and Film*. Ithaca: Cornell University Press, 1972.

Kearney, P. "Creation and Liturgy: The P Redaction of Ex 25-40." *ZAW* 89 (1977): 375-87.

Keil, C. F. and Delitzsch, F. *Commentary on the Old Testament I*. 1962. Reprint. Grand Rapids: Eerdmans, 1981.

Kellerman, U. "Erwägungen zum Esragesetz." *ZAW* 80 (1968): 373-85.

Kingsbury, E.C. "The Theophany Topos and the Mountain of God." *JBL* 86 (1967): 205-10.

Knapp, D. *Deuteronomium 4: Literarische Analyse und Theologische Interpretation.* Göttingen Theologische Arbeiten 35. Göttingen: Vanderhoeck und Ruprecht, 1986.

Knierim, R. "The Composition of the Pentateuch." SBLASP 24 (1985): 399-406.

Knutson, J. B. "Literary Genres in PRU IV." *Ras Shamra Parallels II.* AnOr 50. Edited by L.R. Fisher. Rome: Pontificium Institutum Biblicum, 1975: 180-94.

Koch, K. "Die Eigenart der priesterschriftlichen Sinaigesetzgebung." *ZTK* 55 (1958): 36-51.

—— "P -Kein Redacktor!: Erinnerung an zwei Eckdaten der Quellenscheidung." *VT* 37 (1987): 446-67.

—— *Die Priesterschrift von Exodus 25- bis Leviticus 16: Ein überlieferungsgeschichtliche und literarkritische Untersuchung.* FRLANT 71. Göttingen: Vanderhoeck und Ruprecht, 1963.

Koehler, L. and Baumgartner, W. *Lexicon in Veteris Testamenti Libros.* Leiden: E.J. Brill, 1958.

Kraetzschmar, R. *Die Bundesvorstellung im Alten Testament in ihrer geschichtlichen Entwickelung.* Marburg: Elwert'sche Verlagsbuchlandlung, 1896.

Kraus, H.-J. "Das Heilige Volk: Zur alttestamentlichen Bezeichnung ʿam qādôš." In *Freude Am Evangelium: Festschrift für A. de Quervain,* edited by J. J. Stamm, pp. 50-61. BEvT 44. Munchen: Chr. Kaiser, 1966.

Kuhl, C. "Die 'Wiederaufnahme'—ein literarkritisches Prinzip?" *ZAW* 64 (1952): 1-11.

Kutsch, E. "Gesetz und Gnade: Probleme des alttestamentlichen Bundesbegriffs." *ZAW* 79 (1967): 18-3.

—— "Der Kalender des Jubiläenbuch und das Alte Testament." *VT* 11 (1961): 39-47.

—— "Das sog. 'Bundesblut' in Ex xxiv 8 und Sach ix 11." *VT* 23 (1973): 25-30.

———— *Verheissung und Gesetz: Untersuchungen zum sogenannten 'Bund' im Alten Testament.* BZAW 131. Berlin: de Gruyter, 1973.

Laughlin, J. C. "The 'Strange Fire' of Nadab and Abihu." *JBL* 95 (1976): 559-565.

Lehming, S. "Versuch zu Ex. XXXII." *VT* 10 (1960): 16-50.

Levenson, J.D. "From Temple to Synagogue: 1 Kings 8." In *Traditions in Transformation: Turning Points in Biblical Faith,* edited by B. Halpern and J. D. Levenson, pp. 143-92. Winona Lake, IN: Eisenbrauns, 1981.

———— *Sinai and Zion: An Entry into the Jewish Bible.* New York: Winston Press, 1985.

Levin, C. "Der Dekalog am Sinai." *VT* 35 (1985): 165-91.

Levine, B. "Priestly Writers." In *IDBSup,* edited by K. Crim, pp. 683-87. Nashville: Abingdon, 1976.

Lindblom, J. "Theophanies in Holy Places in Hebrew Religion." *HUCA* 32 (1961): 91-106.

Lohfink, N. *Das Hauptgebot: Eine Untersuchung literarischer Einleitungsfragen zu Dtn 5-11.* AnBib 20. Rome: E. Pontificio Instituto Biblico, 1963.

———— *Höre, Israel! Auslegung von Texten aus den Buch Deuteronomium.* Die Welt der Bibel 18. Düsseldorf: Patmos, 1965.

Loretz, O. "Der Torso eines kanaanäische israelitischen Tempelweihspruches in 1 Kg 8, 12-13." *UF* 6 (1974): 478-80.

Lotman, J. *The Structure of the Artistic Text.* Michigan Slavic Contributions 7. Translated by G. Lenhoff and R. Vroon. Ann Arbor: University of Michigan Press, 1977.

Maier, J. *Von Kultus zur Gnosis: Studien zur Vor- und Frühgeschichte der "jüdischen Gnosis."* Religionswissenschaftliche Studien 1. Salzburg: Kairos, 1964.

Mann, T. W. *Divine Presence and Guidance in Israelite Traditions. The Typology of Exaltation.* JHNES. Baltimore: Johns Hopkins University Press, 1977.

Mayes, A. D. H. *Deuteronomy.* NCB. London: Oliphants, 1979.

—— "Deuteronomy 4 and the Literary Criticism of Deuteronomy." *JBL* 100 (1981): 23-51.

—— *The Story of Israel Between Settlement and Exile: A Redactional Study of the Deuteronomistic History*. London: SCM Press, 1983.

McBride, S. D. *The Deuteronomic Name Theology*. Ph.D. dissertation, Harvard University, 1969.

McCarthy, D. J. *Old Testament Covenant: A Survey of Current Options*. Oxford: Basil Blackwell, 1972.

—— *Treaty and Covenant: A Study in Form in the Ancient Oriental Documents and in the Old Testament*. 2d rev. ed. AnBib 21a. Rome: Pontifical Biblical Institute, 1978.

McConville, J. G. *Law and Theology in Deuteronomy*. JSOT-Sup 33. Sheffield: JSOT Press, 1984.

McNeile, A. H. *The Book of Exodus*. Westminster Commentaries. London: Methuen, 1908.

Mendenhall, G. E. *Law and Covenant in Israel and the Ancient Near East*. Pittsburgh: The Biblical Colloquium, 1955.

—— *The Tenth Generation: The Origins of the Biblical Tradition*. Baltimore: Johns Hopkins Press, 1973.

Mettinger, T. N. D. *The Dethronement of Sabaoth: Studies in the Shem and Kabod Theologies*. ConBOT 18. Translated by F. H. Cryer. Lund: CWK Gleerup, 1982.

Metzger, M. "Himmlische und irdische Wohnstatt." *UF* 2 (1970): 13-9-55.

Michaeli, F. *Le livre de l'Exode*. CAT 2. Paris: Delachaux and Niestle, 1974.

Mickelsen, D. "Types of Spatial Structure in Narrative." In *Spatial Form in Narrative*, edited by J. R. Smitten and A. Daghistany, pp. 64-67. Ithaca: Cornell University, 1981.

Milgrom, J. *Cult and Conscience*. Leiden: Brill, 1976.

—— "Sacrifices and Offerings." In *IBDSup*, edited by K. Crim, pp. 763-70. Nashville: Abingdon, 1976.

—— *Studies in Levitical Terminology*. Berkeley: University of California Press, 1970.

Miller, J. Hillis. *Fiction and Repetition: Seven English Novels*. Cambridge: Harvard University Press, 1982.

Mittmann, S. *Deuteronomium 1,1-6,3: Literarkritisch und traditionsgeschichtlich Untersucht*. BZAW 139. Berlin: de Gruyter, 1975.

Moberly, R. W. L. *At the Mountain of God: Story and Theology in Exodus 32-34*. JSOTSup 22. Sheffield: JSOT Press, 1983.

Moran, W. L. "A Kingdom of Priests." *The Bible in Current Catholic Thought*, edited by J. L. McKenzie, pp. 7-20. New York: Herder and Herder, 1962.

Morgenstern, J. "Biblical Theophanies." *ZA* 25 (1911): 139-93.

——— "Biblical Theophanies." *ZA* 28 (1914): 15-60.

Mosis, R. "Ex 19,5b.6a: Syntaktischer Aufbau und lexikalische Semantik." *BZ* 22 (1978): 1-25.

Mowinckel, S. *Der Actungsechzigste Psalm*. Avhandlinger utgitt an det Norske Videnskaps-Akademi 1. Oslo: Jacob Debwad, 1953.

——— *Studien zu dem Buche Ezra-Nehemia I-III*. Oslo: Universitetsforlaget, 1964.

Muilenburg, J. "The Form and Structure of the Covenantal Formulations," *VT* 9 (1959): 347-65.

——— "The Intercession of the Covenant Mediator (Exod 33:1a, 12-17)." In *Words and Meanings: Essays Presented to David Winton Thomas*, edited by P. R. Ackroyd and B. Lindars, pp. 159-81. Cambridge: University Press, 1968.

——— "The Linguistic and Rhetorical Usages of the Particle *ki* in the Old Testament." *HUCA* 32 (1961): 146.

——— "A Study of Hebrew Rhetoric: Repetition and Style." *Congress Volume: Copenhagen 1953*. VTSup 1 (1953): 97-111.

——— "Form Criticism and Beyond." *JBL* 88 (1969): 1-18.

Myers, J. M. *Ezra-Nehemiah*. AB 14. Garden City, NY: Doubleday, 1965.

Nelson, R. D. *The Double Redaction of the Deuteronomistic History*. JSOTSup 18. Sheffield: JSOT Press, 1981.

Nicholson, E. W. "The Antiquity of the Tradition in Exodus XXIV 9-11." *VT* 25 (1975): 69-79.

—— "The Centralization of the Cult in Deuteronomy." *VT* 13 (1963): 380-89.

—— "The Covenant Ritual in Exodus XXIV 3-8." *VT* 32 (1982): 74-86.

—— "The Decalogue as the Direct Address of God." *VT* 27 (1977): 422-33.

—— *Exodus and Sinai in History and Tradition.* Growing Points in Theology. Richmond: John Knox Press, 1973.

—— "The Interpretation of Exodus XXIV 9-11." *VT* 24 (1974): 77-97.

—— "The Meaning of the Expression *'am hā 'āreṣ* in the Old Testament." *JSS* 10 (1965): 59-66.

—— "The Origin of the Tradition in Exodus XXIV 9-11." *VT* 26 (1976): 148-60.

—— *God and His People. Covenant and Theology in the Old Testament.* Oxford: Clarendon, 1986.

Nielsen, E. "Moses and the Law." *VT* 32 (1982): 87-98.

—— *The Ten Commandments in New Perspective. A Traditio-historical Approach.* Studies in Biblical Theology 7. London: SCM Press, 1968.

Noth, M. *Exodus.* OTL. Translated by J. S. Bowden. Philadelphia: Westminster Press, 1962.

—— *A History of Pentateuchal Traditions.* Translated by B. W. Anderson. Chico: Scholars Press, 1981.

—— *Leviticus.* OTL. Translated by J. E. Anderson. Philadelphia: Westminster Press, 1965.

—— *Numbers.* OTL. Translated by J. D. Martin. Philadelphia: Westminster Press, 1968.

—— *Überlieferungsgeschichtliche Studien I: Die Sammelnden und bearbeitenden Geschichtswerke im Alten Testaments.* Schriften der Königsberger Gelehrten Gesellschaft 18/2. 2d. ed. Tübingen: Max Niemeyer Verlag, 1957.

Ollenburger, B. C. *Zion, the City of the Great King: A Theolog-*

ical Symbol for the Jerusalem Cult. JSOTSup 41. Sheffield: JSOT Press, 1987.

Parrot, A. *Ziqqurats et Tour de Babel.* Paris: Machel, 1949.

Patrick, D. "The Covenant Code Source." *VT* 27 (1977): 145-57.

Paul, S. M. *Studies in the Book of the Covenant in the Light of Cuneiform and Biblical Law.* VTSup 18. Leiden: E. J. Brill, 1970.

Perlitt, L. *Bundestheologie im Alten Testament.* WMANT 36. Neukirchen-Vluyn: Neukirchener Verlag, 1969.

—— "Sinai und Horeb." In *Beiträge zur alttestamentlichen Theologie: Festschrift für W. Zimmerli,* edited by H. Donner, R. Hanhart, and R. Smend, pp. 302-22. Göttingen: Vanderhoeck und Ruprecht, 1977.

Phillips, A. "A Fresh Look at the Sinai Pericope." *VT* 34 (1984): 39-52.

Polzin, R. *Moses and the Deuteronomist: A Literary Study of the Deuteronomic History.* New York: Seabury Press, 1980.

Pritchard, J. B. *Ancient Near Eastern Texts Relating to the Old Testament.* 3d. ed. Princeton: Princeton University Press, 1969.

Rad, G. von. *Deuteronomy.* OTL. Translated by D. Barton. Philadelphia: Westminster Press, 1966.

—— "The Form-Critical Problem of the Hexateuch." In *The Problem of the Hexateuch,* translated by E. W. Trueman Dicken, pp. 1-78. London: Oliver and Boyd, 1966.

—— *Das Gottesvolk im Deuteronomium.* BWANT 47. Stuttgart: W. Kohlhammer, 1929.

—— *Studies in Deuteronomy.* SBT 9. Translated by D. Stalker. Chicago: Henry Regnery Co., 1953.

—— "Literarkritische und überlieferungsgeschichtliche Forschung," *VF* 48 (1947): 172-94.

Rendsburg, G. "Late Biblical Hebrew and the Date of P." *JANESCU* 12 (1980): 65-80.

Rendtorff, R. "The Concept of Revelation in Ancient Israel." In

Revelation as History, edited by W. Pannenberg, pp. 25-53. Translated by D. Granskou. New York: Macmillan, 1968.

———— *Die Gesetze in der Priesterschrift: Eine gattungsgeschichtliche Untersuchung*. 2d. ed. FRLANT 44. Göttingen: Vanderhoeck und Ruprecht, 1962.

———— *Studien zur Geschichte des Opfers im Alten Israel*. WMANT 24. Neukirchen-Vluyn: Neukirchener Verlag, 1967.

———— *Das überlieferungsgeschichtliche Problem des Pentateuch*. BZAW 147. Berlin: de Gruyter, 1977.

———— "The 'Yahwist' as Theologian? The Dilemma of Pentateuchal Criticism." *JSOT* 3 (1977): 2-9 = "Der 'Jahwist' als Theologe? Zum Dilemma der Pentateuchkritik." *Congress Volume: Edinburgh 1974*. VTSup 28 (1975): 158-66.

Richards, I. A. *The Philosophy of Rhetoric*. Oxford: Oxford University Press, 1936.

Ricoeur, P. *The Rule of Metaphor: Multidisciplinary Studies of the Creation of Meaning in Language*. University of Toronto Romance Series 37. Translated by R. Czerny. Toronto: University of Toronto Press, 1977.

Rivard, R. "Pour une Relecture d'Ex 19 et 20; Analyse Sémiotique d'Ex 19,1-8." *ScEs* 33 (1981): 335-56.

Roberts, J. J. M. "Zion in the Theology of the Davidic-Solomonic Empire." In *Studies in the Period of David and Solomon and Other Essays: Papers Read at the International Symposium for Biblical Studies, Tokyo, 5-7 December, 1979*, edited by T. Ishida, pp. 93-108. Winona Lake, IN: Eisenbrans, 1982.

Robertson, E. "The Altar of Earth (Ex 20,24-26)." *JSS* 1 (1948): 12-21.

Rose, M. *Der Ausschliesslichkeitanspruch Jahwes. Deuteronomische Schultheologie und die Volksfrömmigkeit in der späten Königszeit*. BWANT 106. Stuttgart: W. Kohlhammer, 1975.

Rudolf, W. "Der Aufbau von Exodus 19-34." In *Werden und Wesen des Alten Testaments*, edited by P. Volz, F. Stummer and J. Hempel, pp. 41-48. BZAW 66. Berlin: Töpelmann, 1935.

———— *Der 'Elohist' von Exodus bis Joshua.* BZAW 68. Berlin: A. Töpelmann, 1938.

Ruppert, L. "Das Motiv der Versuchung durch Gott in vordeuteronomischer Tradition." *VT* 22 (1972): 55-63.

Rupprecht, K. *Der Temple von Jerusalem.* BZAW 144. Berlin: de Gruyter, 1976.

Ruprecht, E. "Exodus 24,9-11 als Beispiel lebendiger Ezrähltradition aus der Zeit des babylonischen Exil." In *Werden und Wirken des Alten Testaments: Festschrift für Westermann,* edited by R. Albertz, pp. 139-73. Neukirchen-Vluyn: Neukirchener Verlag, 1978.

Sanders, J. A. *Torah and Canon.* Philadelphia: Fortress Press, 1972.

———— *From Sacred Story to Sacred Text.* Philadelphia: Fortress Press, 1987.

Schmid, H. H. *Der sogenannte Jahwist: Beobachtungen und Fragen zur Pentateuchforschung.* Zürich: Theologischer Verlag, 1976.

Schmid, H. "Gottesbild, Gottesschau und Theophanie." *Judaica* 23 (1967): 241-54.

———— *Moses: Überlieferung und Geschichte.* BZAW 110. Berlin: A. Topelmann, 1968.

———— *Die Gestalt des Mose: Probleme alttestamentlicher Forschung unter Beruchsichtigung der Pentateuchkrise.* Ertrage der Forschung 237. Darmstadt: Wissenschaftliche Buchsellschaft, 1986.

Schmid, R. *Das Bundesopfer in Israel: Wesen, Ursprung und Bedeutung der Alttestamentlichen Schelamim.* München: Kösel-Verlag, 1964.

Schmidt, J. M. "Erwägungen zum Verhältnis von Auszugs- und Sinaitradition." *ZAW* 82 (1970): 1-31.

Schmidt, W. H. *Exodus, Sinai, und Mose. Erwagungen zu Ex 1-19 und 24.* Ertrage der Forschung 191. Darmstadt: Wissenschaftliche Buchgesellschaft, 1983.

Schmitt, H.- C. "Redaktion des Pentateuch im Geiste der Prophetie." *VT* 32 (1982): 170-89.

Schnutenhaus, F. "Das Kommen und Erscheinen Gottes im Alten Testament." *ZAW* 76 (1964): 1-22.

Scott, R. B. Y. "A Kingdom of Priests (Exodus xix 6)." *OTS* 8 (1950): 213-219.

Seebass, H. *Mose und Aaron, Sinai und Gottesberg.* Abhandlungen zur Evangelischen Theologie 2. Bonn: H. Bouvier, 1962.

Seeligmann, I. L. "Voraussetzungen der Midraschexegese." *Congress Volume: Copenhagen 1953.* VTSup 1 (1953): 150-81.

Sheppard, G. T. "Canonization: Hearing the Voice of the Same God through Historically Dissimilar Traditions." *Int* 36 (1982): 21-33.

———— *Wisdom as a Hermeneutical Construct: A Study in the Sapientializing of the Old Testament.* BZAW 151. Berlin: de Gruyter, 1980.

Smend, R. "Essen und Trinken—ein Stuck Weltlichkeit des Alten Testaments." In *Beiträge zur alttestamentlichen Theologie: Festschrift für W. Zimmerli*, edited by H. Donner, R. Hanhart, and R. Smend, pp. 446-59. Göttingen: Vanderhoeck und Ruprecht, 1977.

———— *Das Mosebild von Heinrich Ewald bis Martin Noth*, Tübingen: J.C.B. Mohr (Paul Siebeck), 1959.

Smith, M. *Palestinian Parties and Politics that Shaped the Old Testament.* American Council of Learned Societies 1. New York: Columbia University Press, 1971.

Smitten, J. R. and Daghistany, A. "Editor's Preface." In *Spatial Form in Narrative*, edited by J. R. Smitten and A. Daghistany, pp. 2-5. Ithaca: Cornell University, 1981.

Soskice, J. M. *Metaphor and Religious Language.* Oxford: Clarendon Press, 1985.

Spiegelberg, W. *Die sogenannte Demotische Chronik des Pap. 215 der Bibliothèque Nationale zu Paris.* Demotische Studien 7. Leipzig: J.C. Hinrichs'sche Buchhandlung, 1914.

Steuernagel, C. "Der jehovistische Bericht uber den Bundesschluss am Sinai." *TSK* 72 (1899): 319-50.

Talmon, Sh. "Ezra and Nehemiah." In *IDBSup*, edited by K. Crim, pp. 317-28. Nashville: Abingdon, 976.

———— "har." In *TDOT III*, edited by G. J. Botterweck and H. Ringgren, pp. 427-47. Grand Rapids: Eerdmans, 1978.

Terrien, S. *The Elusive Presence: The Heart of Biblical Theology*. Religious Perspectives 26. New York: Harper and Row, 1978.

Thompson, T. L. *The Historicity of the Patriarchal Narratives: The Quest for the Historical Abraham*. BZAW 133. Berlin: de Gruyter, 1974.

———— *The Origin Tradition of Ancient Israel I: The Literary Formation of Genesis and Exodus 1-23*. JSOTSup 55. Sheffield: JSOT Press, 1988.

Todorov, T. *Theories of Symbol*. Translated by C. Porter. Ithaca: Cornell University Press, 1982.

———— *The Poetics of Narrative*. Translated by R. Howard. Ithaca: Cornell University Press, 1977.

Van der Leeuw, G. *Religion in Essence and Manifestation*. 2d. ed. Translated by J. E. Turner. Princeton: Princeton University Press, 1986.

Van Seters, J. *Abraham in History and Tradition*. New Haven: Yale University Press, 1975.

———— *In Search of History: Historiography in the Ancient World and the Origins of Biblical History*. New Haven: Yale University Press, 1983.

Valentin, H. *Aaron: Eine Studie zur vor-priesterschriftlichen Aaron-Überlieferung*. OBO 18. Göttingen: Vanderhoeck und Ruprecht, 1978.

Valeton, J. J. P. "Das Wort *berit* in den jehovistischen und deuteronomistischen Stucken des Hexateuchs, sowie in den verwandten historischen Bücher." *ZAW* 12 (1892): 224-60.

Vaux, R. de. *Ancient Israel: Its Life and Institutions*. New York: McGraw-Hill, 1961.

Vink, J. G. "The Date and Origin of the Priestly Code in the Old Testament." *OTS* 15 (19699): 1-144.

Volz, P. *Moses und sein Werk*. 2d. ed. Tübingen: J. C. B. Mohr (Paul Siebeck), 1932.

Vriezen, Th. C. "The Exegesis of Exodus xxiv 9-11." *OTS* 17 (1972): 100-33.

Wanke, G. *Die Ziontheologie der Korachiten in ihrem Traditionsgeschichtlichen Zusammenhang.* BZAW 97. Berlin: de Gruyter, 1966.

Weinfield, M. *Deuteronomy and the Deuteronomic School.* Oxford: Clarendon Press, 1972.

Weingreen, J. *From Bible to Mishna: The Continuity of Tradition.* Manchester: Manchester University Press, 1976.

Wellek, R. and Warren, A. *Theory of Literature.* 3d. ed. New York: Harcourt Brace Jovanovich, 1975.

Wellhausen, J. *Die Composition des Hexateuchs und der Historischen Bücher des Alten Testament.* 3d. ed. Berlin: Georg Reimer, 1899.

——— *Prolegomena to the History of Ancient Israel.* 1883. Reprint. New York: Meridian Books, 1957.

Westermann, C. "Die Herrlichkeit Gottes in der Priesterschrift." In *Wort-Gebot-Glaube: Beiträge zur Theologie des Alten Testaments: Festschrift für W. Eichrodt,* edited by H. J Stoebe, pp. 227-47. Zurich: Zwingli, 1970.

Whybray, R. N. *The Making of the Pentateuch: A Methodological Study.* JSOTSup 53. Sheffield: JSOT Press, 1987.

Wildberger, H. *Jahwes Eigentumsvolk: Eine Studie zur Traditionsgeschichte und Theologie des Erwählungsgedankens.* Zürich: Zwingli Verlag, 1960.

Wilms, F. E. *Das Jahwistische Bundesbuch in Exodus 34.* SANT 32. München: Kösel-Verlag, 1973.

Winnet, F. V. *The Mosaic Tradition.* Toronto: University of Toronto Press, 1949.

Wolff, H. W. "The Kerygma of the Deuteronomic Historical Work." In *The Vitality of Old Testament Traditions,* by W. Brueggemann and H. W. Wolff, pp. 83-100. 2nd ed. Translated by F. C. Prussner. Atlanta: John Knox Press, 1976=ZAW 73 (1961): 171-86.

Zenger, E. *Israel am Sinai: Analysen und Interpretationen zu Exodus 17-34 2d. ed. Altenberge: Akademische Bibliothek, 1984.*

────── *Die Sinaitheophanie: Untersuchungen zum jahwistischen und elohistischen Geschichtswerk.* Forschung zur Bibel. Würzburg: Echter Verlag, 1971.

Zevit, Z. "Converging Lines of Evidence Bearing on the Date of P." *ZAW* 94 (1982): 481-511.

Zimmerli, W. *Ezekiel I.* Hermeneia. Translated by R. E. Clements. Philadelphia: Fortress Press, 1979.